TEACHER GUIDE

James P. Stobaugh

Junior High
2 Credits – Grammar and Writing

Includes: Answer Keys
Instruction Guide
Daily Concept Builders
Daily Assignments

Skills for LANGUAGE Arts

Lessons in Grammar and Communication

First printing: April 2015

Master Books®, P.O. Box 726, Green Forest, AR 72638
Master Books® is a division of the New Leaf Publishing Group, Inc.

ISBN: 978-0-89051-860-1
ISBN: 978-1-61458-445-2 (ebook)

Cover design by Diana Bogardus.
Interior design by Terry White.

Printed in the United States of America

Please visit our website for other great titles:
www.masterbooks.com

For information regarding author interviews, please contact the publicity department at (870) 438-5288.

Acknowledgments

I thank my four children and my distance-learning students who so graciously allowed me to use their essays. Over the last 15 years it has been my great honor to teach some of the best writers in America. Finally, and most of all, I want to thank my best friend and lifelong editor, my wife, Karen. I also want to thank the students who have contributed to this book as well: J.B. Rutlemann, Joseph Stahl, Emily Miller, Benjamin Cobb, Rebecca Holscher, Sheridan Swathmore, Catelyn Mast, Ian Elliott Smith, Hannah Huynh, Daphnide McDermet, John Micah Braswell, Faith Baumann, Bethany Rishell, Anna Grace Knudsten, Stacia Hiramine, Megan Norman, Austin Allen, James Grinalds, Daniel Greenidge, Claire Atwood, Jaime Schimmer, Chris Loyd, Alouette Greenidge, and Josiah Keiter.

Everything is from God, who . . . gave us the ministry of reconciliation (2 Corinthians 5:18).

Master Books®
A Division of New Leaf Publishing Group
www.masterbooks.com

Contents

Using Your Teacher Guide

How this course has been developed:

1. **Chapters:** This course has 34 chapters (representing 34 weeks of study).
2. **Lessons:** Each chapter has five instructive lessons, taking approximately 45 to 60 minutes each, with an exam due on Friday.
3. **Grading:** Depending on the grading option chosen, the parent/educator will grade the daily concept builders, and the weekly tests and/or essays, as well as the final project (novella).
4. **Course credit:** If a student has satisfactorily completed all assignments for this course, it is equivalent to one credit of writing and one credit of literature.

Throughout this course, you will find the following:

1. **Chapter learning objectives:** Always read the "First Thoughts" and "Chapter Learning Objectives" to comprehend the scope of the material to be covered in a particular week.
2. **Concept builders:** Students should complete a daily concept builder Monday through Friday. These activities take 15 minutes or less and emphasize a particular concept that is vital to that particular chapter topic. These will relate to a subject covered in the chapter, though not necessarily in that day's lesson. Answers are available in this teacher guide with each lesson.
3. **Weekly tests:** Students have weekly evaluations. These are available to remove and give to the student at the back of this teacher guide, with the answers at the end of each chapter.
4. **Daily prayer journal:** Students are encouraged to write in a prayer journal every day. A parent/educator may include this in the overall grade. If so, it is encouraged that the grade be based on participation rather than on the content, since this is a deeply personal expression of a student's walk with God.
5. **Novella:** Students will write a novella over the course of the year.
6. **Warm-ups:** Daily warm up exercises will start each lesson, setting the tone of thought for the day. These are not meant to be graded.

Grading Record Options (See chart on following page.)

This course has been developed to allow two grading options for a parent/educator. This allows one the flexibility to adjust the usage of the course content to individual situations and varying requirements. For ease of grading, **Option A** includes the grading of the weekly test and novella. **Option B** includes the grading of the weekly test, novella, and concept builders. Dividing the total score at the end of the course by 35 will provide a percentage grade for the student. You may use the standard system (90-100 = A, 80-89 = B, 70-79 = C, 60-69 = D, below 60 = F), or you may use your own personal grading system. An additional option includes additional credit for the student's prayer journal, which can be done at the educator's discretion and be added into the overall score of Option A or Option B. An additional 10 percent bonus can be awarded for the prayer journal, in the extra credit column. **Novella** When grading the novella at the end of the course, we suggest awarding: 25 points for creativity and ability to engage reader interest; 25 points for structure of the story, including paragraphs and sentences that are coherent and well-written; 25 points for neatness and any additional research that the student may have done to make the novella's subject more realistic; and 25 points for factors like well-reasoned dialogue, use of vocabulary words learned during the course, and work done to create a well-described setting or points of storyline interest. Or if you choose, you may consider the completion of the novella worth 100 points and deduct 2 points for any spelling or structural problems that are found.

week	Option A	Option B	
	Weekly Test (100 points each)	Weekly Test (100 points each)	CB (25 points)
1			
2			
3			
4			
5			
6			
7			
8			
9			
10			
11			
12			
13			
14			
15			
16			
17			
18			
19			
20			
21			
22			
23			
24			
25			
26			
27			
28			
29			
30			
31			
32			
33			
34			
Subtotal			
Novella (200 points)			
Extra Credit (optional)	Divide by 36 for grade	Divide by 34 for grade	
Final Grade			

Preface

This course will teach you how to read well. Good readers read with a pen. One does not read unless one is marking up the text. Competent readers ask pertinent questions and predict as they read. For instance, when they read *The Yearling*, they will predict the ending. This skill will enhance comprehension. Furthermore, good readers look for the author's purpose, the intended audience, the development and support of the main idea, and the structure/coherence of the work. Finally, good readers read a lot.

This course will teach you how to write well. Great writers are always great readers. Writing is never easy. It is very difficult to do well. It takes planning, courage, and energy. I know this to be true—writing is my vocation. I am occasionally inspired when I write, and inspiration does make writing more pleasant, but it does not make it any easier to do. Writing is, and will always be, difficult for you to do well.

This book will teach you how to write. It will show you how to write with competency and inspiration. It will show you how to connect with your audience. Writing is not about making friends with your audience. Its main purpose is to communicate. Most of the writing you will be doing will be literary analysis. Literary analysis is literary criticism. They are the same.

What is literary criticism? Literary criticism is talking and writing about literature. Any literature, at any age. In that sense, literary analysis is a critical discussion of literature. To be "critical" is not necessarily to be "negative." It is to be intentional in one's evaluation of literature. Indeed, "evaluation" is the highest form of thoughtful analysis.

When children growing up read Margaret Wise Brown's *Runaway Bunny* and ask, "Do I like this book?" and "Why?" they are, in effect, analyzing the literary piece. They are doing literary criticism. As they get more adept, students ask, "Who are the central characters? What conflict do they face? Where is the climax? Is there a theme?" But further sophistication and advanced metacognition in no way diminishes the intentional, informed opinions of the most unsophisticated readers.

You will learn how to do all these things. Literary critics, no matter what their age, use a special "language" to talk about literature. For example, in *The Runaway Bunny* the protagonist (the main character), a little runaway bunny, is pursued by his loving mother, a mother bunny, an important foil (a character who develops the main character). The protagonist experiences several layers of internal conflict as he tries to escape his mother. Along the way, the author, Margaret Wise Brown, uses several setting changes to develop her characters. And so forth. Now readers have a way to discuss this literary work.

As you read great literature, you will find they share similar themes and plot patterns. For instance, as the mother bunny pursues her runaway, likewise God pursues Jonah (Book of Jonah). Different characters. Similar theme. Similar plot.

Finally, young people, learning to read and to write well is critical to the future. Literary analysis or criticism is the first cousin of Christian apologetics. Christian apologetics is the considered defense of Christian dogma, Scripture, and worldview. Learning to evaluate literature, literary analysis, prepares readers to be Christian apologists. After all, it is no coincidence that the greatest apologists are not theologians: they are English teachers! C. S. Lewis did not teach systematic theology: he taught literature.

Besides, literary analysis helps readers to evaluate and to reclaim the "metaphor." What I mean by metaphor is "a comparison between something completely different from something else." In literature, a metaphor enables readers to understand very difficult things by illustrating those things with other simple things more familiar to the audience. Christians desperately need to reclaim the metaphor! Again, a metaphor is a literary concept where the author compares a dissimilar thing to a similar thing so that readers will grasp the meaning and importance of the dissimilar thing. Jesus calls himself the "Good Shepherd." If readers and listeners grasp the importance and meaning of "Good Shepherd," they will be on the way to understanding the role of Jesus Christ. When Jesus spoke these metaphors, he knew that he was using images and concepts that were familiar to his agrarian, pastoral audience.

What we Christians need to do is to take age-old Christian dogmas of "faith," "love," "forgiveness," and especially "hope" and find contemporary metaphors to make these concepts come alive in our post-Christian, sorry world.

Fundamentally, literary criticism, then, will help readers reclaim the metaphor in their psyche, language, and writing. This will presage laudable outcomes in the kingdom of God. My goodness, it will presage laudable outcomes in the kingdom of man!

Therefore, amid so many competing media options, you must learn to analyze, to evaluate, to appreciate great literature. The propagation of the gospel will not be enhanced by how quickly we can appreciate and text messages to one another; however, it will be enhanced by how well we grasp the critical nuances of Bible stories. We cannot suppose that our unsaved world will grasp concepts like "love" and "faith" unless we have words, rhetoric, to tell them what these things are. If we learn how to do literary analysis well, we will be better able to create and to share vital truths to future generations.

Reading 1

"Elijah Confronts the Baals"

Chapter 1

First Thoughts

Communication is a very important part of every Christian's life. We need to do it well. We should write well, speak well, and read well. This first chapter introduces all these components.

Chapter Learning Objectives

In chapter 1 we will . . .

1. Understand and use nouns properly in sentences.
2. Compare spoken language to written language.
3. Implement reading strategies that will help you read better.
4. Analyze the characters in "Elijah Confronts the Baals."
5. Begin writing a novella.
6. List the characters in your novella.

Look Ahead for Friday

- Turn in all assignments.
- List and describe the characters in your novella.

Daily Assignment

- Warm-up: Pretend that you are King Ahab's advisor. What would you say? Use at least two proper nouns, two common nouns, and two collective nouns. (Read 1 Kings 18 if you need a refresher of the account.)
- Students will complete Concept Builder 1-A.
- Prayer journal: students are encouraged to write in their prayer journal every day.
- Finish the next book you have been assigned.
- Students should systematically review their vocabulary words daily.

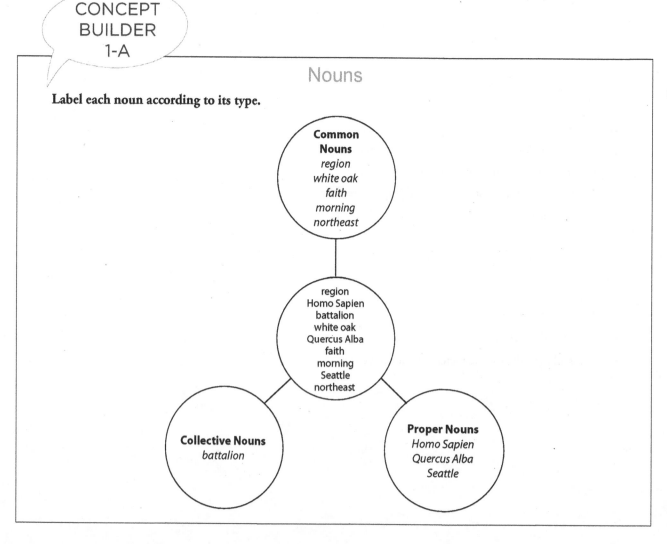

CONCEPT BUILDER 1-A

Nouns

Label each noun according to its type.

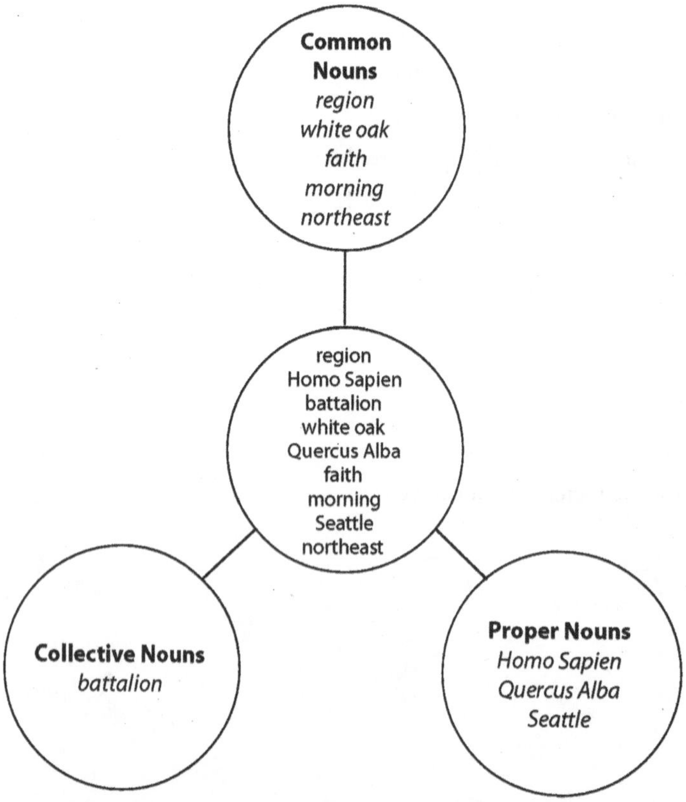

Identify examples of common, proper, and collective nouns in the sentence below.

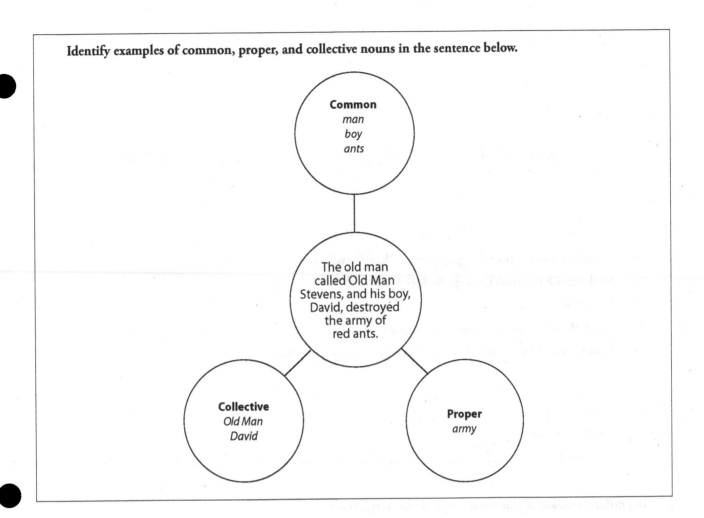

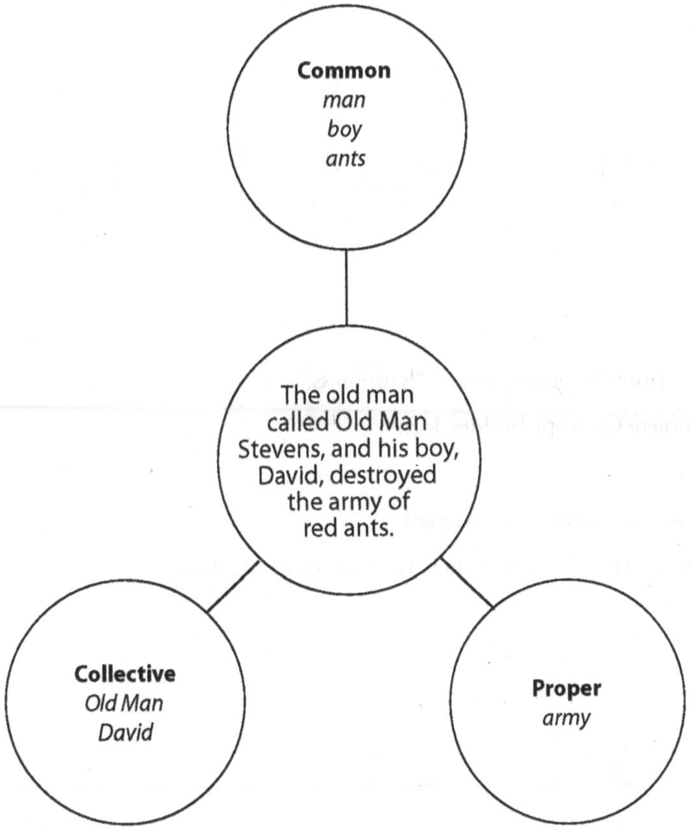

Writing Skills: Spoken Language vs. Word Language

Daily Assignment

- Warm-up: Using written language, define "happiness."
- Students will complete Concept Builder 1-B.
- Prayer journal
- Finish the next book you have been assigned.
- Students should systematically review their vocabulary words daily.

CONCEPT BUILDER 1-B

Nouns

Using different means of communication, define forgiveness.

Written Language

Understanding clemency

Picture

Answers will vary.

Lesson 3

Writing Skills: Reading Basics

Daily Assignment

- Warm-up: What is your favorite book? Why?
- Students will complete Concept Builder 1-C.
- Prayer journal: students are encouraged to write in their prayer journal every day.
- Finish the next book you have been assigned.
- Students should systematically review their vocabulary words daily.

CONCEPT BUILDER 1-C

Nouns

Describe Predestination to a five-year-old child in three ways:

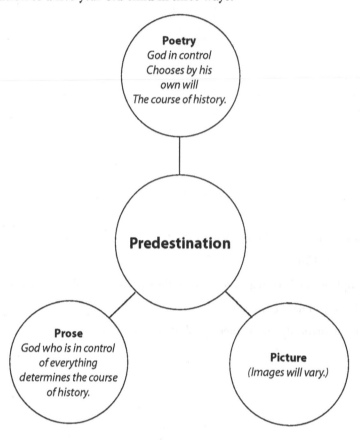

Predestination

Poetry
God in control
Chooses by his
own will
The course of history.

Prose
God who is in control of everything determines the course of history.

Picture
(Images will vary.)

Paraphrase this passage.

Surrounded by leviathan whales, ship crews will throw out a tub in order to divert the attention of their behemoth sentinels. The whales amuse themselves by tossing the tub into the air, as children do with a soccer ball. While their attention is diverted, the formerly endangered ships sail away. Hence, "Throwing a tub to the whales!" (James P. Stobaugh, *Growing Up White* (NY:Harvard Square Editions, 2014).

The author is describing how he distracts people from bigger problems he has by revealing to them smaller problems.

Writing a Novella: Characters in "Elijah Confronts the Baals" (1 Kings 18)

Daily Assignment

- Warm-up: Imagine you are King Ahab. Re-write the same story from his perspective.
- Students will complete Concept Builder 1-D.
- Prayer journal: students are encouraged to write in their prayer journal every day.
- Finish the next book you have been assigned.
- Students should systematically review their vocabulary words daily.

CONCEPT BUILDER 1-D

Reading Well

See passage in student book.

K What I KNOW	W What I WANT to Know	L What I LEARNED
This passage is about a group of people eating dinner together. In fact, the central theme is about the Last Supper.	*There is some tension here. Why? What will happen next?*	*Jesus is celebrating a common ritual meal — Passover — but adding a lot of new twists. These plot changes (e.g., washing the disciples' feet) are important symbolic gestures of Jesus' ministry now and in the future.*

Book Study:
Active Reading (1 Kings 18)

Daily Assignment

- Warm-up: The climax is the turning point in every story. If you had to identify a climax in your life, where and what would that climax be?
- Students will complete Concept Builder 1-E.
- Prayer journal: students are encouraged to write in their prayer journal every day.
- Finish the next book you have been assigned.
- Students should systematically review their vocabulary words daily.

How does the author increase suspense?
Elijah is going to his arch enemy to tell him that rain will fall!

How does he develop the main character Elijah?
We see that Elijah is a man who will not be thwarted by personal relationships or dangerous obstacles.

Discuss the relationship between Elijah and Ahab.
Ahab, while being reprehensible, is presented in a more sympathetic light than Jezebel.

How does the author increase the action and tension anticipating the climax?
So they shouted louder and slashed themselves with swords and spears, as was their custom, until their blood flowed.

Predict what will happen next.
Answers will vary.

CONCEPT BUILDER 1-E

Illustrated Book Review

Create an illustrated booklet using three of the most important scenes from 1 Samuel 18. Skim through the chapter to select the three most important scenes. Illustrate each by drawing, painting, or using magazine or computer pictures. On each page write a paragraph explaining why this is one of the most significant scenes in the account.

Answers will vary.

Chapter 1 Review Questions

Writing a Novella

You should decide upon which characters you will develop in your novella. Choose four or five. Identify the protagonist, one antagonist, and several foils. Write a brief description about each one.

Literary Analysis

Describe Obadiah's role in this biblical narrative.

Obadiah is a foil. His role is to develop Elijah. As Elijah comes, Obadiah disappears from history.

Biblical Application

Pretend that you are writing a sermon on 1 Kings 18. What theological points will you develop?

Answers will vary. Suggestions: Discuss the faithfulness and omnipotence of God.

Chapter 1 Test

Discussion Question (100 points)

Compare these two Bible passages to the Elijah passage (1 Kings 18).

Exodus 7:8–13

The LORD said to Moses and Aaron, "When Pharaoh says to you, 'Perform a miracle,' then say to Aaron, 'Take your staff and throw it down before Pharaoh,' and it will become a snake." So Moses and Aaron went to Pharaoh and did just as the LORD commanded. Aaron threw his staff down in front of Pharaoh and his officials, and it became a snake. Pharaoh then summoned wise men and sorcerers, and the Egyptian magicians also did the same things by their secret arts: Each one threw down his staff and it became a snake. But Aaron's staff swallowed up their staffs. Yet Pharaoh's heart became hard and he would not listen to them, just as the LORD had said.

1 Samuel 17:45–50

David said to the Philistine, "You come against me with sword and spear and javelin, but I come against you in the name of the LORD Almighty, the God of the armies of Israel, whom you have defied. This day the LORD will deliver you into my hands, and I'll strike you down and cut off your head. This very day I will give the carcasses of the Philistine army to the birds and the wild animals, and the whole world will know that there is a God in Israel. All those gathered here will know that it is not by sword or spear that the LORD saves; for the battle is the LORD's, and he will give all of you into our hands." As the Philistine moved closer to attack him, David ran quickly toward the battle line to meet him. Reaching into his bag and taking out a stone, he slung it and struck the Philistine on the forehead. The stone sank into his forehead, and he fell facedown on the ground. So David triumphed over the Philistine with a sling and a stone; without a sword in his hand he struck down the Philistine and killed him.

	Plot (Story)	Theme(s)	Setting
1 Kings 18	A moody prophet reveals the apostasy of Israel.		
Exodus 17	Moses confronts Pharaoh and God frees the people.		
1 Samuel 17	A young, unspectacular boy kills Israel's opponent and saves the nation.		

Chapter 1 Test Answer Sample

	Plot (Story)	Theme(s)	Setting
1 Kings 18	A moody prophet reveals the apostasy of Israel.	*All passages exhibit a courageous man of God facing a much more powerful opponent. God intervenes and helps the hero win.*	*Elijah faces the Baals and King Ahab in the divided Kingdom.*
Exodus 17	Moses confronts Pharaoh and God frees the people.	⇩	*Moses frees the Israelites from captivity under Pharaoh.*
1 Samuel 17	A young, unspectacular boy kills Israel's opponent and saves the nation.	*All three passages offer a didactic lesson that God is powerful and good and that He will deliver His people.*	*This passage occurs during the reign of King Saul.*

Reading 2

"Elijah Confronts the Baals"

Chapter 2

First Thoughts

We will focus on characterization and how it is used in literature, specifically, the story of Elijah confronting the Baals.

Chapter Learning Objectives

In chapter 2 we will . . .

1. Work to understand the concepts for protagonist, antagonist, internal conflict, external conflict.
2. Discuss protagonists who change.
3. Analyze nonpersonal antagonists.
4. Implement what you learned in your novella.

Look Ahead for Friday

- Turn in all assignments
- Work on your characters this week

Novella: Developing a Robust Protagonist

Daily Assignment

- Warm-up: Describe three well-developed protagonists in the Bible.
- Students will complete Concept Builder 2-A.
- Prayer journal: students are encouraged to write in their prayer journal every day.
- Finish the next book you have been assigned.
- Students should systematically review their vocabulary words daily.

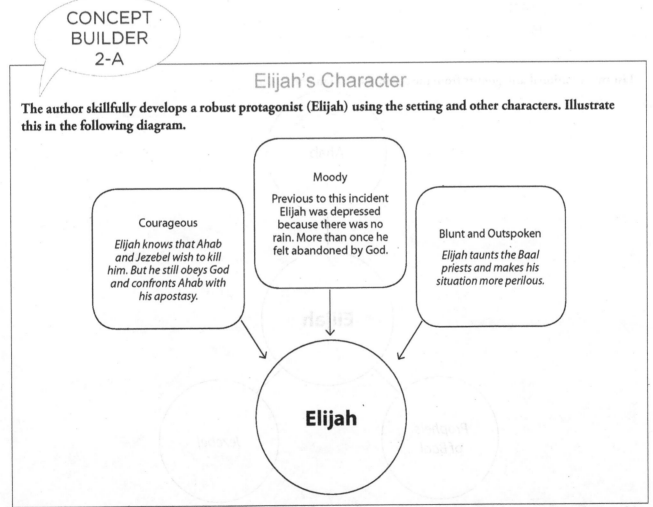

CONCEPT BUILDER 2-A

Elijah's Character

The author skillfully develops a robust protagonist (Elijah) using the setting and other characters. Illustrate this in the following diagram.

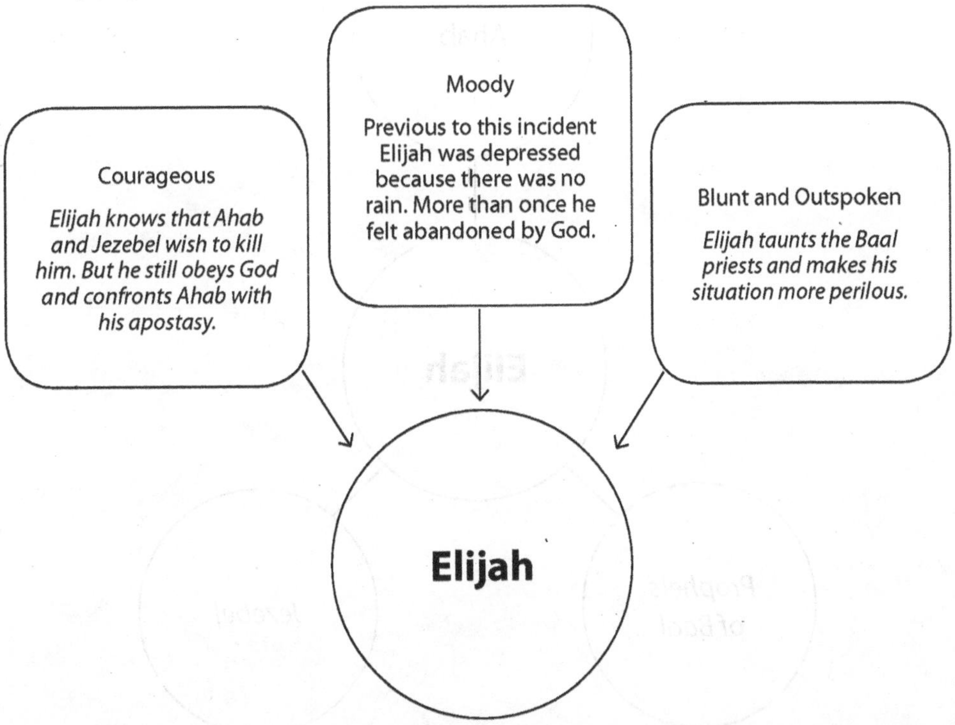

Moody
Previous to this incident Elijah was depressed because there was no rain. More than once he felt abandoned by God.
Courageous
Elijah knows that Ahab and Jezebel wish to kill him. But he still obeys God and confronts Ahab with his apostasy.
Blunt and Outspoken
Elijah taunts the Baal priests and makes his situation more perilous.
Elijah

Lesson 2

Antagonists

Daily Assignment

- Warm-up: Describe a scary antagonist from a movie you've seen.
- Students will complete Concept Builder 2-B.
- Prayer journal: students are encouraged to write in their prayer journal every day.
- Finish the next book you have been assigned.
- Students should systematically review their vocabulary words daily.

CONCEPT BUILDER 2-B

Antagonists

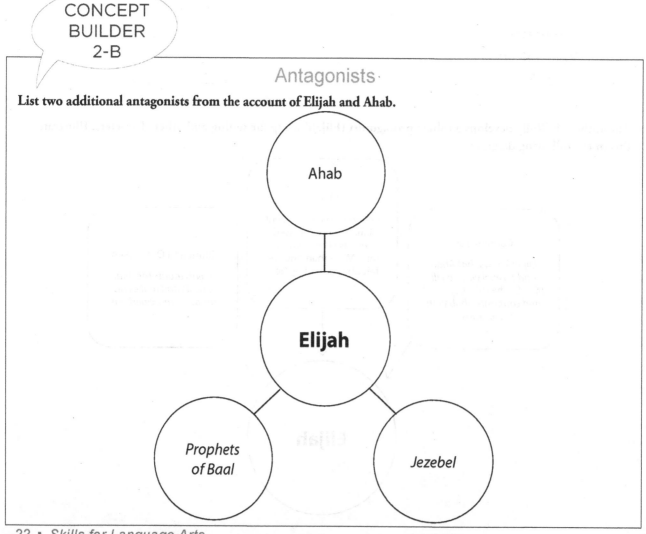

List two additional antagonists from the account of Elijah and Ahab.

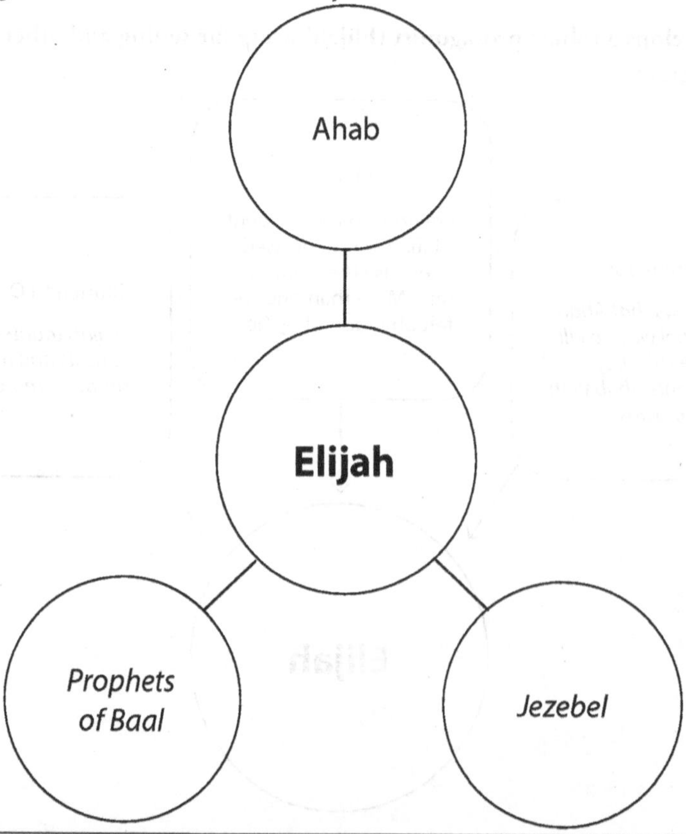

Obadiah: A Vital Foil

Daily Assignment

- Warm-up: How is John the Baptist a foil in the gospel story?
- Students will complete Concept Builder 2-C.
- Prayer journal: students are encouraged to write in their prayer journal every day.
- Finish the next book you have been assigned.
- Students should systematically review their vocabulary words daily.

CONCEPT BUILDER 2-C

Foils

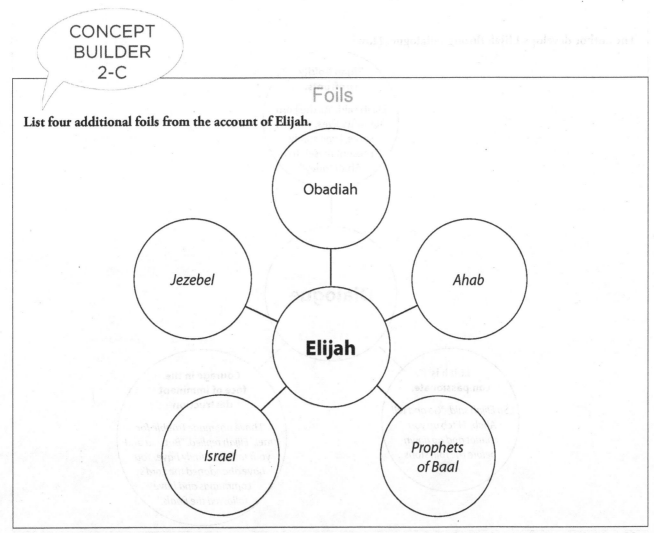

List four additional foils from the account of Elijah.

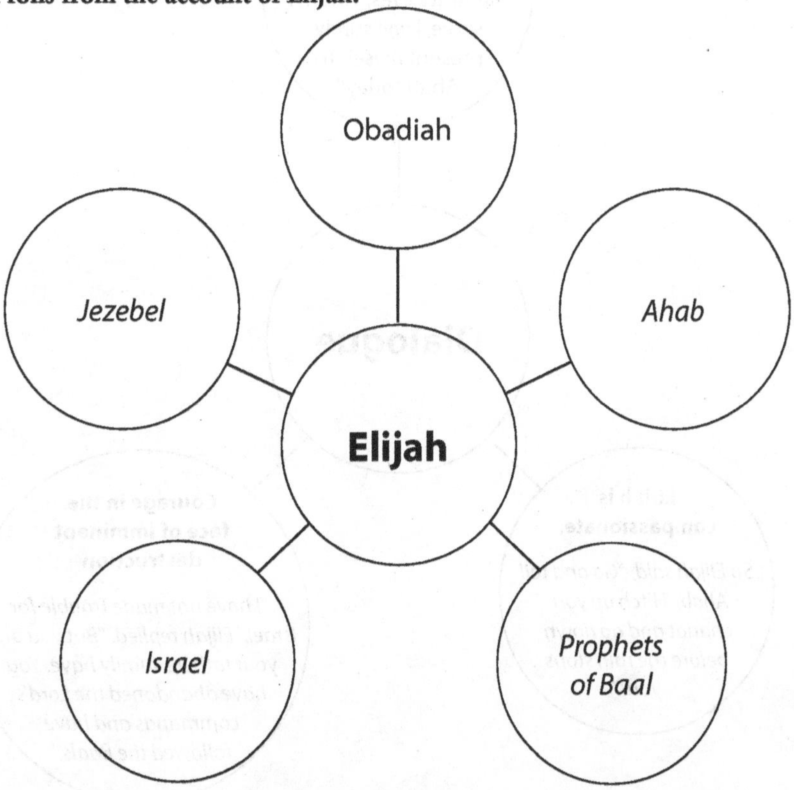

Lesson 4

Protagonists Who Change

Daily Assignment

- Warm-up: Describe a friend or family member who changed over time.
- Students will complete Concept Builder 2-D.
- Prayer journal: students are encouraged to write in their prayer journal every day.
- Finish the next book you have been assigned.
- Students should systematically review their vocabulary words daily.

CONCEPT BUILDER 2-D

Dialogue

The author develops Elijah through dialogue. How?

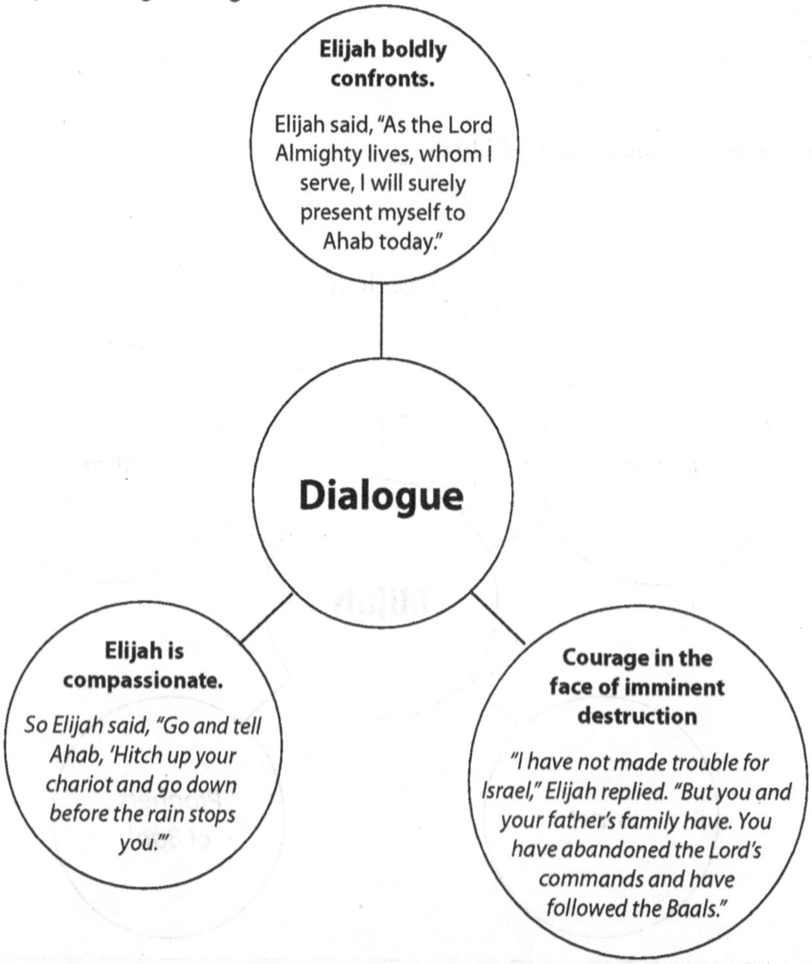

Elijah boldly confronts.
Elijah said, "As the Lord Almighty lives, whom I serve, I will surely present myself to Ahab today."
Dialogue
Elijah is compassionate.
So Elijah said, "Go and tell Ahab, 'Hitch up your chariot and go down before the rain stops you.'"
Courage in the face of imminent destruction
"I have not made trouble for Israel," Elijah replied. "But you and your father's family have. You have abandoned the Lord's commands and have followed the Baals."

Lesson 5

Nonpersonal Antagonists

Daily Assignment

- Warm-up: Describe someone you know who had to endure nonpersonal obstacles.
- Students will complete Concept Builder 2-E.
- Prayer journal: students are encouraged to write in their prayer journal every day.
- Finish the next book you have been assigned.
- Students should systematically review their vocabulary words daily.

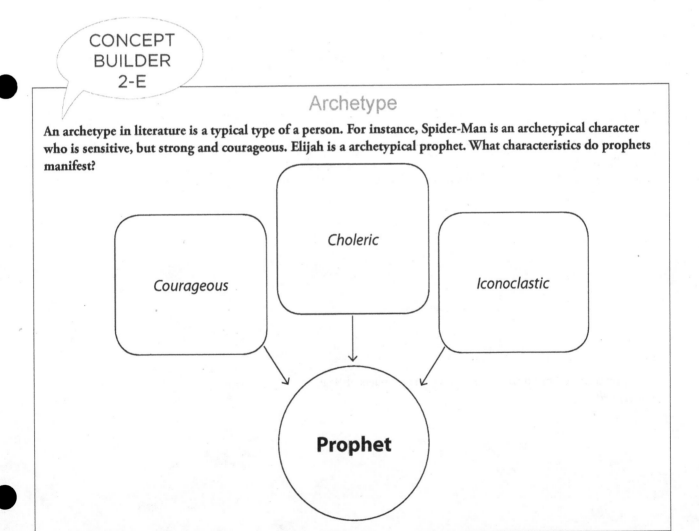

CONCEPT BUILDER 2-E

Archetype

An archetype in literature is a typical type of a person. For instance, Spider-Man is an archetypical character who is sensitive, but strong and courageous. Elijah is a archetypical prophet. What characteristics do prophets manifest?

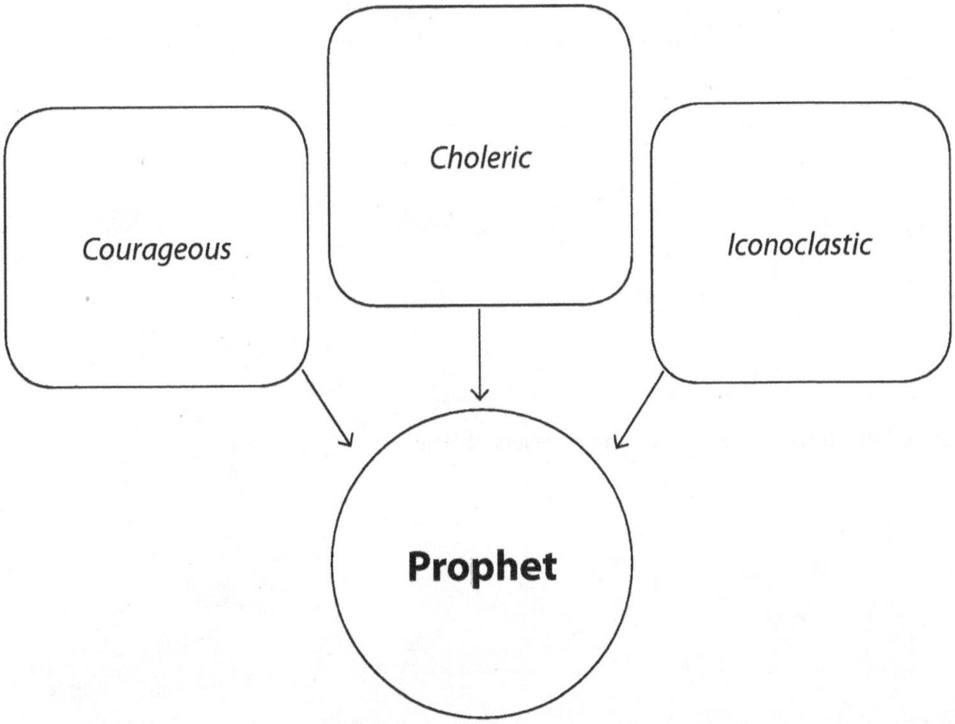

Chapter 2 Review Questions

Writing a Novella

First, you will list and develop your characters. Who is your protagonist? Antagonist? Foils? Describe each one carefully, making sure that readers clearly know who these characters are. Notice the way a novel I wrote introduces an important foil:

> Anna descended with a certainty in Providence that gave her gait a strong assurance — there was no creak on the stairs when she descended. Anna approached the new day with more than a modicum of caution though. She was unwilling to commit to unbridled optimism until she identified and measured the obstacles before her and the resources that she could marshal to meet them. Anna was disinclined to embrace luck, or chance, for my careful wife did not believe in such things. Her God controlled her future and He would show her the path to follow this new day. She trusted her God, but her husband, Jake Stevens, was an entirely different matter. God only knew what he would do, especially on his birthday.

Readers learn a lot about this important character, Anna, by these descriptions and narrative insights. We know that Anna is a careful, godly woman. She loves and trusts God but not necessarily her husband. Since her husband is the narrator, this makes this passage humorous.

Literary Analysis

Jezebel and Ahab are two of the most despicable characters in Scripture. How does the author of 1 Kings develop these villains?
Like Macbeth, Ahab is manipulated and controlled by Jezebel. She is a ruthless, vindictive, godless ruler.

Biblical Application

Does God seem too harsh when He destroys the prophets of Baal?
Answers will vary.

Chapter 2 Test

Matching (40 points)

A. Protagonist	_____ Elijah
B. Foil	_____ King Ahab
C. Antagonist	_____ Obadiah
D. Non-Personal Antagonist	_____ God
	_____ Baals
	_____ Fire

Letter (60 points total)

In spite of recent triumphs, Elijah is discouraged. Write him a letter encouraging him. Your letter will be evaluated in these three areas:

- Syntax and diction: grammar and style (10 points)
- Organization: paragraphs, transitions, introduction, et al. (20 points)
- Argument (30 points)

Chapter 2 Test Answer Sample

Matching (40 points)

A. Protagonist	*A*	Elijah
B. Foil	*C*	King Ahab
C. Antagonist	*B*	Obadiah
D. Non-Personal Antagonist	*B*	God
	C	Baals
	D	Fire

Letter (60 points total)

In spite of recent triumphs, Elijah is discouraged. Write him a letter encouraging him. Your letter will be evaluated in these three areas:

- Syntax and diction: grammar and style (10 points)
- Organization: paragraphs, transitions, introduction, et al. (20 points)
- Argument (30 points)

Answers will vary.

Reading 3

"Elijah Confronts the Baals"

Chapter 3

First Thoughts

Nouns as well as sentences are the building blocks of writing. Writing is difficult; good writing is very difficult. We will spend all year improving our writing. It begins as we grasp the fundamentals of the writing process.

Chapter Learning Objectives

In chapter 3 we will . . .

1. Recognize different uses of gerunds.
2. Identify different sentences.
3. Write with clarity.
4. Understand and implement the SQ3R Reading Strategy.
5. Outline the plot of your novella.

Look Ahead for Friday

- Turn in all assignments
- Outline the plot in your novella

Lesson 1

Grammar Review: Gerunds

Daily Assignment

- Warm-up: Write a paragraph with a gerund used as a subject, direct object, predicate nominative, and object of a preposition.
- Students will complete Concept Builder 3-A.
- Prayer journal: students are encouraged to write in their prayer journal every day.
- Finish the next book you have been assigned.
- Students should systematically review their vocabulary words daily.

CONCEPT BUILDER 3-A

Match

Match

A. Gerund used as a subject	1. *B* You really should stop running in the house.
B. Gerund used as a direct object	2. *A* Running is great exercise.
C. Gerund used as a predicate nominative	3. *D* Compare this to running.
D. Gerund used as an object of a preposition	4. *C* You are faking.

Writing Skills: Sentences

Daily Assignment

- Warm-up: Write a paragraph or two using declarative, interrogative, imperative, and exclamatory sentences.
- Students will complete Concept Builder 3-B.
- Prayer journal: students are encouraged to write in their prayer journal every day.
- Finish the next book you have been assigned.
- Students should systematically review their vocabulary words daily.

CONCEPT BUILDER 3-B

Sentence Building

Rewrite this paragraph with at least one example of a declarative, interrogative, and exclamatory sentence.

Around the time of the Great Flood (2347 B.C.), mankind stopped merely herding sheep and guarding cattle, and settled into small, farming communities. The first place this settlement occurred was in the Tigris and Euphrates River Valley. This development marked the genesis of culture, or that which separates human beings from other species. Art, literature, science, and mathematics emerged from these agrarian communities. Before long, with improved agrarian methods (e.g., the invention of the plow) and improved transportation, cities, like Babylon, were formed. Great masses of people could live in these relatively comfortable and safe places. Farmers provided food; craftsmen provided goods; and priests provided succor to the soul. Agricultural societies, by their nature, were also more cognizant of time. They formed the "week," the first artificial division of time that was not based on natural phenomenon (e.g., the month was based on phases of the moon). With basic needs met, mankind began to look to the cosmos to find answers about critical things like birth and death, fate and peace. Only the Hebrews, neighbors to the southwest, really found the answer, but that did not stop Mesopotamian sages from searching. (James Stobaugh, *Studies in World History, Vol. 1*, Master Books, p. 9).

*What important event happened around the time of the Great Flood (2347 B.C.)? (**interrogative**) Man stopped merely herding sheep and guarding cattle, and settled into small, farming communities. (**declarative**) The first place this settlement occurred was in the Tigris and Euphrates River Valley. This development marked the genesis of culture, or that which separates human beings from other species. Art, literature, science, and mathematics emerged from these agrarian communities. Before long, with improved agrarian methods (e.g., the invention of the plow) and improved transportation, cities like Babylon were formed. Great masses of people could live in these relatively comfortable and safe places. Farmers provided food; craftsmen provided goods; and priests provided succor for the soul. Agricultural societies, by their nature, were also more cognizant of time. They formed the "week," the first artificial division of time that was not based on natural phenomenon (e.g., the month was based on phases of the moon). With basic needs met, mankind began to look to the cosmos to find answers about critical things like birth and death, fate and peace. Only the Hebrews, neighbors to the southwest, really found the answer, but that did not stop Mesopotamians from searching! (**exclamatory**)*

Lesson 3

Writing Skills: Sentence Clarity

Daily Assignment

- Warm-up: Explain to a child something about your favorite games and sports.
- Students will complete Concept Builder 3-C.
- Prayer journal: students are encouraged to write in their prayer journal every day.
- Finish the next book you have been assigned.
- Students should systematically review their vocabulary words daily.

CONCEPT BUILDER 3-C

Sentence Order

In order to improve the clarity of your paragraph, place these sentences in the order in which they should occur.

3 Grace is unmerited favor.

2 When you are forgiven for something you did wrong, and you do not deserve it, it is grace.

1 Did you do something very wrong and you were caught?

4 The Bible teaches us that grace is a gift from God, undeserved and freely given.

Place the following paragraphs in the right order:

4 Jim's descriptions add much suspense by showing his own experience with the captain. They show that he could feel it all around him. He doesn't specifically describe suspense but instead describes what causes it. "He was a very silent man by custom. All day he hung round the cove or upon the cliffs with a brass telescope; all evening he sat in a corner of the parlour next the fire and drank rum and water very strong. He had taken me aside one day and promised me a silver fourpenny on the first of every month if I would only keep my 'weather-eye open for a seafaring man with one leg' and let him know the moment he appeared."

1 In chapter 1 of *Treasure Island*, Robert Lewis Stevenson uses dialogue, setting, and Jim Hawkins's descriptions to develop suspense that lasts through the whole book. Jim is not just scared, he and other characters in the story can feel the suspense like a heavy cloud hanging over them.

5 Stevenson, in just one chapter, uses setting, dialogue and other methods to create suspense that amplifies the adventure throughout *Treasure Island.*

3 He also uses dialogue between the captain and Jim's father to show how mysterious and strange a character the captain is. He reveals very little about himself and is happy to keep it that way. He is plain and straightforward, giving Jim's father no unnecessary information, yet speaking in a way that shows he has things to hide. "'This is a handy cove,' says he at length; 'and a pleasant sittyated grog-shop. Much company, mate?' My father told him no, very little company, the more was the pity. 'Well, then,' said he, 'this is the berth for me.'"

2 "And hearing ours well-spoken of, I suppose, and described as lonely, had chosen it from the others for his place of residence. And that was all we could learn of our guest." Stevenson uses the setting of the lonely Admiral Benbow Inn to create a sense of mystery. It leads to questions that make a suspenseful storyline such as: Why does the captain want to stay at a lonely inn? What does he have to hide? Why is he avoiding other "seafaring men"?

Lesson 4

Reading Skills: SQ3R

Daily Assignment

- Warm-up: Assuming that the above passage ("With strong purpose . . .") is the beginning of a book, write the next page.
- Students will complete Concept Builder 3-D.
- Prayer journal: students are encouraged to write in their prayer journal every day.
- Finish the next book you have been assigned.
- Students should systematically review their vocabulary words daily.

CONCEPT BUILDER 3-D

Using the SQ3R Technique

Employ the SQ3R technique in this passage:

An economy consists of the economic system of a nation or other political entity. An economy includes labor, capital (money), and land resources. It also includes the manufacturing, trade, and consumption of goods and services. Goods and services are exchanged according to demand and supply between participants by barter or a money exchange with a credit value accepted within the contracted groups.

The economy involves all aspects of a society: history and social organization, as well as its geography and natural resources. These factors give context to a developing economy and they set the conditions and parameters in which an economy functions.

Much of what we think of as human history inevitably revolves around agriculture. It is mostly farmers who build cities, write books, and develop culture. Sometime before the Great Flood, Mesopotamia evolved into an agrarian society (a society of farmers).

Farmers develop a concept of time, a concept of "the week." The week, contrasted to the concept of a "month" (which is based on the stages of the moon), is an entirely human constructed phenomenon. Weeks were started or stopped by religious events, market days, and other non-agrarian events.

Agriculture spawned ancillary economies such as cottage industries (small entities that produced products in their homes) and a religious class. Agriculture and improved transportation enabled cities separated from adjacent farms to emerge.

Agricultural societies were usually very religious and were very focused on male leadership. Men ruled agricultural societies.

Farming communities had much higher birth and survival rates than nomadic, herding communities. It is estimated that only 5 to 8 million people lived when the Great Flood struck. When farming began in earnest, around 1600 B.C., world population mushroomed to 60 to 70 million people [see Peter N. Stearns, *World History in Brief* (NY: Pearson Publishing Co., 2010), pp. 13-14.].

Survey: *Clearly this is an essay about the concept "economy."*

Question: *How do economies affect human society? How did different economies emerge?*

Read: *A few challenging vocabulary words include "ancillary" and "nomadic."*

Recite: *As nomads gained new technologies (e.g., the plow), they settled down and became farmers. This had a very positive impact on society.*

Review: *After the Great Flood, more and more cities emerged because people learned how to grow food in stable agricultural communities.*

Lesson 5

Writing a Novella: Plot in "Elijah Confronts the Baals"

Daily Assignment

- Warm-up: What defining crisis has helped form you into the person you are?
- Students will complete Concept Builder 3-E.
- Prayer journal: students are encouraged to write in their prayer journal every day.
- Finish the next book you have been assigned.
- Students should systematically review their vocabulary words daily.

CONCEPT BUILDER 3-E

The Plot

Identify different components of the plot in Elijah's account.

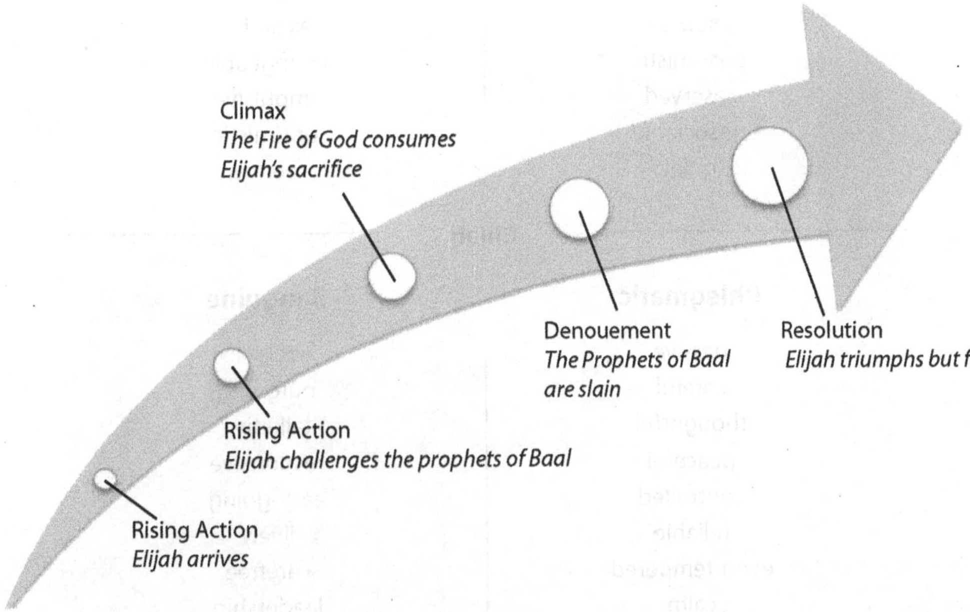

Climax
The Fire of God consumes Elijah's sacrifice
Denouement
The Prophets of Baal are slain
Resolution
Elijah triumphs but flees
Rising Action
Elijah challenges the prophets of Baal
Rising Action
Elijah arrives

Chapter 3 Review Questions

Writing a Novella

You should roughly outline your novella. Use this outline:

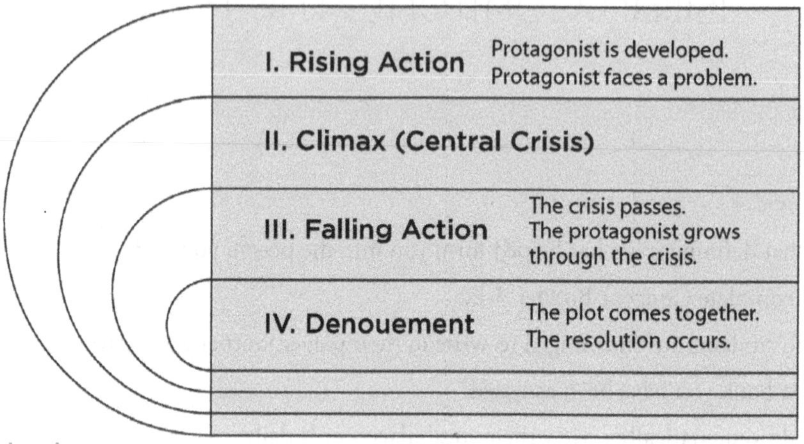

I. Rising Action
Protagonist is developed.
Protagonist faces a problem.
II. Climax (Central Crisis)
III. Falling Action
The crisis passes.
The protagonist grows through the crisis.
IV. Denouement
The plot comes together.
The resolution occurs.

Literary Analysis

Analyze Elijah. Circle words below that describe him. Which category captures his personality?

A. Choleric
B. Melancholic
C. Sanguine
D. Phlegmatic

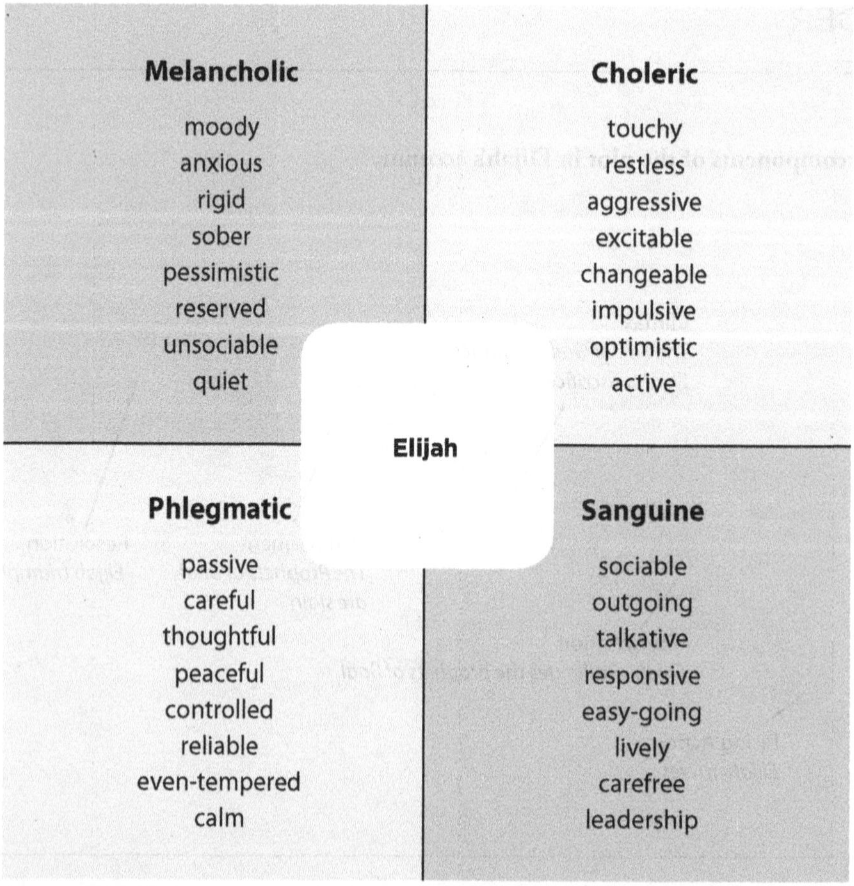

Biblical Application

Both Jezebel and Ahab are very "modern" in their faith expression. Explain.

They are both "good" Jewish believers and "good" Baal worshipers. They pursue at least two politically correct paths to God — but it does not work, of course, and they appear foolish and manipulative.

Chapter 3 Test

ESSAY (100 POINTS TOTAL)

I. Circle words that describe Elijah. Box words that describe Jezebel. What does this tell you about these sworn enemies?

Character

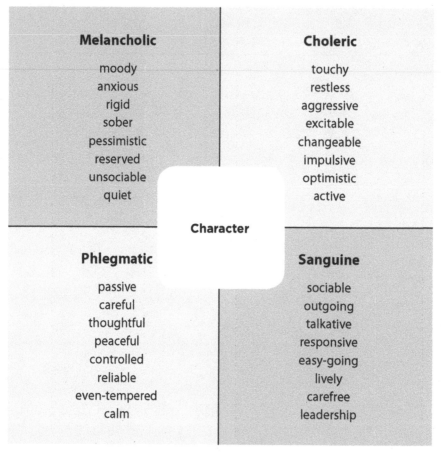

Melancholic	**Choleric**
moody	touchy
anxious	restless
rigid	aggressive
sober	excitable
pessimistic	changeable
reserved	impulsive
unsociable	optimistic
quiet	active
Phlegmatic	**Sanguine**
passive	sociable
careful	outgoing
thoughtful	talkative
peaceful	responsive
controlled	easy-going
reliable	lively
even-tempered	carefree
calm	leadership

II. Take the same box and star words that describe your novella protagonist.

III. Take the same box and check words that describe your personality.

IV Now write a one-page essay comparing Elijah, Jezebel, your novella protagonist, and yourself. What did you learn about each character?

Your essay will be evaluated in these three areas:

- Syntax and diction: grammar and style (25 points)
- Organization: paragraphs, transitions, introduction, et al. (25 points)
- Argument (50 points)

Chapter 3 Test Answer Sample

I–IV. Answers will vary.

Composition Evaluation

Based on 100 points: 85/B

I. Grammar and Syntax: Is the composition grammatically correct?

(25 points) Comments: 25/25 Rarely use first person and never use second person. Your diction and syntax are excellent.

II. Organization: Does this composition exhibit well-considered organization? Does it flow? Transitions? Introduction and a conclusion?

(25 points) Comments: 20/25 See comments. Use transitions. Restate your argument as the essay develops. Your introduction was excellent. Conclusion was bad — a summary would be safer. Focus on one topic, one argument, and one thesis.

III. Content: Does this composition answer the question, argue the point well, and/or persuade the reader?

(50 points) 40/50

Reading 1

The Yearling, by Marjorie Rawlings

Chapter 4

First Thoughts

Every sentence must have a verb. Sentences, composed with verbs, are at the heart of all writing. Sentences, though, need to be written carefully and correctly. As you write better and better, you develop a common sense about sentences that helps you recognize, and then correct mistakes. Finally, our novella has characters who are living in a story or plot. Now we will examine which narrative point of view to choose to write this novella.

Chapter Learning Objectives

In chapter 4 we will . . .

1. Understand, identify, and use active and passive voice verb forms.
2. Identify number and agreement in verbs.
3. Understand and choose a point of view narration for your novella.
4. Actively read the first chapter of *The Yearling*.

Look Ahead for Friday

- Turn in all assignments
- Outline the plot in your novella

Grammar Review: Verbs

Daily Assignment

- Warm-up: Write a paragraph using two action verbs that have actions you cannot see.
- Students will complete Concept Builder 4-A.
- Prayer journal: students are encouraged to write in their prayer journal every day.
- Finish the next book you have been assigned.
- Students should systematically review their vocabulary words daily.

CONCEPT BUILDER 4-A

Match

Match these collective nouns and verbs. Collective nouns are normally used with plural verbs when you refer to individual parts acting separately, or singular verbs when they are used as a group. For example, "The team disagree among themselves about the issue" or "The team agrees about the issue."

1. The audience (*speaks*) with one voice on the issue.
2. The public (*argue*) about the very important tax question.
3. The army (*needs*) new recruits.
4. The jury (*argue*) among themselves.
5. The swarm of bees (*attacks*) the lion.

Choose the correct form of the verb.

1. Mathematics (*is*) my favorite subject.
2. My chief worry (*is*) my growing debt.
3. My family (*disagree*) about where to take their vacation.
4. *Great Expectations* (*is*) a great novel.
5. Mom and Dad (*are*) coming.
6. Neither Mom nor Dad (*is*) coming.
7. One hundred dollars (*is*) a lot to pay for shoes.
8. Every player on our team (*is*) vital to our success.
9. One problem with friends (*is*) how to spend time with all of them.
10. Neither my dad nor my four siblings (*are*) ready to leave.

Grammar: More Verbs

Daily Assignment

- Warm-up: In the book you are reading, *The Yearling*, the protagonist (main character) matures throughout the novel. Using only active voice verbs, describe a defining moment that matured you.
- Students will complete Concept Builder 4-B.
- Prayer journal: students are encouraged to write in their prayer journal every day.
- Finish the next book you have been assigned.
- Students should systematically review their vocabulary words daily.

CONCEPT BUILDER 4-B

Active Voice

Rewrite this essay with active voice only.

If we were asked to name the most interesting country in the world, I suppose most people would say Israel — above all because it was the birthplace of Christ, not because there is anything in the geography so very noteworthy, as it isn't very large, and a good portion is desert, but because of all the great things that have happened there. But after Israel, Egypt would be my choice. For one thing, the story of Joseph in the Old Testament and Moses who brought Israel out of Egypt into the Promised Land is linked to it. Egypt is a wondrous land. Our imaginations are populated by powerful pharaohs, exotic plants, deadly snakes, and mighty pyramids.

If we were asked to name the most interesting country in the world, I suppose most people would say Israel — not because there is anything in the geography so very noteworthy, as it isn't very large, and a good portion is desert, but because of all the great things that have happened there, and above all because it was the birthplace of Christ. But after Israel, Egypt would be my choice. For one thing, it is linked to the story of Joseph in the Old Testament, and Moses brought Israel out of Egypt into the Promised Land. Egypt is a wondrous land. Powerful pharaohs, exotic plants, deadly snakes, and mighty pyramids all populate our imaginations.

Lesson 3

Writing Skills: Sentence Common Sense

Daily Assignment

- Warm-up: Write a run-on sentence about a summer vacation you remember.
- Students will complete Concept Builder 4-C.
- Prayer journal: students are encouraged to write in their prayer journal every day.
- Finish the next book you have been assigned.
- Students should systematically review their vocabulary words daily.

CONCEPT BUILDER 4-C

Making Sense

Correct these sentences:

1. In Sunday school class we are studying Genesis Mr. Smith is my teacher.
   Mr. Smith, my Sunday school teacher, is leading a study on Genesis.

2. The phonograph was invented by Edison. A great inventor.
   Edison, a great inventor, invented the phonograph.

3. I don't know how to cook a pie. Without ruining the crust.
   I can't cook a pie without ruining the crust.

4. My automobile can drive in all sorts of weather. Including a snowstorm.
   My automobile can drive in all sorts of weather including a snowstorm.

5. Louis Pasteur discovered that germs cause disease. Including how to kill them too.
   Louis Pasteur discovered that germs cause disease and then he discovered how to kill them.

Lesson 4

Point of View

Daily Assignment

- Warm-up: Most of the story *The Yearling* is told from Jody's perspective. Is he a reliable source? Can readers believe his viewpoint?
- Students will complete Concept Builder 4-D.
- Prayer journal: students are encouraged to write in their prayer journal every day.
- Finish the next book you have been assigned.
- Students should systematically review their vocabulary words daily.

CONCEPT BUILDER 4-D

Point of View

Identify the point of view of each passage.

D First Person Narration	A. Penny Baxter was at the wood-pile. He still wore the coat of the broadcloth suit that he had been married in, that he now wore as badge of his gentility when he went to church, or off trading. The sleeves were too short, not because Penny had grown, but because the years of hanging through the summer dampness, and being pressed with the smoothing iron and pressed again, had somehow shrunk the fabric. Jody saw his father's hands, big for the rest of him, close around a bundle of wood.
A Objective Third Person	B. Penny Baxter was at the wood-pile. He still wore the coat of the broadcloth suit that he had been married in, that he now wore as badge of his gentility when he went to church, or off trading. He knew that the sleeves were too short, not because he had grown, but because the years of hanging through the summer dampness, and being pressed with the smoothing iron and pressed again, had somehow shrunk the fabric. Jody thought the same thing when he saw his father's hands, big for the rest of him, close around a bundle of wood.
C Limited Omniscient Narration	C. Penny Baxter was at the wood-pile. He still wore the coat of the broadcloth suit that he had been married in, that he now wore as badge of his gentility when he went to church, or off trading. He knew that the sleeves were too short, not because he had grown, but because the years of hanging through the summer dampness, and being pressed with the smoothing iron and pressed again, had somehow shrunk the fabric. Jody saw his father's hands, big for the rest of him, close around a bundle of wood.
B Omniscient Narration	D. I was at the wood-pile. I still wore the coat of the broadcloth suit that he had been married in, that I now wore as badge of his gentility when I went to church, or off trading. The sleeves were too short, not because I had grown, but because the years of hanging through the summer dampness, and being pressed with the smoothing iron and pressed again, had somehow shrunk the fabric. Jody saw my hands, big for the rest of me, close around a bundle of wood.

Book Study: Active Reading

The Yearling by Margorie Rawlings

Chapter I

Why would Rawlings start her novel with an image from nature and then place an unknown boy, Jody, in this setting?
The setting is a powerful force in this novel. It is the place where Jody finds Fawn, and ultimately its demand is Fawn's undoing. But nature is not a malevolent force. It is a place of wonder and of life. Jody is only one character, albeit an important one, in the drama that will unfold.

What is the literary purpose of Old Julia?
This old dog suggests that there are things that are immutable (unchangeable), but of course that is not true, as Jody discovers.

Predict the ending of this novel.
Answers will vary.

Daily Assignment

- Warm-up: Do you think that Jody Baxter's parents are too strict?
- Students will complete Concept Builder 4-E.
- Prayer journal: students are encouraged to write in their prayer journal every day.
- Finish the next book you have been assigned.
- Students should systematically review their vocabulary words daily.

CONCEPT BUILDER 4-E

Internal Conflict

Jody experiences a lot of internal conflict, especially when Flag dies. When you develop your characters for your novella, be sure and provide a lot of internal conflict. It is a great way to build the interest of your readers. Name a character from a story you know or have written, and four losses they suffered.

Answers will vary.

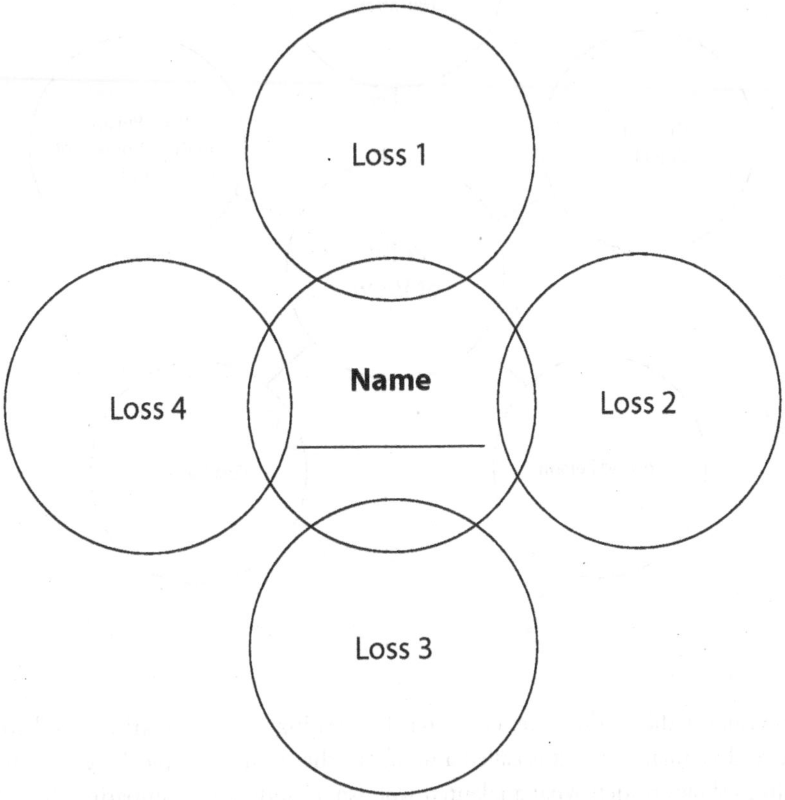

Chapter 4 Review Questions

Writing a Novella

What point of view will you employ in your novella? Why? Write one chapter at least this week.

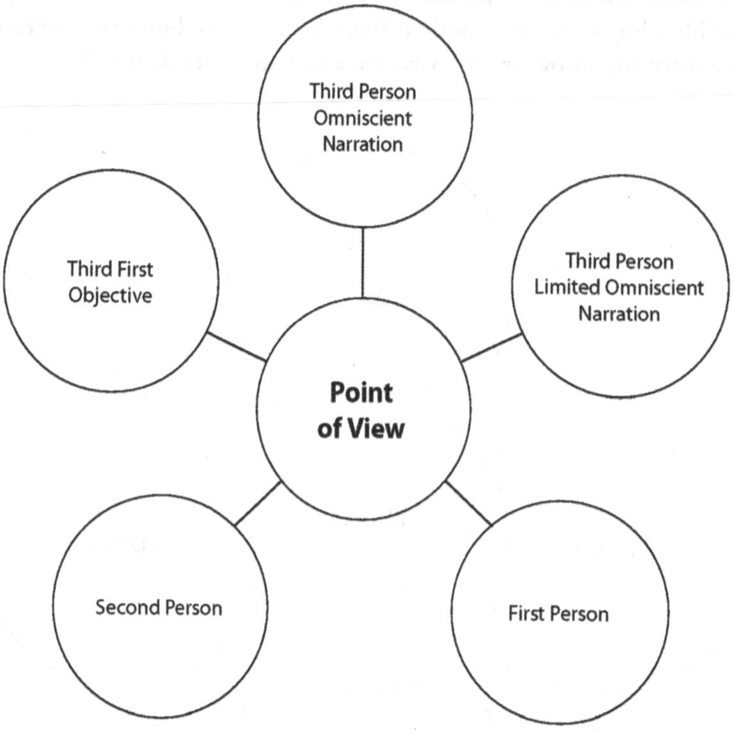

Literary Analysis

Rawlings helps readers visualize the world of her characters by creating vivid comparisons. When the words *like* or *as* are used to compare two dissimilar things it is called a *simile*. In the simile example, "He . . . cut a twig as even as a polished pencil," Rawlings shows readers what a talented woodsman Jody is by comparing the twig that he cut to a pencil. Rawlings also uses *personification*. Personification is figurative language in which an idea or inanimate object is given human characteristics, as in "The dusky glen laid cool hands on him." Jody's dogs "watched after him indifferently. They were a sorry pair, he thought, good for nothing but the chase, the catch and the kill. They had no interest in him except when he brought them their plates of table scraps night and morning." Dogs are not "indifferent." People are. And so forth. Would you like to live close to Jody? Why or why not?

Jody lived in a rural area in an innocent, carefree era. I would love to live where he lived!

Biblical Application

Write a eulogy for Flag.

Answers will vary.

Chapter 4 Test

Grammar (25 points)

I. Circle the linking verbs in the following sentences.

A. I am a teacher.

B. I appear to be sick.

C. You were not ready!

D. They seem to be nearly finished.

E. The soldiers are brave.

II. Identify the point of view in these passages (25 points)

A. First Person	_____ Over the years, though, Margaret grew comfortable with her God. And that was all right too. They talked to each other and no doubt they loved each other, but practically speaking, she now wondered what sort of relationship that they had. Compatibility, though, did not inevitably lead to passion. And that was what she felt toward her God now: passion.
B. Third Person Objective	_____ Over the years, though, Margaret appeared to grow comfortable with her God. And that was all right too. Many saw her praying out loud.
C. Omniscient Narration	_____ I grew comfortable with God. And that was all right with me. I talked with Him. I trusted Him.

III. Explain what point of view you are choosing for your novella and explain why. (50 points total)

Your essay will be evaluated in these three areas:

Syntax and diction: grammar and style (10 points)

Organization: paragraphs, transitions, introduction, et al. (15 points)

Argument (25 points)

Chapter 4 Test Sample Answer

Grammar (25 points)

I. Circle the linking verbs in the following sentences.

A. I (am) a teacher.

B. I (appear) to be sick.

C. You (were) not ready!

D. They (seem) to be nearly finished.

E. The soldiers (are) brave.

II. Identify the point of view in these passages (25 points)

A. First Person	*C*	Over the years, though, Margaret grew comfortable with her God. And that was all right too. They talked to each other and no doubt they loved each other, but practically speaking, she now wondered what sort of relationship that they had. Compatibility, though, did not inevitably lead to passion. And that was what she felt toward her God now: passion.
B. Third Person Objective	*B*	Over the years, though, Margaret appeared to grow comfortable with her God. And that was all right too. Many saw her praying out loud.
C. Omniscient Narration	*A*	I grew comfortable with God. And that was all right with me. I talked with Him. I trusted Him.

III. Explain what point of view you are choosing for your novella and explain why. (50 points total)

Your essay will be evaluated in these three areas:

Syntax and diction: grammar and style (10 points)

Organization: paragraphs, transitions, introduction, et al. (15 points)

Argument (25 points)

Answers will vary.

Reading 2

The Yearling, by Marjorie Rawlings

Chapter 5

First Thoughts

Verbs are words that express action or state of condition. They link one thing to another. The verb is the epicenter of the writing universe. The Second Edition of the *Oxford English Dictionary* claims that there are 171,476 active English words with about another 100,000 that are archaic. It is virtually impossible to memorize every one of these words. Therefore, we are going to examine ways that we can increase our vocabulary through *sentence context clues* and *roots* and *prefixes*. Finally, you will clarify the setting of your novella and write one chapter.

Chapter Learning Objectives

In chapter 5 we will . . .

1. Understand, identify, and conjugate verbs.
2. Avoid gratuitously using different verb tenses.
3. Define vocabulary words in context.
4. Discuss the setting in *The Yearling.*
5. Determine the setting for your novella.

Look Ahead for Friday

- Turn in all assignments
- Outline the plot in your novella

Lesson 1

Grammar Review: The Correct Use of Verbs

Daily Assignment

- Warm-up: Referring to the two charts above, use five verb forms in sentences.
- Students will complete Concept Builder 5-A.
- Prayer journal: students are encouraged to write in their prayer journal every day.
- Finish the next book you have been assigned.
- Students should systematically review their vocabulary words daily.

CONCEPT BUILDER 5-A

Match

Complete this chart for the regular verb dance.

Infinitive	Present Participle	Past	Past Participle
to dance	*dancing*	*danced*	*have danced*

Complete this chart for the irregular verb *lie*.

Infinitive	Present Participle	Past	Past Participle
to lie	*lying*	*lay*	*have laid*

Lesson 2

Grammar: Verb Tenses

Daily Assignment

- Warm-up: Discuss an incident in the *The Yearling* from the perspective of 50-year-old Jody.
- Students will complete Concept Builder 5-B.
- Prayer journal: students are encouraged to write in their prayer journal every day.
- Finish the next book you have been assigned.
- Students should systematically review their vocabulary words daily.

CONCEPT BUILDER 5-B

Conjugating Verbs

Conjugate the verb run.

Present Tense

Singular	Plural
I run	*We run*
You run	*You run*
He, She, It runs	*They run*

Past Tense

Singular	Plural
I ran	*We ran*
You ran	*You ran*
He, She, It ran	*They ran*

Future Tense

Singular	Plural
I will run	*We will run*
You will run	*You will run*
He, She, It will run	*They will run*

Present Perfect Tense

Singular	Plural
I have run	*We have run*
You have run	*You have run*
He, She, It has run	*They have run*

Past Perfect Tense

Singular	Plural
I had run	*We had run*
You had run	*You had run*
He, She, It had run	*They had run*

Future Perfect Tense

Singular	Plural
I will have run	*We will have run*
You will have run	*You will have run*
He, She, It will have run	*He, She, It will have run*

Correct this reading passage:

For Christmas, my dad's brother, Uncle Ray gave me an illustrated Howard Pyle's The Story of the Champions of the Round Table. "Son forget not that you are a king's son and your lineage is as noble as anyone's on earth. . . ." It was all true and Sir Lancelot made me noble as I read it. Like the Holy Scriptures, to this nine year old, to read about someone made me that someone. Howard Pyle, and the disciples gifted me, "Silver or gold I do not have, but what I do have I give you. In the name of Jesus Christ of Nazareth, walk (Acts 3:6)."

Brave Sir Lancelot and Sir Percival will protect coy ladies from duplicitous wizards and fierce dragons. Duplicitous wizards and fierce dragons had been in short supply in southeast Arkansas. Uncorrupted, intrepid, and felicitous, in the face of imminent butchery, fanciful in the early morning light, my knighted champions slashed through the early morning, like the four horsemen of the Apocalypse. "I watched as the Lamb opened the first of the seven seals," St. John wrote, "Then I heard one of the four living creatures say in a voice like thunder, 'Come!' I looked, and there before me was a white horse! Its rider held a bow, and he was given a crown, and he rode out as a conqueror bent on conquest" (Revelation 6:1-2).

For Christmas, my dad's brother, Uncle Ray gave me an illustrated Howard Pyle's The Story of the Champions of the Round Table. *"Son forget not that you are a king's son and your lineage is as noble as anyone's on earth. . . ." It was all true and Sir Lancelot made me noble as I read it. Like the Holy Scriptures, to this nine year old, to read about someone made me that someone. Howard Pyle, and the disciples gifted me, "Silver or gold I do not have, but what I do have I give you. In the name of Jesus Christ of Nazareth, walk (Acts 3:6)."*

Brave Sir Lancelot and Sir Percival protected coy ladies from duplicitous wizards and fierce dragons. Duplicitous wizards and fierce dragons were in short supply in southeast Arkansas. Uncorrupted, intrepid, and felicitous, in the face of imminent butchery, fanciful in the early morning light, my knighted champions slashed through the early morning, like the four horsemen of the Apocalypse. "I watched as the Lamb opened the first of the seven seals," St. John wrote, "Then I heard one of the four living creatures say in a voice like thunder, 'Come!' I looked, and there before me was a white horse! Its rider held a bow, and he was given a crown, and he rode out as a conqueror bent on conquest (Revelation 6:1–2)."

Reading Skills: Vocabulary

Daily Assignment

- Warm-up: Write a letter of sympathy to a friend who has lost someone. In your letter use these words: *commiserate, pejorative, predilection,* and *anxiety*.
- Students will complete Concept Builder 5-C.
- Prayer journal: students are encouraged to write in their prayer journal every day.
- Finish the next book you have been assigned.
- Students should systematically review their vocabulary words daily.

CONCEPT BUILDER 5-C

Definitions

Define the words in bold. If possible, try to determine their meaning by the context of the passage.

Evan Nash was born next to Bayou Bartholomew. Celebrated by **scion** ***(Must be "rich people" because this word is contrasted with "pauper")*** and pauper alive, Evan grew up on an **antebellum** ***("ante" means before and "bellum" means war so it must mean "before the Civil War")*** plantation, Willow Lane. Massive in design and expectation, it was a fitting testimony to the Nash legacy. Willow Lane appeared to belong to a king or a duke or the **Caliph** ***(This word is connected to "king" or "duke" so it must mean "a high official," or "king")*** of Egypt, but not to a prosperous Delta planter. A brick walk escorted visitors into a massive hallway that was larger than most sharecropper cabins. There were eight bedrooms, each remodeled with its own bath during the 1920s. When a toilet was flushed, bubbles emerged from the depth of Bayou Bartholomew. Young Nash tied bacon to cotton twine and caught scores of crawdads enjoying the **noisome** ***(considering the context, it must mean "bad")*** deposits. Hooks were optional.

Lesson 4

Writing: Accepted Standards

Daily Assignment

- Warm-up: Most readers love Jody. Why is he such an appealing character?
- Students will complete Concept Builder 5-D.
- Prayer journal: students are encouraged to write in their prayer journal every day.
- Finish the next book you have been assigned.
- Students should systematically review their vocabulary words daily.

CONCEPT BUILDER 5-D

Internal Conflict: Loss

An important theme (the main purpose or meaning) of this book is "loss." List four major losses that Jody experiences.

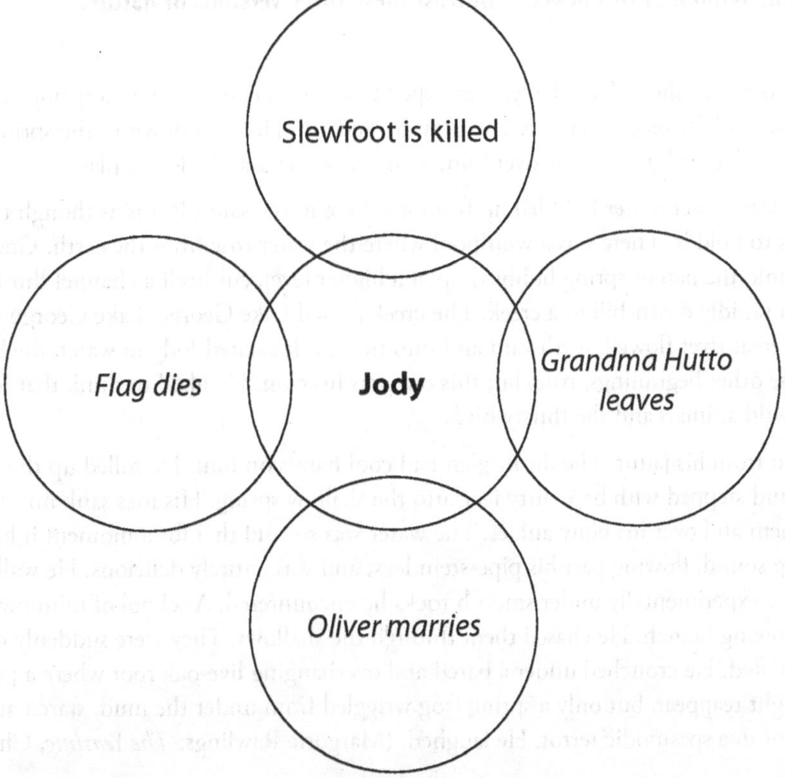
Slewfoot is killed
Flag dies
Jody
Grandma Hutto leaves
Oliver marries

Lesson 5

The Setting

Daily Assignment

- Warm-up: Describe where you live (your setting) and how it has affected the way you look at things.
- Students will complete Concept Builder 5-E.
- Prayer journal: students are encouraged to write in their prayer journal every day.
- Finish the next book you have been assigned.
- Students should systematically review their vocabulary words daily.

CONCEPT BUILDER 5-E

Setting: Nature

Nature is a ubiquitous symbol in this novel. Contrast these three versions of nature.

A. The east bank of the road shelved suddenly. It dropped below him twenty feet to a spring. The bank was dense with magnolia and loblolly bay, sweet gum and gray-barked ash. He went down to the spring in the cool darkness of their shadows. A sharp pleasure came over him. This was a secret and a lovely place.

A spring as clear as well water bubbled up from nowhere in the sand. It was as though the banks cupped green leafy hands to hold it. There was a whirlpool where the water rose from the earth. Grains of sand boiled in it. Beyond the bank, the parent spring bubbled up at a higher level, cut itself a channel through white limestone and began to run rapidly down-hill to a creek. The creek joined Lake George, Lake George was a part of the St. John's River, the great river flowed northward and into the sea. It excited Jody to watch the beginning of the ocean. There were other beginnings, true, but this one was his own. He liked to think that no one came here but himself and the wild animals and the thirsty birds.

He was warm from his jaunt. The dusky glen laid cool hands on him. He rolled up the hems of his blue denim breeches and stepped with bare dirty feet into the shallow spring. His toes sank into the sand. It oozed softly between them and over his bony ankles. The water was so cold that for a moment it burned his skin. Then it made a rippling sound, flowing past his pipe-stem legs, and was entirely delicious. He walked up and down, digging his big toe experimentally under smooth rocks he encountered. A school of minnows flashed ahead of him down the growing branch. He chased them through the shallows. They were suddenly out of sight as though they had never existed. He crouched under a bared and overhanging live-oak root where a pool was deep, thinking they might reappear, but only a spring frog wriggled from under the mud, stared at him, and dove under the tree root in a spasmodic terror. He laughed. (Margorie Rawlings, *The Yearling*, Ch. 1)

B. The cold passed reluctantly from the earth, and the retiring fogs revealed an army stretched out on the hills, resting. As the landscape changed from brown to green, the army awakened, and began to tremble with eagerness at the noise of rumors. It cast its eyes upon the roads, which were growing from long troughs of liquid mud to proper thoroughfares. A river, amber-tinted in the shadow of its banks, purled at the army's feet; and at night, when the stream had become of a sorrowful blackness, one could see across it the red, eyelike gleam of hostile camp-fires set in the low brows of distant hills. (Stephen Crane, *Red Badge of Courage*, Ch. 1)

C. Sometimes, after staying in a village parlor till the family had all retired, I have returned to the woods, and, partly with a view to the next day's dinner, spent the hours of midnight fishing from a boat by moonlight, serenaded by owls and foxes, and hearing, from time to time, the creaking note of some unknown bird close at hand. These experiences were very memorable and valuable to me—anchored in forty feet of water, and twenty or thirty rods from the shore, surrounded sometimes by thousands of small perch and shiners, dimpling the surface with their tails in the moonlight, and communicating by a long flaxen line with mysterious nocturnal fishes which had their dwelling forty feet below, or sometimes dragging sixty feet of line about the pond as I drifted in the gentle night breeze, now and then feeling a slight vibration along it, indicative of some life prowling about its extremity, of dull uncertain blundering purpose there, and slow to make up its mind. At length you slowly raise, pulling hand over hand, some horned pout squeaking and squirming to the upper air. It was very queer, especially in dark nights, when your thoughts had wandered to vast and cosmogonal themes in other spheres, to feel this faint jerk, which came to interrupt your dreams and link you to Nature again. It seemed as if I might next cast my line upward into the air, as well as downward into this element, which was scarcely more dense. Thus I caught two fishes as it were with one hook. (Henry David Thoreau, *Walden*, "The Pond")

Matching

B Nature is ominous.

C Nature is a place of refuge, preferably to human company.

A Nature is not friendly, nor impartial. It is important as it is connected to human experience.

Chapter 5 Review Questions

Writing a Novella

What is the setting of your story? Remember: the setting is both the time and place where a written work occurs. Write at least one chapter for your novella.

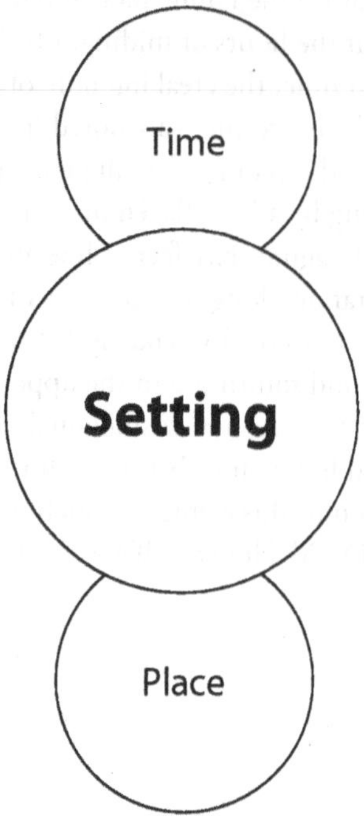

Literary Analysis

Write a letter to a friend or relative recommending this book. What makes it such a great book? In your letter include a greeting, a body (the main part), and a conclusion (a farewell statement).

Answers will vary.

Biblical Application

Have you ever experienced the death of a loved one? If so, write that person a letter telling him/her why you miss him/her.

Answers will vary.

Chapter 5 Test

I. Choose the best word for the vocabulary word in context (30 points, 6 points/word).

The pejorative comment hurt my feelings.

A. Friendly

B. Gentle

C. Negative

D. Thoughtless

His perspicuity helped us solve the knotty problem.

A. Insightful . . . difficult.

B. Stupidity . . . easy.

C. Enthusiasm . . . potential.

D. Laziness . . . impossible.

The aplomb of the dancer allowed her to recover from her injury quicker.

A. Skill

B. Mood

C. Smile

D. Composure

The criminal did break the law, but he showed no malfeasance toward his victim.

A. Hard feelings

B. Evil

C. Love

D. Calmness

II. Verb Tenses

Every verb has six tenses: present tense, past tense, future tense, present perfect tense, past perfect tense, and future perfect tense. Complete the following chart (36 points, 2 points each):

Present Tense

Singular	Plural
I sing	We _____
You _____	You _____
He, She, It _____	They _____

Past Tense

Singular	Plural
I _____	We _____
You _____	You _____
He, She, It _____	They _____

Future Tense

Singular	Plural
I will _____	We will ________
You will ________	You will ________
He, She, It will ________	They will ________

Present Perfect Tense

Singular	Plural
I have ________	We have ________
You have ________	You have ________
He, She, It has _____	They have ________

Past Perfect Tense

Singular	Plural
I had ________	We had ________
You had ________	You had ________
He, She, It had ________	They had ________

Future Perfect Tense

Singular	Plural
I will have ________	We will have ________
You will have ________	You will have ________
He, She, It will have ________	He, She, It will have ________

III. How important is the setting to *The Yearling*? Could the story occur, say, in your hometown? Why or why not? (34 points total)

Your essay will be evaluated in these three areas:

Syntax and diction: grammar and style (10 points)

Organization: paragraphs, transitions, introduction, et al. (10 points)

Argument (14 points)

Chapter 5 Test Answer Sample

I. Choose the best word for the vocabulary word in context (30 points, 6 points/word).

The pejorative comment hurt my feelings.

A. Friendly

B. Gentle

<u>C. Negative</u>

D. Thoughtless

His perspicuity helped us solve the knotty problem.

<u>A. Insightful . . . difficult.</u>

B. Stupidity . . . easy.

C. Enthusiasm . . . potential.

D. Laziness . . . impossible.

The aplomb of the dancer allowed her to recover from her injury quicker.

A. Skill

B. Mood

C. Smile

<u>D. Composure</u>

The criminal did break the law, but he showed no malfeasance toward his victim.

A. Hard feelings

<u>B. Evil</u>

C. Love

D. Calmness

II. Verb Tenses – Every verb has six tenses: present tense, past tense, future tense, present perfect tense, past perfect tense, and future perfect tense. Complete the following chart (36 points, 2 points each):

Present Tense

Singular	Plural
I sing	We *sing*
You *sing*	You *sing*
He, She, It *sings*	They *sing*

Past Tense

Singular	Plural
I *sang*	We *sang*
You *sang*	You *sang*
He, She, It *sang*	They *sang*

Future Tense

Singular	Plural
I will *sing*	We will *sing*
You will *sing*	You will *sing*
He, She, It will *sing*	They will *sing*

Present Perfect Tense

Singular	Plural
I have *sung*	We have *sung*
You have *sung*	You have *sung*
He, She, It has *sung*	They have *sung*

Past Perfect Tense

Singular	Plural
I had *sung*	We had *sung*
You had *sung*	You had *sung*
He, She, It had *sung*	They had *sung*

Future Perfect Tense

Singular	Plural
I will have *sung*	We will have *sung*
You will have *sung*	You will have *sung*
He, She, It will have *sung*	He, She, It will have *sung*

III. How important is the setting to *The Yearling*? Could the story occur, say, in your hometown? Why or why not? (34 points total)

Your essay will be evaluated in these three areas:

Syntax and diction: grammar and style (10 points)

Organization: paragraphs, transitions, introduction, et al. (10 points)

Argument (14 points)

While the setting is important — raising a deer in the city would be impossible — the themes in the novel — forgiveness, maturation, et al. — could be developed at any number of different places.

Reading 1

Les Miserables, by Victor Hugo

Chapter 6

First Thoughts

Victor-Marie Hugo was born on February 26, 1802, in France during the Napoleonic Era. In fact, his father, Joesph-Leopold-Sigisbert Hugo, was a general under Napoleon. His parents separated — a scandalous thing in the early 19th century. He lived with his mother in Corsica, Elba, Italy, and Spain. Therefore, he never had a stable home and often received ridicule from insensitive adults and classmates who teased Hugo for being part of a single family. Victor Hugo, however, knew the pleasure of God: he was a gifted writer. At the age of 15, he was already writing and throughout his career was a prolific writer. While most critics saw him as a mediocre writer, like Charles Dickens and Henry David Longfellow — both mediocre writers — the public adored Victor Hugo and bought everything he wrote. He was a wealthy man. He was a sort of "John Grisham" of his age!

Chapter Learning Objectives

In chapter 6 we will . . .

1. Identify and use pronouns in the correct case and tense.
2. Understand agreement between different parts of speech.
3. Review your progress with the novella.

Look Ahead for Friday

- Turn in all assignments.
- Rewrite your novella.

Structure

Daily Assignment

- Warm-up: In our reading assignment, the protagonist was forgiven for a crime he committed. Using three nominative and three objective pronouns, describe a time when you were forgiven for something that you did. How did you react? How should you have reacted?
- Students will complete Concept Builder 6-A.
- Prayer journal: students are encouraged to write in their prayer journal every day.
- Finish the next book you have been assigned.
- Students should systematically review their vocabulary words daily.

CONCEPT BUILDER 6-A

Pronouns

Complete the Chart.

Pronoun	Answer
1. First Person Nominative Singular	*I*
2. Third Person Objective Plural	*Them*
3. Second Person Possessive Plural	*Your, yours*
4. Third Person Objective Singular	*Him, her, it*
5. First Person Possessive Singular	*My, mine*

Lesson 2

Grammar Review: Parts of a Sentence

Daily Assignment

- Warm-up: Some counselors argue that the most important component of mental health is a person's unequivocal knowledge that he/she is loved. It is not so important that we love as that we know we are loved. Give an example of that sort of love in your own life.
- Students will complete Concept Builder 6-B.
- Prayer journal: students are encouraged to write in their prayer journal every day.
- Finish the next book you have been assigned.
- Students should systematically review their vocabulary words daily.

CONCEPT BUILDER 6-B

Identifying Parts of a Sentence

Identify the part of each sentence.

1. Subject
2. Predicate
3. Clause
4. Phrase
5. Modifier

A. *1* Edgar Allan Poe's famous short story "The Fall of the House of Usher,"

B. *2* is a fantastical portrayal of the decrepit human condition.

C. *4* Offering lurid details, Poe lures his reader into a web of suspense

D. *3* as events cascade to a tumultuous and lurid finale.

E. *3* Poe creates the uncertain and suspenseful gothic mood of his stories; Poe draws them on toward the end of his tale.

Lesson 3

Characters and Conflict

Daily Assignment

- Warm-up: Write a letter of appreciation to Javert explaining why Javert should be pardoned.
- Students will complete Concept Builder 6-C.
- Prayer journal: students are encouraged to write in their prayer journal every day.
- Finish the next book you have been assigned.
- Students should systematically review their vocabulary words daily.

CONCEPT BUILDER 6-C

Choosing Verbs

Write the subject of each sentence and select the correct verb.

1. None of us really (know, **knows**) what is happening.
2. Some of the soldiers (**seem**, seems) tired from the drill.
3. Somebody in the crowd (raise, **raises**) his hand.
4. (Has, **Have**) all of the students returned from the field trip?
5. Few of the chocolate cookies (was, **were**) left.

Read each sentence. If it is correct mark it "C." If it is incorrect, mark it "X."

1. *X* All poets like Henry Wadsworth Longfellow was the greatest poets in American History.
2. *C* Those who critique him are really not fair.
3. *X* Everybody like him because he was simple.
4. *C* Even though I don't have the same agenda, I still side with the commoners.
5. *X* So in a nutshell no one says that Henry Wadsworth Longfellow were not a great poet.

Lesson 4

Tone

Daily Assignment

- Warm-up: Analyze the tone in *Les Miserables* and discuss how Hugo creates this tone. Give an example.
- Students will complete Concept Builder 6-D.
- Prayer journal: students are encouraged to write in their prayer journal every day.
- Finish the next book you have been assigned.
- Students should systematically review their vocabulary words daily.

CONCEPT BUILDER 6-D

Tone

Evaluate the way Hugo weaves together the tone into the introduction of Jean Valjean.

How does Hugo develop the tone in this passage?

Jean Valjean was "thoughtful but not gloomy disposition." But he "lost his mother and father at an early age."

Jean Valjean is a lonely, sad figure. How does Hugo show this?

He has to take care of his family and he had not even had time "to fall in love." The sympathy of the readers is evoked.

Hugo wants his theistic readers to do a very interesting thing. What?

Readers are invited to feel sorry for a criminal.

Notice that Hugo changes his narration completely and intrudes his own voice into the narrative. Why?

Hugo makes a political statement. "This is the second time, during his studies on the penal question and damnation by law, that the author of this book has come across the theft of a loaf of bread as the point of departure for the disaster of a destiny."

Lesson 5

Writing: Ethos, Logos, Pathos

Daily Assignment

- Warm-up: Write a letter using ethos (emotional appeal) to your parents asking them for something you know they will probably not give you.
- Students will complete Concept Builder 6-E.
- Prayer journal: students are encouraged to write in their prayer journal every day.
- Finish the next book you have been assigned.
- Students should systematically review their vocabulary words daily.

CONCEPT BUILDER 6-E

Ethos, Logos, Pathos

Match each passage to its purpose in this letter.

C Pathos A. Let us consider a more concrete example of just and unjust laws. An unjust law is a code that a numerical or power majority group compels a minority group to obey but does not make binding on itself. This is difference made legal. By the same token, a just law is a code that a majority compels a minority to follow and that it is willing to follow itself. This is sameness made legal. Let me give another explanation. A law is unjust if it is inflicted on a minority that, as a result of being denied the right to vote, had no part in enacting or devising the law.

A Logos B. Never before have I written so long a letter. I'm afraid it is much too long to take your precious time. I can assure you that it would have been much shorter if I had been writing from a comfortable desk, but what else can one do when he is alone in a narrow jail cell, other than write long letters, think long thoughts and pray long prayers?

B Ethos C. There was a time when the church was very powerful--in the time when the early Christians rejoiced at being deemed worthy to suffer for what they believed. In those days the church was not merely a thermometer that recorded the ideas and principles of popular opinion; it was a thermostat that transformed the mores of society. Whenever the early Christians entered a town, the people in power became disturbed and immediately sought to convict the Christians for being "disturbers of the peace" and "outside agitators." But the Christians pressed on, in the conviction that they were "a colony of heaven," called to obey God rather than man. Small in number, they were big in commitment.

Chapter 6 Review Questions

Writing a Novella

How is your novella progressing? Are you exhibiting ethos, logos, and pathos in your story? Review what you have written so far. Rewrite any sections that need work.

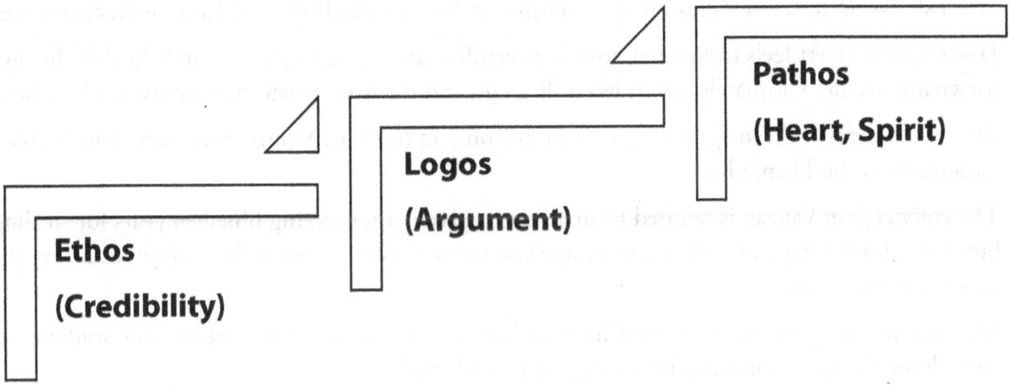

Literary Analysis

Most critics argue that *Les Miserables* is full of predictable plots and subplots and populated with weak, archetypical characters. Do you agree? Do you think it is a great novel? Why or why not?

It is one of the most popular novels of all time. The theme of redemption is strong and appealing. However, this reader finds the characters to be predictable and at time too monolithic.

Biblical Application

Javert is one of the enigmatic figures in Western literature. Is he bad? Good? He obeys the law and enforces the law, but Hugo makes him into a villain. Or is he? Discuss Javert.

Javert represented unforgiveness, mercilessness. He was obsessed with obeying the law and felt that if this was ignored society would collapse.

Chapter 6 Test

I. Organize the events in the order in which they occur. (65 points)

Organize the events in the novel in the order in which they occur.

_____ Thénardier's daughter Eponine, who is in love with Marius, helps Marius discover Cosette's whereabouts.

_____ Javert shows up to arrest Valjean while Valjean is at Fantine's bedside, and Fantine dies from the shock.

_____ Javert agrees. Javert feels tormented, torn between his duty to his profession and the debt he owes Valjean for saving his life. Ultimately, Javert lets Valjean go and throws himself into the river, where he drowns.

_____ After a few years, Valjean again escapes from prison and heads to Montfermeil, where he is able to buy Cosette from the Thénardiers.

_____ The convict Jean Valjean is released from a French prison after serving nineteen years for stealing a loaf of bread and for subsequent attempts to escape from prison. Myriel covers for Valjean, claiming that stolen silverware was a gift.

_____ Marius Pontmercy moves out of Gillenormand's house and lives as a poor young law student. While in law school, Marius associates with a group of radical students.

_____ The Thénardiers agree to look after Cosette as long as Fantine sends them a monthly allowance.

_____ Valjean manages to intercept a note and sets out to save the life of the man his daughter loves.

_____ Valjean arrives at the barricade and volunteers to execute Javert. When alone with Javert, however, Valjean instead secretly lets him go free.

_____ Marius and Cosette rush to dying Valjean's side. Valjean dies in peace.

_____ When Valjean emerges hours later, Javert immediately arrests him. Valjean pleads with Javert to let him take the dying Marius to Marius's grandfather.

_____ Marius sees Cosette at a public park. It is love at first sight, but the protective Valjean does his utmost to prevent Cosette and Marius from ever meeting.

_____ Marius decides to join his radical student friends, who have started a political uprising. Armed with two pistols, Marius heads for the barricades.

II. Discussion Question (35 points)

Why does Javert take his own life?

Chapter 6 Test Answer Sample

I. Organize the events in the order in which they occur. (65 points)

Organize the events in the novel in the order in which they occur.

7 Thénardier's daughter Eponine, who is in love with Marius, helps Marius discover Cosette's whereabouts.

3 Javert shows up to arrest Valjean while Valjean is at Fantine's bedside, and Fantine dies from the shock.

12 Javert agrees. Javert feels tormented, torn between his duty to his profession and the debt he owes Valjean for saving his life. Ultimately, Javert lets Valjean go and throws himself into the river, where he drowns.

4 After a few years, Valjean again escapes from prison and heads to Montfermeil, where he is able to buy Cosette from the Thénardiers.

1 The convict Jean Valjean is released from a French prison after serving nineteen years for stealing a loaf of bread and for subsequent attempts to escape from prison. Myriel covers for Valjean, claiming that stolen silverware was a gift.

5 Marius Pontmercy moves out of Gillenormand's house and lives as a poor young law student. While in law school, Marius associates with a group of radical students.

2 The Thénardiers agree to look after Cosette as long as Fantine sends them a monthly allowance.

9 Valjean manages to intercept a note and sets out to save the life of the man his daughter loves.

10 Valjean arrives at the barricade and volunteers to execute Javert. When alone with Javert, however, Valjean instead secretly lets him go free.

13 Marius and Cosette rush to dying Valjean's side. Valjean dies in peace.

11 When Valjean emerges hours later, Javert immediately arrests him. Valjean pleads with Javert to let him take the dying Marius to Marius's grandfather.

6 Marius sees Cosette at a public park. It is love at first sight, but the protective Valjean does his utmost to prevent Cosette and Marius from ever meeting.

8 Marius decides to join his radical student friends, who have started a political uprising. Armed with two pistols, Marius heads for the barricades.

II. Discussion Question (35 points)

Why does Javert take his own life?

Javert, a traditionalist, a "pharisee," is confronted with "grace" and unconditional love, and is unable either to make the transition to this new place or to reject it altogether. In a real way, then, Javert could not accept the biblical concepts of love and forgiveness that were central to the rehabilitation and vitality of vital characters in Les Miserables.

Reading 2

Les Miserables, by Victor Hugo

Chapter 7

First Thoughts

Hugo was writing his novel to a target audience: upper middle class, educated males, who, in the middle of the 19th century, bought most of the reading material in France. Hugo knew that a novel that celebrated Judeo-Christian morality, that honored the sanctify of the family, would appeal to his audience. He, also, knowing the French penchant (tendency) to embrace revolution, included a revolutionary scene that celebrated the 1848 French uprising. Hugo explained his novel in this way:

> So long as there shall exist, by virtue of law and custom, decrees of damnation pronounced by society, artificially creating hells amid the civilization of earth, and adding the element of human fate to divine destiny; so long as the three great problems of the century — the degradation of man through pauperism, the corruption of woman through hunger, the crippling of children through lack of light — are unsolved; so long as social asphyxia is possible in any part of the world — in other words, and with a still wider significance, so long as ignorance and poverty exist on earth, books of the nature of *Les Misérables* cannot fail to be of us. (Preface)

To what target audience are you writing your novella?

Chapter Learning Objectives

In chapter 7 we will . . .

1. Examine special verb uses.
2. Understand the use of pronouns.
3. Evaluate themes in *Les Miserables.*
4. Gain new reading skills as you complete the Book Study: Active Reading exercises.

Look Ahead for Friday

- Turn in all assignments.
- Consider symbolism in *Les Miserables.*

Grammar Review: Pronoun Usage

Daily Assignment

- Warm-up: If you could be one character in a movie of *Les Miserables*, who would that be?
- In your essay, use the words who and whom.
- Students will complete Concept Builder 7-A.
- Prayer journal: students are encouraged to write in their prayer journal every day.
- Finish the next book you have been assigned.
- Students should systematically review their vocabulary words daily.

CONCEPT BUILDER 7-A

Troublesome Verbs

Sit, Set, Lie, Lay, Rise, Raise

Choose the correct verb:

1. If the phenomena which (lie, **lay**) before him will not suit his purpose, all history must be ransacked.
2. He (**sat**, set) with his eyes fixed partly on the ghost and partly on Hamlet, and with his mouth open.
3. The days when his favorite volume (sat, **set**) him upon making wheelbarrows and chair.
4. To make the jacket (**sit**, set) yet more closely to the body, it was gathered at the middle by a broad leathern belt.
5. For more than two hundred years his bones (**lay**, laid) undistinguished.
6. The author (lay, **laid**) the whole fault on the audience.
7. (Raise, **Rise**) up oh men and give God the Glory!
8. The man (**raised**, rises) the puppies from birth.
9. Your job is to (sit, **set**) the table and then (**sit**, set) next to your sister, and do not (raise, **rise**) up without permission.

Themes

Daily Assignment

- Warm-up: What sort of themes predominate in your life?
- Students will complete Concept Builder 7-B.
- Prayer journal: students are encouraged to write in their prayer journal every day.
- Finish the next book you have been assigned.
- Students should systematically review their vocabulary words daily.

CONCEPT BUILDER 7-B

Theme

List three themes in this novel.

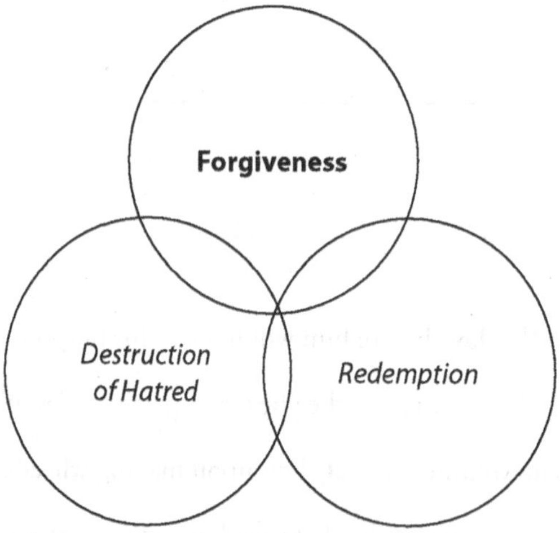

Similar Themes in Biblical Stories

Which of these stories have similar themes to *Les Miserables*?

The Woman at the Well (John 4)

The Woman Caught in Adultery (John 8)

The Prodigal Son (Luke 15)

The Story of Samson (Judges 13-16)

Both the Samaritan Woman (at the well) and the woman caught in adultery, have very similar themes: forgiveness for offenses for which they were guilty. The Prodigal Son, too, is forgiven for offenses he committed. Samson, alone, would be the aberrant story (although a very good one!).

Setting Of *Les Miserables*

Daily Assignment

- Warm-up: In what place, in what time, and in what situation, were you the happiest? Why?
- Students will complete Concept Builder 7-C.
- Prayer journal: students are encouraged to write in their prayer journal every day.
- Finish the next book you have been assigned.
- Students should systematically review their vocabulary words daily.

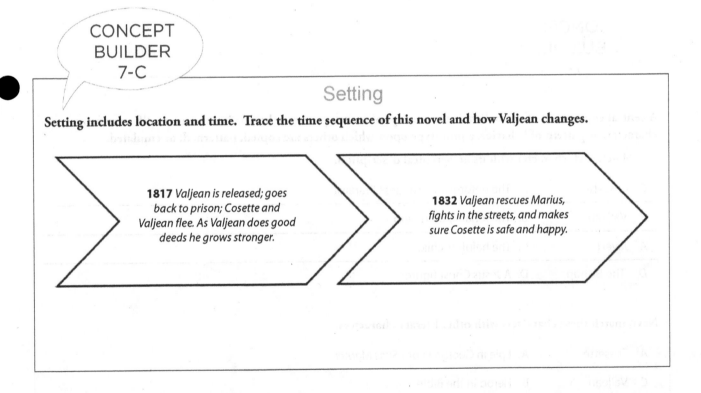

CONCEPT BUILDER 7-C

Setting

Setting includes location and time. Trace the time sequence of this novel and how Valjean changes.

1817 *Valjean is released; goes back to prison; Cosette and Valjean flee. As Valjean does good deeds he grows stronger.*

1832 *Valjean rescues Marius, fights in the streets, and makes sure Cosette is safe and happy.*

Symbolism

Daily Assignment

- Warm-up: Write a defense for poor Javert.
- Students will complete Concept Builder 7-D.
- Prayer journal: students are encouraged to write in their prayer journal every day.
- Finish the next book you have been assigned.
- Students should systematically review their vocabulary words daily.

CONCEPT BUILDER 7-D

Archetypes

A central component of symbolism is the concept of archetype. An archetype is a theme, motif, statement, character, or pattern of behavior, a prototype upon which others are copied, patterned, or emulated.

Match each character with its archetypical description.

C Cossette	A. The unforgiving, ruthless literalist
B Valjean	B. The rehabilitated hero
A Javert	C. The helpless child
D The Bishop	D. A Jesus Christ figure

Next, match these characters with other literary characters.

A Cossette	A. Epie in George Eliot's *Silas Marner*
C Valjean	B. Herod in the Bible
B Javert	C. The Apostle Paul in the Bible
D The Bishop	D. Billy Budd in Herman Mellville's *Billy Budd*

Lesson 5

Student Essay: Symbolism in *Les Miserables*

Daily Assignment

- Warm-up: Describe a song or movie that symbolizes your life.
- Students will complete Concept Builder 7-E.
- Prayer journal: students are encouraged to write in their prayer journal every day.
- Finish the next book you have been assigned.
- Students should systematically review their vocabulary words daily.

CONCEPT BUILDER 7-E

Use of Dialogue in Developing Protagonist

Chapter XII

Read the following and answer questions.

How does Hugo move the action forward by dialogue?

Conversation propels the action from the garden to the visit by the solders to the final conversation between Valjean and the Monseigneur.

Hugo strictly uses dialogue—no omniscient narration—to reveal his character's evolution into a hero. Why?

Hugo wants to surprise his reader. He wants his reader to "experience" not merely to "hear about" the transformation of Valjean.

Chapter 7 Review Questions

Writing a Novella

Write another chapter in your novella.

Literary Analysis

How does Hugo address social ills of his time?

He took issue with the way that the poor were treated and the social justice system in France.

Biblical Application

Does Hugo present a biblical view of human nature?

Not really. Hugo believed that people are naturally good. He did not argue for a view of original sin. This would somewhat diminish his theme of redemption!

Chapter 7 Test

I. Matching (30 points)

A. Ethos	_______	emotional appeal, persuades readers by appealing to their emotions
B. Pathos	_______	the appeal to logic, convinces an audience through the use of logic or reason
C. Logos	_______	the ethical appeal, means to convince an audience of the author's credibility or character

II. Choose the correct pronoun. (60 points)

1. Each of the criminals had (his, their) motivation.
2. John and Mary planned (his and her, their) vacation.
3. Did Smith or Jones announce (his, their) intent to run for governor?
4. Neither my baseball nor my bat was returned to (its, their) original location.
5. Everyone turned in (his or her, their) assignments.
6. All of the lawyers turned in (his or her, their) briefs to the judge.
7. If any one of the students has misplaced (his or her, their) library card, (he or she, they) can pay a fine and get a replacement.
8. In the 19th century many states did not treat (its, their) public employees fairly.
9. Both of the children have made (her, their) desires known.
10. Every one of the female debaters knows (her, their) arguments by heart.
11. Either Sharon or her sisters will reveal (her, their) plans.
12. The losing captains thanked (his, their) special unit.
13. Mark's parents asked Mark if everything was in (its, their) place.
14. Neither of the workers wore clothing suitable for (his or her, their) job.

III. Discuss an example of symbolism in *Les Miserables*. (10 points)

There are several instances of symbolism. Probably the most famous is the candlesticks, which represent the redemption and grace of God that Javert himself experiences, and then gives to others.

Chapter 7 Test Answer Sample

I. Matching (30 points)

A. Ethos	*B*	emotional appeal, persuades readers by appealing to their emotions
B. Pathos	*C*	the appeal to logic, convinces an audience through the use of logic or reason
C. Logos	*A*	the ethical appeal, means to convince an audience of the author's credibility or character

II. Choose the correct pronoun. (60 points)

1. Each of the criminals had (**his**, their) motivation.
2. John and Mary planned (his and her, **their**) vacation.
3. Did Smith or Jones announce (**his**, their) intent to run for governor?
4. Neither my baseball nor my bat was returned to (**its**, their) original location.
5. Everyone turned in (**his or her**, their) assignments.
6. All of the lawyers turned in (his or her, **their**) briefs to the judge.
7. If any one of the students has misplaced (**his or her**, their) library card, (**he or she**, they) can pay a fine and get a replacement.
8. In the 19th century many states did not treat (its, **their**) public employees fairly.
9. Both of the children have made (her, **their**) desires known.
10. Every one of the female debaters knows (**her**, their) arguments by heart.
11. Either Sharon or her sisters will reveal (**her**, their) plans.
12. The losing captains thanked (his, **their**) special unit.
13. Mark's parents asked Mark if everything was in (**its**, their) place.
14. Neither of the workers wore clothing suitable for (**his or her**, their) job.

III. Discuss an example of symbolism in *Les Miserables.* (10 points)

There are several instances of symbolism. Probably the most famous is the candlesticks, which represent the redemption and grace of God that Javert himself experiences, and then gives to others.

Answers will vary.

Reading 1

Great Expectations by Charles Dickens

Chapter 8

First Thoughts

Charles Dickens was one of the world's most prolific and best-loved writers. *Great Expectations* was his most autobiographical work. Charles Dickens, like Pip, was a smorgasbord of inferiority complexes, shame, and, later, confidence.

Chapter Learning Objectives

In chapter 8 we will . . .

1. Review pronoun and pronoun antecedent agreement
2. Review subjects and verbs
3. Review writing: paragraphs
4. Analyze the style of *Great Expectations*
5. Analyze the style in your novella

Look Ahead for Friday

- Turn in all assignments.
- Evaluate the style of your novella.

Lesson 1

Grammar Review: Pronoun and Pronoun Antecedent Agreement

Daily Assignment

- Warm-up: Unrequited love, unfulfilled love, is a common motif or theme in literature. Unrequited love or one-sided love is love that is not openly reciprocated or understood. The beloved may or may not be aware of the admirer's deep and strong romantic affections. Have you ever wanted something that you could not have? How did it feel?
- In your essay, use the words who and whom.
- Students will complete Concept Builder 8-A.
- Prayer journal: students are encouraged to write in their prayer journal every day.
- Finish the next book you have been assigned.
- Students should systematically review their vocabulary words daily.

CONCEPT BUILDER 8-A

Pronouns

Choose the correct pronoun:

1. My mother takes a great deal of pride in (**her**, his) gardens.
2. Nobody puts (**his**, their) books in the backpack without making sure there is room.
3. Each of these famous people put (**his**, their) mark on history.
4. Mary nor David completed (**his**, their) task.
5. Mary and David completed (his, **their**) task.
6. Several of them (was, **were**) unhappy.
7. None of the apples (**tastes**, taste) good.

Characters are either flat (undeveloped) or round (developed). They are static (unchanged) or dynamic (changing). Trace round, dynamic Estella's development as a character.

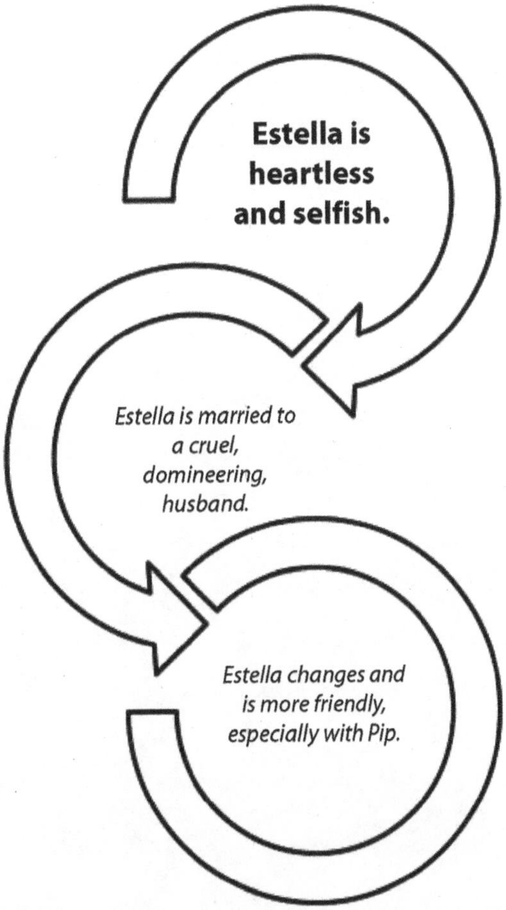
Estella is heartless and selfish.
Estella is married to a cruel, domineering, husband.
Estella changes and is more friendly, especially with Pip.

Lesson 2

Grammar: Subject Follows the Verb

Daily Assignment

- Warm-up: How is *Great Expectations* autobiographical?
- Students will complete Concept Builder 8-B.
- Prayer journal: students are encouraged to write in their prayer journal every day.
- Finish the next book you have been assigned.
- Students should systematically review their vocabulary words daily.

CONCEPT BUILDER 8-B

Unrequited Love in Other Literary Works

Pip is in love with a young lady he can never have. Unrequited love is a theme that has been popular in western literature forever. Romeo and Juliet, for one, may be the most famous example. Identify the elements of unrequited love in the Samson narrative.

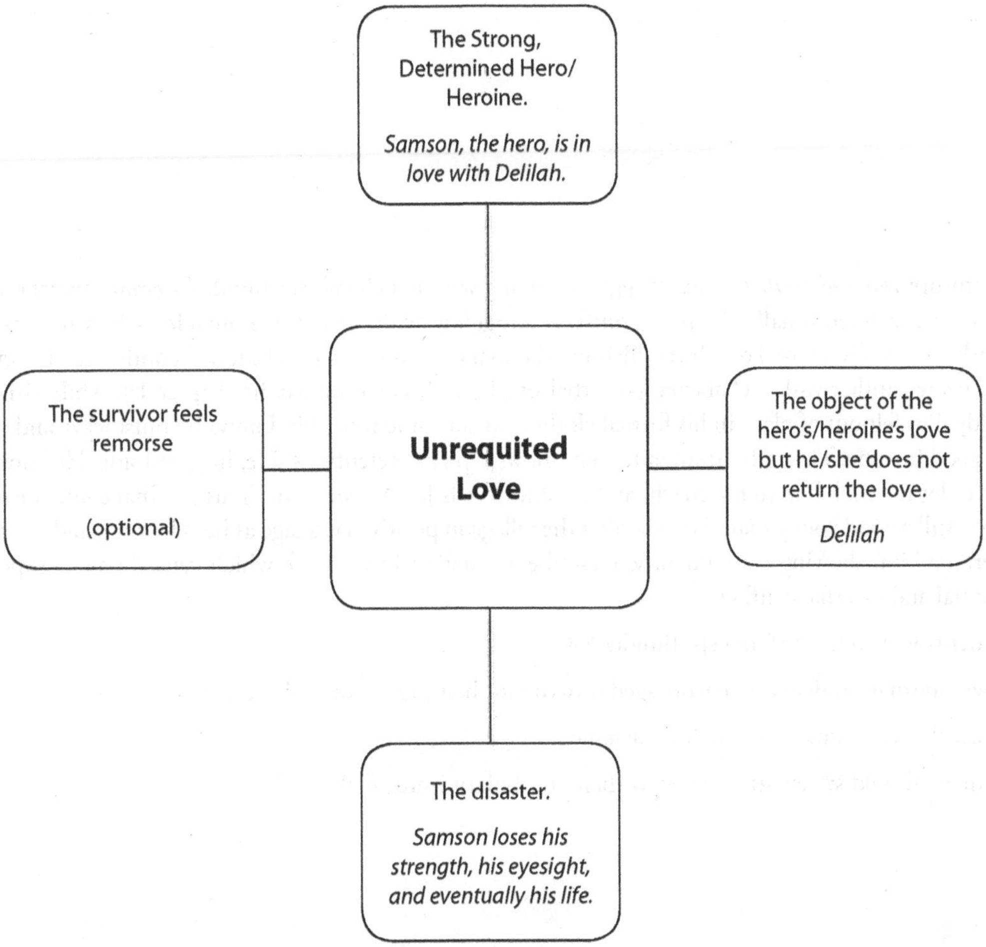

The Strong, Determined Hero/ Heroine.
Samson, the hero, is in love with Delilah.
The survivor feels remorse
(optional)
Unrequited Love
The object of the hero's/heroine's love but he/she does not return the love.
Delilah
The disaster.
Samson loses his strength, his eyesight, and eventually his life.

Grammar Review

Choose the correct verb form.

1. One hundred dollars (**was**, were) not enough.
2. *Romeo and Juliet* (**was**, were) one of Shakespeare's most famous tragedies.
3. Taxes (**is**, are) always unpopular

Lesson 3

Setting Of *Les Miserables*

Daily Assignment

- Warm-up: *Internal conflict* is the struggle occurring within a character's mind. *External conflict* is a conflict in which a character, usually the protagonist, is struggling with some force outside of him or herself. Internal conflict is usually a moral or ethical dilemma the character must resolve. External conflict can be several things, like overt conflict with a character — verbal or physical. For instance, in chapter 19, while visiting Joe and Biddy, Pip felt out of place in his formal clothes. At the same time, Pip knows he must leave and this presages his good fortune. The embarrassment, then, shows Pip's unpretentious side, his good side. He knows it's selfish not to let Joe walk him to the coach, and he almost tells Joe he can come. This internal conflict evidences that Pip is still a good young man. He describes the village in positive language as he is leaving, and tears of emotion overtake him, showing his humanity. Describe a situation in your life which caused you to experience both internal and external conflict.
- Students will complete Concept Builder 8-C.
- Prayer journal: students are encouraged to write in their prayer journal every day.
- Finish the next book you have been assigned.
- Students should systematically review their vocabulary words daily.

CONCEPT BUILDER 8-C

Internal & External Conflict

Characters are created and they create by experiencing and inflicting conflict. Pip in particular matures as a character as he overcomes adversity. Identify four internal/external conflicts that form Pip as a character.

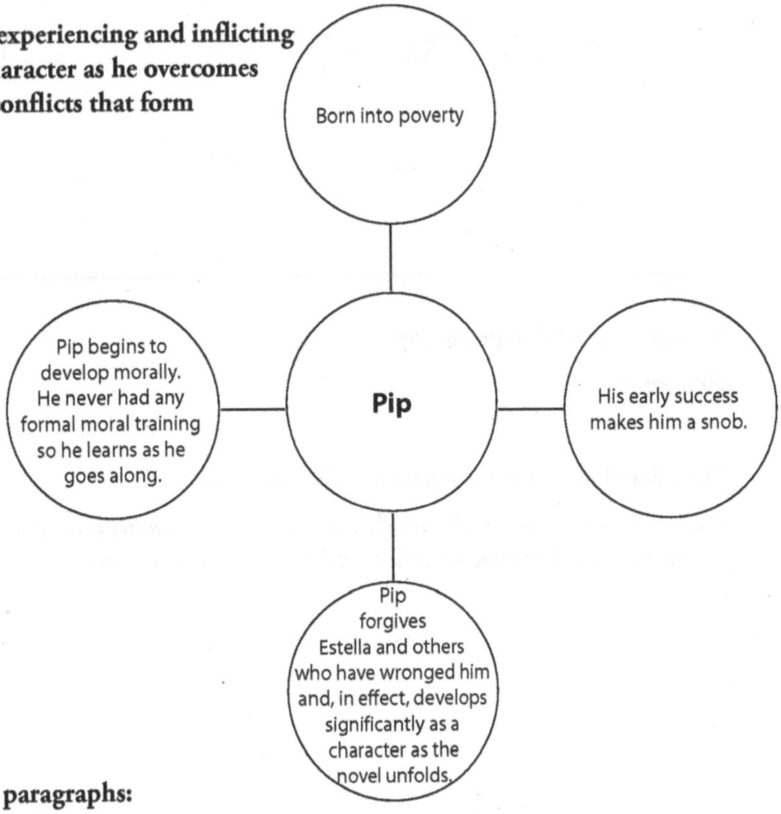

Born into poverty
Pip begins to develop morally. He never had any formal moral training so he learns as he goes along.
Pip
His early success makes him a snob.
Pip forgives Estella and others who have wronged him and, in effect, develops significantly as a character as the novel unfolds.

Rewrite the first part of this sermon with paragraphs:

In *The Screwtape Letters,* C.S. Lewis uses humor to discuss a parlous subject. There is an distinction between satire and humor that is important to understand in order to see Lewis's style of humor.

The Merriam-Webster dictionary describes satire as, "Wit, irony or sarcasm used to expose and discredit vice or folly" and humor as, "a funny or amusing quality." Humor is meant for the entertainment of the reader, while satire is intended to make a point and is usually not constructive. In *The Screwtape Letters*, Lewis uses Gilbertian humor by making his serious subject seem wildly comic rather than using satire to "expose the folly" of the demons. In his introduction Lewis says, "I have no intention of explaining how the correspondence which I now offer to the public fell into my hands." He also uses humor similar to the humor that Jonathan Swift uses by addressing the difficult topic of demons in a good natured, yet saturnine way. Lewis uses terms for the devil such as "Our Father Below," the man being tempted as the "patient," and terms for the Lord such as "The Enemy" to remind the reader through humor of the serious fact that demons are enemies of God. "You may know one of them to be a great warrior on the Enemy's side. No matter. Your patient, thanks to Our Father Below, is a fool." (Margo)

In The Screwtape Letters, *C.S. Lewis uses humor to discuss a parlous subject. There is a distinction between satire and humor that is important to understand in order to see Lewis's style of humor.*

The Merriam-Webster dictionary describes satire as, "Wit, irony, or sarcasm used to expose and discredit vice or folly" and humor as, "a funny or amusing quality." Humor is meant for the entertainment of the reader, while satire is intended to make a point and is usually not constructive. In The Screwtape Letters, *Lewis uses Gilbertian humor by making his serious subject seem wildly comic rather than using satire to "expose the folly" of the demons.*

In his introduction Lewis says, "I have no intention of explaining how the correspondence which I now offer to the public fell into my hands." He also uses humor similar to the humor that Jonathan Swift uses by addressing the difficult topic of demons in a good natured, yet saturnine way. Lewis uses terms for the Devil such as "Our Father Below," the man being tempted as the "patient," and terms for the Lord such as "The Enemy" to remind the reader through humor of the serious fact that demons are enemies of God. "You may know one of them to be a great warrior on the Enemy's side. No matter. Your patient, thanks to Our Father Below, is a fool." (Margo)

Book Study: Active Reading

Great Expectations by Charles Dickens

Predict what will happen to Pip.

Answers will vary.

How does Dickens use dialogue to build suspense?

Dickens uses dialogue to advance the plot, to reveal personality traits of the characters. He can maintain first person narration but still explore the minds and motivations of characters.

Daily Assignment

- Warm-up: What was your favorite scene in *Great Expectations*?
- Students will complete Concept Builder 8-D.
- Prayer journal: students are encouraged to write in their prayer journal every day.
- Finish the next book you have been assigned.
- Students should systematically review their vocabulary words daily.

CONCEPT BUILDER 8-D

Foils

Foils are critical to a literary piece. They are the primary means that authors employ to sculpt their protagonists. How does each foil affect Pip?

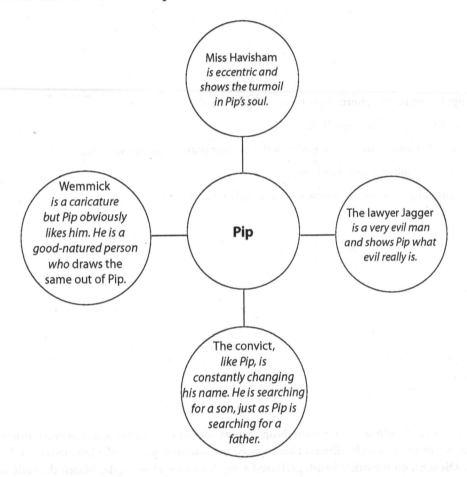

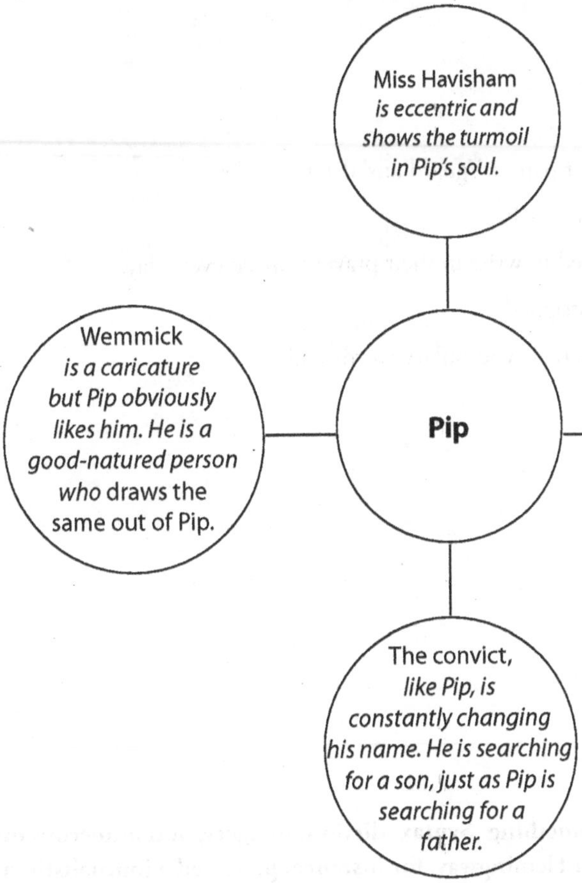

Miss Havisham *is eccentric and shows the turmoil in Pip's soul.*
Wemmick *is a caricature but Pip obviously likes him. He is a good-natured person who* draws the same out of Pip.
Pip
The lawyer Jagger *is a very evil man and shows Pip what evil really is.*
The convict, *like Pip, is constantly changing his name. He is searching for a son, just as Pip is searching for a father.*

Style

Daily Assignment

- Warm-up: Compare and contrast your parents'/guardians' driving styles.
- Students will complete Concept Builder 8-E.
- Prayer journal: students are encouraged to write in their prayer journal every day.
- Finish the next book you have been assigned.
- Students should systematically review their vocabulary words daily.

CONCEPT BUILDER 8-E

Style

Literary style is the way an author creates something. Syntax, diction, imagery, and numerous other literary techniques, conspire to create a style. Ernest Hemingway, for instance, preferred a journalistic style of mostly short sentences. Dickens, on the other hand, preferred a much more verbose style. Match the style for each of these passages. (Student book)

D Dickens offers self-deprecatory comments about himself and his struggles with unrequited love.

C Dickens uses exaggeration (hyperbole) to poke fun at his surroundings.

B Dickens offers insightful and vulnerable reflections about his personal life.

A Dickens offers a satirical picture of a colorful figure in this passage.

Chapter 8 Review Questions

Writing a Novella

Write another chapter in your novella. Pay particular attention to your style this week. Who is your audience? What can you do to make your writing more appealing to this audience?

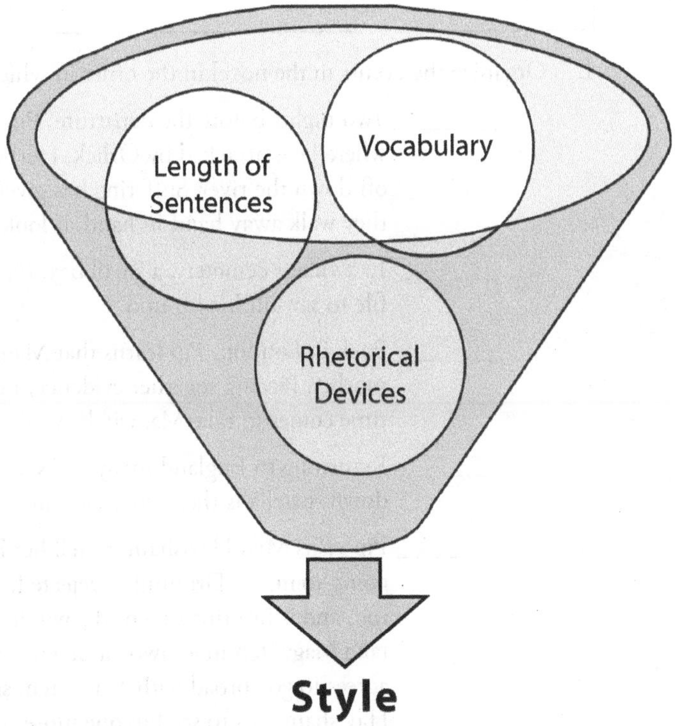

Literary Analysis

Dickens originally wrote two different endings for *Great Expectations*. In this first version, Pip learns that Drummle treated Estella badly, but he died, and she then married a country doctor who treated her better. Pip runs into her in London where he gathers that she has grown to have a heart and regrets how she treated him. Compare and contrast this ending with the actual ending. Which ending do you prefer?

Answers will vary. Dickens was advised by other author friends to write the ending we have. They thought was it was more interesting and believable. It relied less on coincidence.

Biblical Application

G.K. Chesterton wrote "I do not for a moment maintain that [Dickens] enjoyed everybody in his daily life. But he enjoyed everybody in his books. . . . His books are full of baffled villains stalking out or cowardly bullies kicked downstairs. But the villains and the cowards are such delightful people that the reader always hopes the villain will put his head through a side window and make a last remark; or that the bully will say one more thing, even from the bottom of the stairs."[1] Chesterton appreciated that Dickens's villains were entertaining but, at the same time, they were really villains. Today, we are asked to feel sorry for villains. Bad people, cruel people, and evil people are sympathetically presented by screenwriters. Why is this a problem?

Evil is real but the love of God is more real. Dickens, whose faith has never been fully confirmed, often was lighthearted with villains (e.g., Fagin in Oliver Twist).

1 G.K. Chesterton, *The Victorian Age in Literature* (1913) (Notre Dame, IN: University of Notre Dame Press, 1963), p. 60.

Chapter 8 Test

I. Organize the events in the novel in the order in which they occur. (40 points)

_________ Two nights before the departure, Pip receives a mysterious message to go to his own home village, where he is attacked by Orlick. Herbert rescues him, but he's still battered and sore when they set off down the river. Suffering has given Estella human feelings at last, and she is kind to Pip. As they walk away hand in hand, it looks as though they will finally get together.

_________ In a village cemetery, a small boy, Pip, is accosted by a runaway convict who demands food and a file to saw off his leg iron.

_________ Back in London, Pip learns that Magwitch once had a baby girl, but she was abandoned by her mother. Piecing together evidence, Pip realizes with shock that Estella was that baby girl. The time comes to take Magwitch away.

_________ Returning to England many years later, Pip visits Miss Havisham's house, which has been pulled down. Estella is there, too. Her husband Drummle, who treated her badly, has died.

_________ Pip visits Miss Havisham, to tell her he's lost his fortune; Estella is there, and he learns that she's going to marry Drummle. Dejected, Pip returns to London to learn that Compeyson is there, too, and is hunting down Magwitch. Herbert, Pip, and Jaggers' clerk Wemmick hatch a plan to take Magwitch in a rowboat down river, where he can board a ship bound for Germany. Pip agrees to go abroad with Magwitch, since he feels he has no future left in England. Miss Havisham asks to see Pip one more time.

_________ Pip falls in love with Estella and becomes self-conscious about his low social class and unpolished manners. From then on, his abiding dream is to be a gentleman. He is bitterly disappointed when he becomes a teenager and Miss Havisham sees nothing better for him than to become apprenticed to his brother-in-law Joe at his blacksmith's forge.

_________ Miss Havisham was deeply affected by Pip's outburst to Estella, and she is full of remorse for her selfish scheme; she begs Pip to forgive her. He does so, but just as he is leaving, she bends over the fire and then suddenly goes up in a pillar of flame. Pip rescues her, but she never recovers.

_________ Magwitch tells Pip and Herbert his history. The convict Magwitch was fighting with on the marshes was his partner, Compeyson, who gave evidence against Magwitch to save his own skin. Pip and Herbert realize that Compeyson is the same man who deserted Miss Havisham on her wedding day.

II. Discussion Question (60 points)

Pip is one of the most complicated characters in western literature. The different elements of Pip's personality seem to be constantly in conflict. Explain.

Chapter 8 Test Answer Sample

I. Organize the events in the novel in the order in which they occur. (40 points)

7 Two nights before the departure, Pip receives a mysterious message to go to his own home village, where he is attacked by Orlick. Herbert rescues him, but he's still battered and sore when they set off down the river. Suffering has given Estella human feelings at last, and she is kind to Pip. As they walk away hand in hand, it looks as though they will finally get together.

1 In a village cemetery, a small boy, Pip, is accosted by a runaway convict who demands food and a file to saw off his leg iron.

6 Back in London, Pip learns that Magwitch once had a baby girl, but she was abandoned by her mother. Piecing together evidence, Pip realizes with shock that Estella was that baby girl. The time comes to take Magwitch away.

8 Returning to England many years later, Pip visits Miss Havisham's house, which has been pulled down. Estella is there, too. Her husband Drummle, who treated her badly, has died.

4 Pip visits Miss Havisham, to tell her he's lost his fortune; Estella is there, and he learns that she's going to marry Drummle. Dejected, Pip returns to London to learn that Compeyson is there, too, and is hunting down Magwitch. Herbert, Pip, and Jaggers' clerk Wemmick hatch a plan to take Magwitch in a rowboat down river, where he can board a ship bound for Germany. Pip agrees to go abroad with Magwitch, since he feels he has no future left in England. Miss Havisham asks to see Pip one more time.

2 Pip falls in love with Estella and becomes self-conscious about his low social class and unpolished manners. From then on, his abiding dream is to be a gentleman. He is bitterly disappointed when he becomes a teenager and Miss Havisham sees nothing better for him than to become apprenticed to his brother-in-law Joe at his blacksmith's forge.

5 Miss Havisham was deeply affected by Pip's outburst to Estella, and she is full of remorse for her selfish scheme; she begs Pip to forgive her. He does so, but just as he is leaving, she bends over the fire and then suddenly goes up in a pillar of flame. Pip rescues her, but she never recovers.

3 Magwitch tells Pip and Herbert his history. The convict Magwitch was fighting with on the marshes was his partner, Compeyson, who gave evidence against Magwitch to save his own skin. Pip and Herbert realize that Compeyson is the same man who deserted Miss Havisham on her wedding day.

II. Discussion Question (60 points)

Pip is one of the most complicated characters in western literature. The different elements of Pip's personality seem to be constantly in conflict. Explain.

For example, when Pip first learns that he has "expectations" of a great fortune, he was conflicted with multiple emotions: self-centeredness, pleasure, responsibility, misgiving, embarrassment, and fear. Because Dickens isn't trying to make Pip look good. Pip is never a paradigm of virtue. Pip, then, defies all archetypes and becomes a rich, many faceted character.

Reading 2

Great Expectations by Charles Dickens

Chapter 9

First Thoughts

Dickens is one of the most prolific and beloved writers of the 19th century. Yet, today, many young people struggle with Dickens. His descriptions can be tedious and his tone somewhat sentimental. But give him a chance! He is worth the time and effort. He will bless you in new ways, if you will.

Chapter Learning Objectives

In chapter 9 we will . . .

1. Review "Unity in a Paragraph"
2. Learn how to develop paragraphs
3. Discuss the setting in *Great Expectations*
4. Evaluate "Social Reform Literature"
5. Discuss coincidence

Look Ahead for Friday

- Turn in all assignments.
- Work on your novella this week.

Writing: Unity in a Paragraph

Daily Assignment

- Warm-up: Write a unified paragraph describing your favorite vacation spot.
- In your essay, use the words who and whom.
- Students will complete Concept Builder 9-A.
- Prayer journal: students are encouraged to write in their prayer journal every day.
- Finish the next book you have been assigned.
- Students should systematically review their vocabulary words daily.

CONCEPT BUILDER 9-A

Paragraph Unity

Rewrite the following paragraph in your own words. It is an excerpt from the book *Yesterday, Today & Forever* by Maria von Trapp (Green Forest, AR: New Leaf Press, page 5, 1975):

It was in Italian South Tyrol in a primitive little country inn on the edge of a lovely village in the mountains. The year was 1938, and this was the first station on our flight from Naziinvaded Austria. We, that is Father Wasner, my husband, and I, and nine children with the tenth on the way, had just barely arrived at this peaceful little place when it happened. With a terrific wail, Lorli, aged six, discovered that we had forgotten her favorite toy, a worn-out, shapeless, hairless something, formerly a teddy bear. The grief of a child is always terrible. It is bottomless, without hope. A child has no past and no future. It just lives in the present moment — wholeheartedly. If the present moment spells disaster, the child suffers it with his whole heart, his whole soul, his whole strength, and his whole little being. Because a child is so helpless in his grief, we should never take it lightly, but drop all we are doing at the moment and come to his aid.

Answers will vary.

Lesson 2

Writing: Paragraph Development

Daily Assignment

- Warm-up: Write a well-developed paragraph that exhibits lucidity, unity, and adequate development.
- Students will complete Concept Builder 9-B.
- Prayer journal: students are encouraged to write in their prayer journal every day.
- Finish the next book you have been assigned.
- Students should systematically review their vocabulary words daily.

CONCEPT BUILDER 9-B

Paragraph Development

Match each paragraph type with an example.

Paragraph Type	Example
A. Narration	1. *G* The main cause of World War I was . . .
B. Persuasion	2. *B* Ladies and gentlemen of the jury, I am arguing today . . .
C. Exposition	3. *A* Once upon a time there was . . .
D. Definition	4. *E* The apple tree was full of pink blossoms . . .
E. Description	5. *D* Love is kind and forgiving . . . .
F. Process	6. *C* This is my explanation of what happened . . .
G. Cause and Effect	7. *F* Here is how you cook pasta . . .

Lesson 3

The Setting

Daily Assignment

- Warm-up: Describe the setting of your life. How important has your setting been to your formation as a person?
- Students will complete Concept Builder 9-C.
- Prayer journal: students are encouraged to write in their prayer journal every day.
- Finish the next book you have been assigned.
- Students should systematically review their vocabulary words daily.

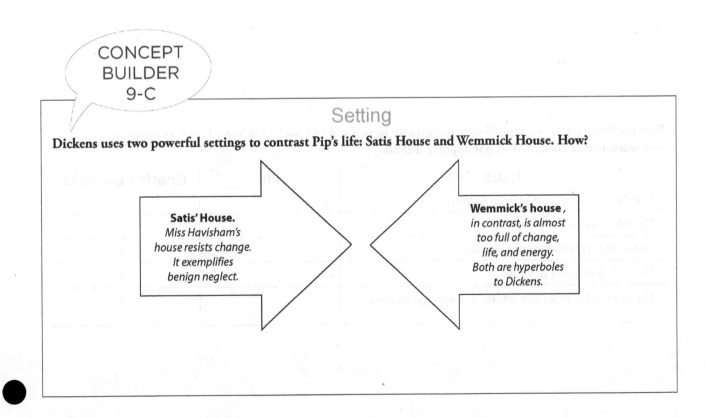

CONCEPT BUILDER 9-C

Setting

Dickens uses two powerful settings to contrast Pip's life: Satis House and Wemmick House. How?

Satis' House. *Miss Havisham's house resists change. It exemplifies benign neglect.*

Wemmick's house, *in contrast, is almost too full of change, life, and energy. Both are hyperboles to Dickens.*

Lesson 4

Social Reform Literature

Daily Assignment

- Warm-up: Write a protest letter to the editor of your local newspaper about something in your town that upsets you.
- Students will complete Concept Builder 9-D.
- Prayer journal: students are encouraged to write in their prayer journal every day.
- Finish the next book you have been assigned.
- Students should systematically review their vocabulary words daily.

CONCEPT BUILDER 9-D

Social Reform Literature

Rate the following issues according to importance to you and to Charles Dickens: 1 — very important, 2 — moderately important, 3 — not important at all.

Issue	Me	Charles Dickens
The way orphans are treated in society.		*1*
The religious faith of people in general.		*3*
The working conditions of the poor.		*1*
The laws governing poverty.		*2*
The required military commitment of average citizens.		*3*

Lesson 5

Coincidence

Daily Assignment

- Warm-up: Describe a coincidental event that changed your life.
- Students will complete Concept Builder 9-E.
- Prayer journal: students are encouraged to write in their prayer journal every day.
- Finish the next book you have been assigned.
- Students should systematically review their vocabulary words daily.

CONCEPT BUILDER 9-E

Coincidence

Find three examples of coincidence. Are they necessary to the development of the plot?

In the dirty, unwelcoming office of Jagger, full of dishonest pretension, Herbert Pocket, Pip's host, turns out to be a kind, young, garrulous, generous friend, his arms full of food and his face full of laughter.

Pip runs into Jaggers in the street, and is invited to dinner at Jaggers' house, where he's given a note from Miss Havisham. This will lead ultimately to his reunion with Estella.

At the end of the novel Pip slips away from Joe and Biddy to go gaze nostalgically at where Satis House used to stand. He has heard that Estella was unhappy with Drummle, but that he recently died. By coincidence, Estella is walking in the old rundown garden that evening too.

Chapter 9 Review Questions

Writing a Novella

Write another chapter in your novella. Use coincidence when necessary, but sparingly and with good cause.

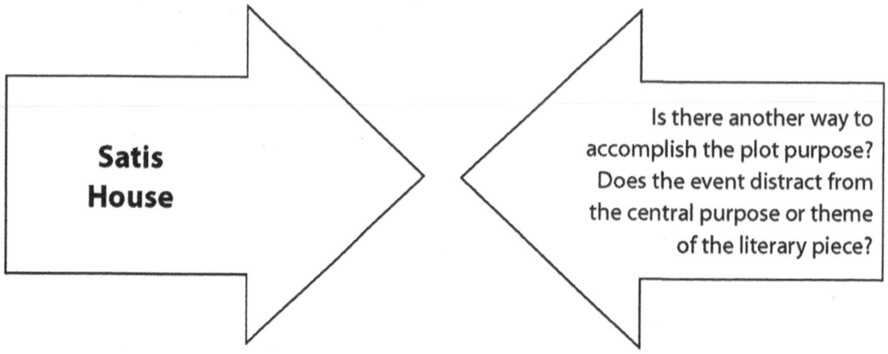

Satis House
Is there another way to accomplish the plot purpose? Does the event distract from the central purpose or theme of the literary piece?

Literary Analysis

Are the women in *Great Expectations* credible, believable characters? Or are they shallow archetypes without depth and complexity? Explain.

All the women in Great Expectations, *as in most Dickens' novels, are archetypical characters who rarely are developed. They are the Madame Defarge-types* (A Tale of Two Cities). *Estella changes somewhat and Nancy, in* Oliver Twist, *is complicated, but even these women are more "types" than real characters.*

Biblical Application

Pip lies a lot throughout the novel. Is this wrong? If it is wrong, is it understandable, even excusable? When are lies acceptable? For instance, if Corrie ten Boom did not lie about hiding Jewish people, she came very close. Should we lie to save someone?

While lying is wrong, certainly, this author would lie if it would save the lives of human beings, like Corrie ten Boom did.

Chapter 9 Test

I. Rewrite the following paragraphs removing unnecessary thoughts and sentences (75 points, 15 points each).

A. Adoption is an important theme in the Bible. I have an adopted sister and brother. The subject of orphans and adoption finds its way into numerous portions throughout both Old and New Testaments. The biblical understanding of adoption is interesting to explore.

B. There are many ways the theme of adoptions roots itself in the Bible. One of these ways is through Moses and Esther. This hero and heroine were both adopted, Moses by the Pharaoh's daughter. In the cartoon I saw, Pharaoh's daughter loved Moses. When the child grew older, she brought him to Pharaoh's daughter, and he became her son. She named him Moses, "Because," she said, "I drew him out of the water" (Exodus 2:10; HCSB), and Esther by Mordecai. Mordecai was the legal guardian of his cousin Hadassah (that is, Esther), because she didn't have a father or mother. . . . When her father and mother died, Mordecai had adopted her as his own daughter (Esther 2:7; HCSB). Much good came out of this, as they were both involved in saving God's people, Israel. Israel, as you know, is the nation with whom God made a covenant.

C. God frequently commands His people, and Christ commands His followers, to care for orphans. In fact, there are approximately 30 references in the New International Version to taking care of "orphans" or "the fatherless." And you should see how many times God tells husbands to love their wives! One of these references is found in Psalm 82:3: "Defend the weak and the fatherless; uphold the cause of the poor and the oppressed." Adoption is a significant way of caring for the fatherless, and is very much in line with God's commands.

D. A young woman in her 20s takes verses like Psalm 82:3 very seriously. She runs an outreach in Uganda for impoverished and orphaned children. It's called Amazima, which means "the truth" in Luganda, one of many languages spoken in Uganda. The program helps kids pay their school tuition, and equips them with school supplies. This woman has also adopted 13 daughters before the age of 21. She also loves to drive a Chevrolet.

E. The New Testament offers us another understanding of adoption. In Galatians 4:4–7, Paul states, "When the time came to completion, God sent His Son, born of a woman, born under the law, to redeem those under the law, so that we might receive adoption as sons. And because you are sons, God has sent the Spirit of His Son into our hearts, crying, 'Abba, Father!' So you are no longer a slave but a son, and if a son, then an heir through God" (HCSB). First John 3:1 says, "See what great love the Father has lavished on us, that we should be called children of God! And that is what we are!" These verses, and others, give us ample reason to believe that God made it possible for us to be adopted into His family through Christ's sacrifice on the Cross. But that does not mean you can have anything you want. No, you have to ask Him for it. He is our perfect father no matter what our family situation is, no matter who we are or where we've come from, or if we're saints or sinners — we are the children of God! This is a life-changing sense of adoption for those with a loving earthly father and those without, to have a Heavenly Father to guide them, love them, "embrace" them when they succeed, and pick them up when they fall. (Margo)

II. When does coincidence work in a novel and when does it not work? (25 points)

Your essay will be evaluated in these three areas:

Syntax and diction: grammar and style (5 points)

Organization: paragraphs, transitions, introduction, et al. (5 points)

Argument (15 points)

Chapter 9 Test Answer Sample

I. Rewrite the following paragraphs removing unnecessary thoughts and sentences (75 points, 15 points each).

A. Adoption is an important theme in the Bible. The subject of orphans and adoption finds its way into numerous portions throughout both Old and New Testaments. The biblical understanding of adoption is interesting to explore.

B. There are many ways the theme of adoptions roots itself in the Bible. One of these ways is through Moses and Esther. This hero and heroine were both adopted, Moses by the Pharaoh's daughter. When the child grew older, she brought him to Pharaoh's daughter, and he became her son. She named him Moses, "Because," she said, "I drew him out of the water" (Exodus 2:10; HCSB). Mordecai was the legal guardian of his cousin Hadassah (that is, Esther), because she didn't have a father or mother. . . . When her father and mother died, Mordecai had adopted her as his own daughter (Esther 2:7). Much good came out of this, as they were both involved in saving God's people, Israel.

C. God frequently commands His people, and Christ commands His followers, to care for orphans. In fact, there are approximately 30 references in the New International Version to taking care of "orphans" or "the fatherless." One of these references is found in Psalm 82:3: "Defend the weak and the fatherless; uphold the cause of the poor and the oppressed." Adoption is a significant way of caring for the fatherless, and is very much in line with God's commands.

D. A young woman in her 20s takes verses like Psalm 82:3 very seriously. She runs an outreach in Uganda for impoverished and orphaned children. It's called Amazima, which means "the truth" in Luganda, one of many languages spoken in Uganda. The program helps kids pay their school tuition, and equips them with school supplies. This woman has also adopted 13 daughters before the age of 21.

E. The New Testament offers us another understanding of adoption. In Galatians 4:4–7 Paul states, "When the time came to completion, God sent His Son, born of a woman, born under the law, to redeem those under the law, so that we might receive adoption as sons. And because you are sons, God has sent the Spirit of His Son into our hearts, crying, 'Abba, Father!' So you are no longer a slave but a son, and if a son, then an heir through God," and 1st John 3:1 says, "See what great love the Father has lavished on us, that we should be called children of God! And that is what we are!." These verses, and others, give us ample reason to believe that God made it possible for us to be adopted into His family through Christ's sacrifice on the Cross. He is our perfect father no matter what our family situation is, no matter who we are or where we've come from, or if we're saints or sinners — we are the children of God! This is a life changing sense of adoption for those with a loving earthly father and those without, to have a Heavenly Father to guide them, love them, "embrace" them when they succeed, and pick them up when they fall. (Margo)

II. When does coincidence work in a novel and when does it not work? (25 points)

Your essay will be evaluated in these three areas:

Syntax and diction: grammar and style (5 points)

Organization: paragraphs, transitions, introduction, et al. (5 points)

Argument (15 points)

Every author uses coincidence. It is necessary to advance the plot; however, when coincidence exists to build suspense only, or to make the reader maudlin, then it is wrong to use.

Reading 1

Winnie the Pooh by A.A. Milne

Chapter 10

First Thoughts

Winnie the Pooh, also called Pooh Bear, is a fictional human-like bear created by A.A. Milne. The first collection of stories about the character was the book *Winnie-the-Pooh* (1926), and this was followed by *The House at Pooh Corner* (1928). Milne also included a poem about the bear in the children's verse book, *When We Were Very Young* (1924) and many more in *Now We Are Six* (1927). All four volumes were illustrated by E.H. Shepard.

Winnie the Pooh, like Tolkien's *Hobbit*, while easy to read is actually quite profound and, like so much of children's literature, is full of wisdom. In fact, this author, a pastor, has used more stories from the escapades of the Pooh Bear than all other sources.

Chapter Learning Objectives

In chapter 10 we will . . .

1. Understand the correct use of modifiers
2. Practice using transitions
3. Analyze dialogue and narration in *Winnie the Pooh*

Look Ahead for Friday

- Turn in all assignments.
- Assess the pathos, logos, ethos of your novella.

Grammar Review: The Correct Use of Modifiers

Daily Assignment

- Warm-up: Describe a good thing that happened to you. Next, describe a better thing that happened to you. Finally, describe the best thing that ever happened to you.
- In your essay, use the words who and whom.
- Students will complete Concept Builder 10-A.
- Prayer journal: students are encouraged to write in their prayer journal every day.
- Finish the next book you have been assigned.
- Students should systematically review their vocabulary words daily.

CONCEPT BUILDER 10-A

The Correct Use of Modifiers

Write the forms for the comparative and superlative forms of these words:

Positive	Comparative	Superlative
harmful	*more harmful*	*most harmful*
loose	*looser*	*loosiest*
lovely	*more lovely*	*most lovely*
gentle	*gentler*	*gentlest*

Writing: Transitional Words

Daily Assignment

- Warm-up: Write a three-paragraph essay with transitions in every paragraph about your favorite character in *Winnie the Pooh.*
- Students will complete Concept Builder 10-B.
- Prayer journal: students are encouraged to write in their prayer journal every day.
- Finish the next book you have been assigned.
- Students should systematically review their vocabulary words daily.

CONCEPT BUILDER 10-B

Transitions

Using transitions make the following paragraphs more coherent.

A. It was during these hard times, hard times when we struggled, that we seemed to grow the most. Lawrence Kohlberg, a child psychologist, and a man under whom I studied while a seminarian at Harvard, argued that human beings grew emotionally, and spiritually when they faced conflict. *For example,* only when we were forced to reevaluate our circumstances were we free to grow. Failures, disappointments, and letdowns all had a purpose. *Therefore,* as we look back on our own Christian lives, the hard times, the broken times, were often the best times. At these moments, as we walked through the "valley of the shadow of death" as we faced conflict, we had to feel the grit of life in our beds and in our hearts. These were the times in which we grew the most.

B. In John 2, we have a picture of Jesus at a wedding in Cana. With His mother and His disciples, we see Him sharing one of the happiest events in Judaism. *For example, then, as today,* a wedding was a notable occasion. It was Jewish law that the wedding should take place on a Wednesday, but the wedding lasted far more than one day. It could last for a week! The wedding ceremony itself occurred late in the evening, usually after a feast. After the ceremony the young couple was conducted to their new home. By then it was dark and they were carried through the village streets by the light of flaming torches with a canopy over their heads. The wedding couple traveled the most circuitous route possible so that as many people as possible could see the happy couple. A newlywed couple did not go away for a honeymoon. Hardly! They stayed at home and hosted a week-long party. They wore crowns and stayed dressed in their bridal gowns. They were king and queen for a week! In a land where life was so unforgiving and harsh, this was a joyous week indeed!

Narration: Second Person

Daily Assignment

- Warm-up: Describe the first time you heard about Winnie the Pooh.
- Students will complete Concept Builder 10-C.
- Prayer journal: students are encouraged to write in their prayer journal every day.
- Finish the next book you have been assigned.
- Students should systematically review their vocabulary words daily.

CONCEPT BUILDER 10-C

Character Foils

Essentially all the characters exist to develop the main character, Winnie the Pooh. He learns something about life through each one. How?

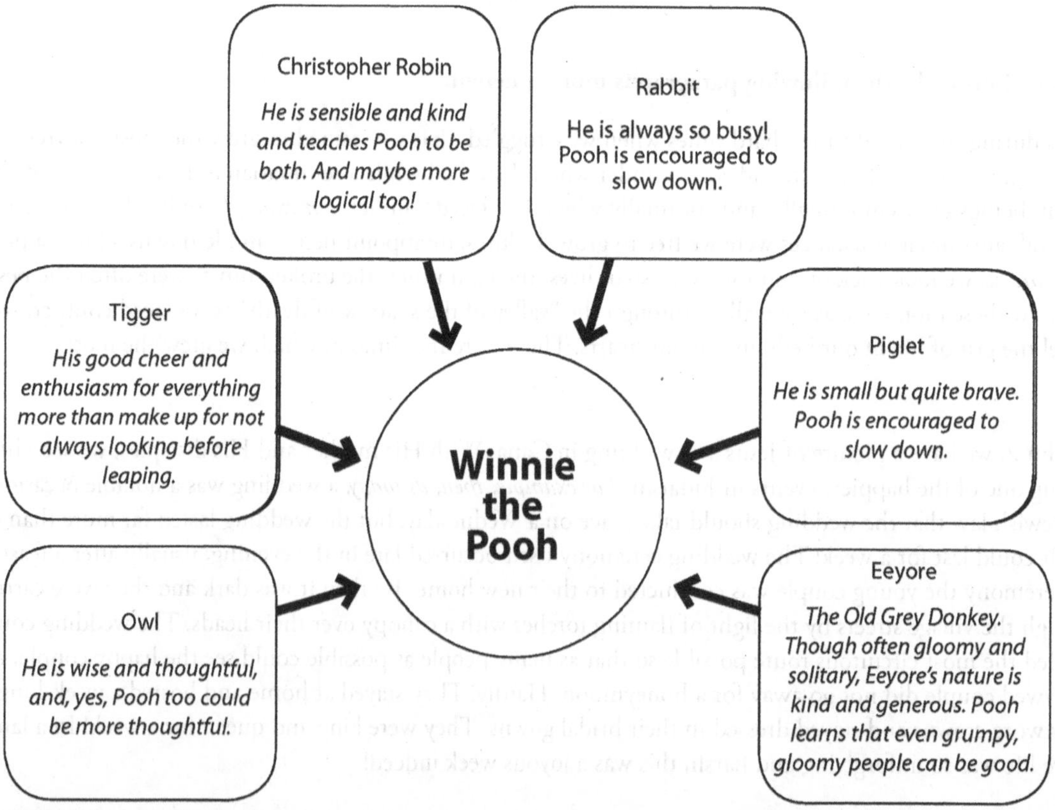
Christopher Robin
He is sensible and kind and teaches Pooh to be both. And maybe more logical too!
Rabbit
He is always so busy! Pooh is encouraged to slow down.
Tigger
His good cheer and enthusiasm for everything more than make up for not always looking before leaping.
Piglet
He is small but quite brave. Pooh is encouraged to slow down.
Winnie the Pooh
Owl
He is wise and thoughtful, and, yes, Pooh too could be more thoughtful.
Eeyore
The Old Grey Donkey. Though often gloomy and solitary, Eeyore's nature is kind and generous. Pooh learns that even grumpy, gloomy people can be good.

Lesson 4

Dialogue

Daily Assignment

- Warm-up: Write an imaginary dialogue between yourself and Winnie the Pooh. Talk about the best way to make Eeyore happy.
- Students will complete Concept Builder 10-D.
- Prayer journal: students are encouraged to write in their prayer journal every day.
- Finish the next book you have been assigned.
- Students should systematically review their vocabulary words daily.

Book Study: Active Reading

Winnie the Pooh, A.A. Milne

Chapter 1

Why does Milne use second person?

To involve his readers, some of whom might be children.

How does Milne use dialogue?

To introduce his characters.

How does Milne help the reader identify with Pooh?

Because, ironically, he is so human!

Predict the outcome of Pooh's plans to use a balloon to get honey.

Answers will vary.

What is Christopher Robin's role?

He is an important foil.

Daily Assignment

- Warm-up: Describe a providential (God-inspired) event that changed your life.
- Students will complete Concept Builder 10-E.
- Prayer journal: students are encouraged to write in their prayer journal every day.
- Finish the next book you have been assigned.
- Students should systematically review their vocabulary words daily.

CONCEPT BUILDER 10-E

Values

Clearly Pooh and his friends share certain values. Compare these values to other cultural icons.

Character	What is okay	What isn't okay
Winnie the Pooh	To Pooh friends are important. He is loyal, kind, and patient.	Pooh does not like to be hurried. He does not like to hurt others' feelings.
Spider-Man	*Spider-Man is a good super hero, albeit, a little whiny. (Other answers will vary.)*	*Evil and anything that hurts someone else are wrong.*
Dora	*Dora is much like Winnie the Pooh. (Other answers will vary.)*	*Much like Winnie the Pooh.*
Prince Caspian	*Caspian loves adventure and good friends.*	*Intense sense of justice and will fight any injustice.*
Bilbo Baggins	*Shy but bold and courageous like Piglet.*	*Prefers to be left alone and will not support unjust positions.*
Cinderella's stepmother	*Selfish, self-centered, mean.*	*Will not tolerate anyone prospering if she is not in control.*

Chapter 10 Review Questions

Writing a Novella

Write another chapter in your novella. Pay particular attention, again, to your narration. Generally speaking, you want to use the same narration point of view throughout your entire novella. Have you?

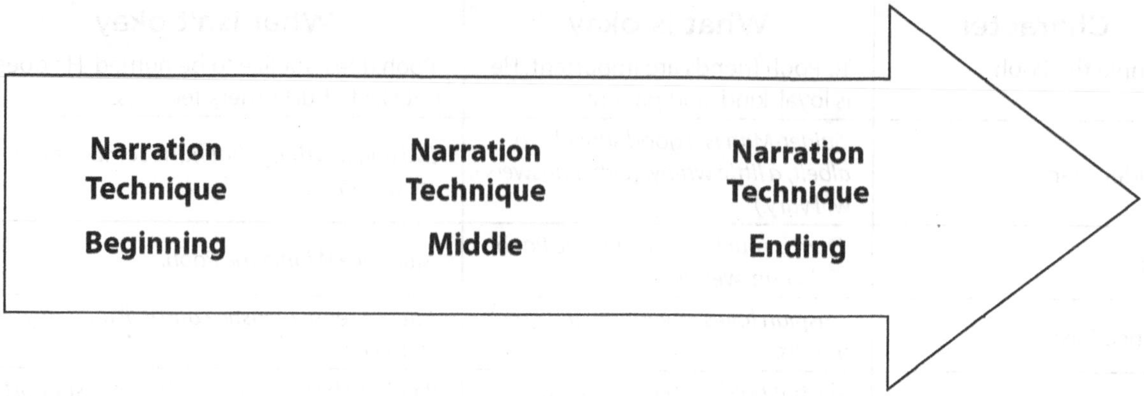

Literary Analysis

What is the function of the character Christopher Robin?

Christopher Robin is a significant foil, and A.A. Milne uses him as a frame story for the whole story. This is an important link to other children, who are, after all, Christopher Robin. Contrast this with the Dr. Seuss stories which connect with the ethos of children but really has no humans in them. Finally, the book concludes with Christopher Robin saying that he hopes his father can think up more stories about Winnie-the-Pooh.

Biblical Application

Read Genesis 1:1–5. How does God, our Creator, begin to bring about our world?

Answers will vary..

Chapter 10 Test

I. Develop at least three biblical themes in *Winnie the Pooh* (25 points).

II. Discuss the use of transitions in every paragraph in this essay (75 points, 12 points each)

In *Cold Sassy Tree,* Olive Ann Burns chooses a young boy to be her narrator. Though the reader may at first have doubts about the neutrality and reliability of this narrator, he is a reliable and trustworthy character. Throughout the book's course, he impartially reveals incidents that hurt him, and makes an effort to leave no detail untold.

____

Cold Sassy Tree carries with it the feel of a personal letter or diary — the narrator, a young boy, makes no effort to hide anything. Indeed, he even relates what is possibly the most embarrassing incident of his youth:

I was kissing Lightfoot! . . . Just then God spoke out loud in the voice of Miss Alice Ann. "Will Tweedy, you ought to be ashamed!" said God. I looked up and there He stood in a pink and white poky-dot dress, pointing His plump forefinger at us.

____

Furthermore, Will Tweedy, the narrator, makes no effort to present himself as the perfect child. Indeed, he narrates all events to the reader with perfect neutrality — both those that flatter him, and those that hurt him. Because of Will's willingness to tell even his most embarrassing tales, the reader feels comfortable trusting him with other details.

____

Through Will, the reader is privy to even the smallest detail of life in *Cold Sassy Tree:*

Grandpa and Miss Love stood there watching me read what it said under the picture: "PIERCE, 8 h.p., Geo. N. Pierce Co., Buffalo, N.Y. Price $900, without top; seats 4 persons, doors in back only; single, water-cooled cylinder; jump spark ignition, planetary transmission, 3 speeds; wt. 1,250 pound."

____

Also, this abundance of detail not only draws the reader into the story, but builds a relationship of trust between the reader and Will, the narrator. After all, if Will tells the reader what kind of ignition and what type of transmission Grandpa's automobile has, surely he can be trusted not to leave out other details important to the plot.

____

In *Cold Sassy Tree,* Olive Ann Burns chooses an ideal narrator. He is unscrupulous in his narration; impartially revealing all of the events in *Cold Sassy Tree* to the reader. Furthermore, he records in meticulous detail every minor incident—both drawing the reader into the story and adding to his reliability. (Daniel)

Chapter 10 Test Answer Sample

I. Develop at least three biblical themes in *Winnie the Pooh* (25 points).

Answers will vary. Common themes include: love, forgiveness, patience.

II. Discuss the use of transitions in every paragraph in this essay (75 points, 12 points each)

In *Cold Sassy Tree*, Olive Ann Burns chooses a young boy to be her narrator. Though the reader may at first have doubts about the neutrality and reliability of this narrator, he is a reliable and trustworthy character. Throughout the book's course, he impartially reveals incidents that hurt him, and makes an effort to leave no detail untold.

The next paragraph picks up the theme of "a young boy" and "the narrator" — both concepts introduced in the previous paragraph.

Cold Sassy Tree carries with it the feel of a personal letter or diary — the narrator, a young boy, makes no effort to hide anything. Indeed, he even relates what is possibly the most embarrassing incident of his youth:

> I was kissing Lightfoot! . . . Just then God spoke out loud in the voice of Miss Alice Ann. "Will Tweedy, you ought to be ashamed!" said God. I looked up and there He stood in a pink and white poky-dot dress, pointing His plump forefinger at us.

"Furthermore" is a transition word, and, again, the author picks up on previous thoughts.

Furthermore, Will Tweedy, the narrator, makes no effort to present himself as the perfect child. Indeed, he narrates all events to the reader with perfect neutrality — both those that flatter him, and those that hurt him. Because of Will's willingness to tell even his most embarrassing tales, the reader feels comfortable trusting him with other details.

"Will" is the thought that draws the reader forward.

Through Will, the reader is privy to even the smallest detail of life in Cold Sassy Tree:

Grandpa and Miss Love stood there watching me read what it said under the picture: "PIERCE, 8 h.p., Geo. N. Pierce Co., Buffaly, N.Y. Price $900, without top; seats 4 persons, doors in back only; single, water-cooled cylinder; jump spark ignition, planetary transmission, 3 speeds; wt. 1,250 pound."

"Also" is a strong transition.

Also, this abundance of detail not only draws the reader into the story, but builds a relationship of trust between the reader and Will, the narrator. After all, if Will tells the reader what kind of ignition and what type of transmission Grandpa's automobile has, surely he can be trusted not to leave out other details important to the plot.

The conclusion/summary pulls everything together.

In *Cold Sassy Tree*, Olive Ann Burns chooses an ideal narrator. He is unscrupulous in his narration; impartially revealing all of the events in *Cold Sassy Tree* to the reader. Furthermore, he records in meticulous detail every minor incident—both drawing the reader into the story and adding to his reliability. (Daniel)

Reading 2

Winnie the Pooh by A.A. Milne

Chapter 11

First Thoughts

The Winnie the Pooh stories are set in Ashdown Forest, Sussex, England, 30 miles south of London. In 1925 Milne, a veteran of World War I, sought solitude and bought a country home a mile to the north of the forest at Cotchford Farm, near Hartfield. As Christopher Milne, A.A. Milne's son, wrote in his autobiography, many locations in the stories can be linked to real places in and around the forest. Tolkien chose Middle Earth to cleanse his soul from the carnage of World War I, while Milne used Ashdown Forest. Both places became places of cleansing, succor, and honor.

Chapter Learning Objectives

In chapter 11 we will . . .

1. Correctly use comparative and superlative forms of adjectives and adverbs.
2. Identify and avoid dangling and misplaced modifiers.
3. Make judgments about literature that will increase comprehension.
4. Identify the themes of this novel.

Look Ahead for Friday

- Turn in all assignments.
- Identify the themes of your novella.

Lesson 1

Grammar Review: Use of Comparative and Superlative Forms

Daily Assignment

- Warm-up: Compare two characters in *Winnie the Pooh*. Be sure to write your comparisons correctly.
- In your essay, use the words who and whom.
- Students will complete Concept Builder 11-A.
- Prayer journal: students are encouraged to write in their prayer journal every day.
- Finish the next book you have been assigned.
- Students should systematically review their vocabulary words daily.

CONCEPT BUILDER 11-A

Use of Comparative and Superlative Forms

Correct these sentences:

1. It is much more hotter today than yesterday.
   It is much hotter today than yesterday.

2. Of all the dogs in the race, the greyhounds were the faster.
   Of all the dogs in the race, the greyhounds were the fastest.

3. George was smarter than any person in class.
   George was smarter than any other person in class.

4. Ice fishing is most fun than fishing in a stream.
   Ice fishing is more fun than fishing in a stream.

5. Mary ran faster than any one.
   Mary ran faster than anyone else.

Lesson 2

Grammar: Dangling Modifiers

Daily Assignment

- Warm-up: Write a three-paragraph essay using modifiers about your favorite scene in *Winnie the Pooh.*
- Students will complete Concept Builder 11-B.
- Prayer journal: students are encouraged to write in their prayer journal every day.
- Finish the next book you have been assigned.
- Students should systematically review their vocabulary words daily.

CONCEPT BUILDER 11-B

Dangling Modifiers

Correct these sentences:

1. At fourteen my dad bought me my first gun.
   When I was 14 my dad bought me my first gun.

2. The mom corrected her children with a smile.
   The mom, with a smile, corrected her children.

3. The fans encouraged the pitch hitter in the stands.
   The fans in the stands encouraged the pitch hitter.

4. Inside the car I notice a light was blinking.
   I noticed that a light inside the car was blinking.

5. A book lay on the sidewalk covered in a frayed book cover.
   A book covered in a frayed book cover lay on the sidewalk.

Writing: Coherence in a Paragraph

Daily Assignment

- Warm-up: Write a coherent paragraph about what you did yesterday. What is your cohesion strategy? (Time? Space? Importance?)
- Students will complete Concept Builder 11-C.
- Prayer journal: students are encouraged to write in their prayer journal every day.
- Finish the next book you have been assigned.
- Students should systematically review their vocabulary words daily.

CONCEPT BUILDER 11-C

Coherence

Choose a coherence strategy for each paragraph:

A. In time	1. *C* The East End, from its beginnings, was full of people who were not searching for the truth of the ages. If they discovered this truth, the wisdom of the ages, maybe they would live some of that truth out. But they were not concerned so much about truth and meaning. They wanted to pay the rent, to buy groceries, to watch a Pirate game. That was mostly the extent of their excursion into the nonconcrete.
B. In space	2. *B* The house was located two miles behind the shopping center but traffic nonetheless was awful.
C. In importance	3. *A* The Civil War ended before Stephen Crane was able to fight.

Reading: Making Judgments

Daily Assignment

- Warm-up: Have you read a book, or seen a movie, that violated your morals?
- Students will complete Concept Builder 11-D.
- Prayer journal: students are encouraged to write in their prayer journal every day.
- Finish the next book you have been assigned.
- Students should systematically review their vocabulary words daily.

CONCEPT BUILDER 11-D

Making Judgments

Rate the following statements from authors 1 to 5 — 1 implies strong agreement and 5 means you completely oppose the comment.

Answers will vary.

Theme

Daily Assignment

- Warm-up: Discuss the theme(s) of your novella.
- Students will complete Concept Builder 11-E.
- Prayer journal: students are encouraged to write in their prayer journal every day.
- Finish the next book you have been assigned.
- Students should systematically review their vocabulary words daily.

CONCEPT BUILDER 11-E

Themes

Discuss briefly the following themes in *Winnie the Pooh*.

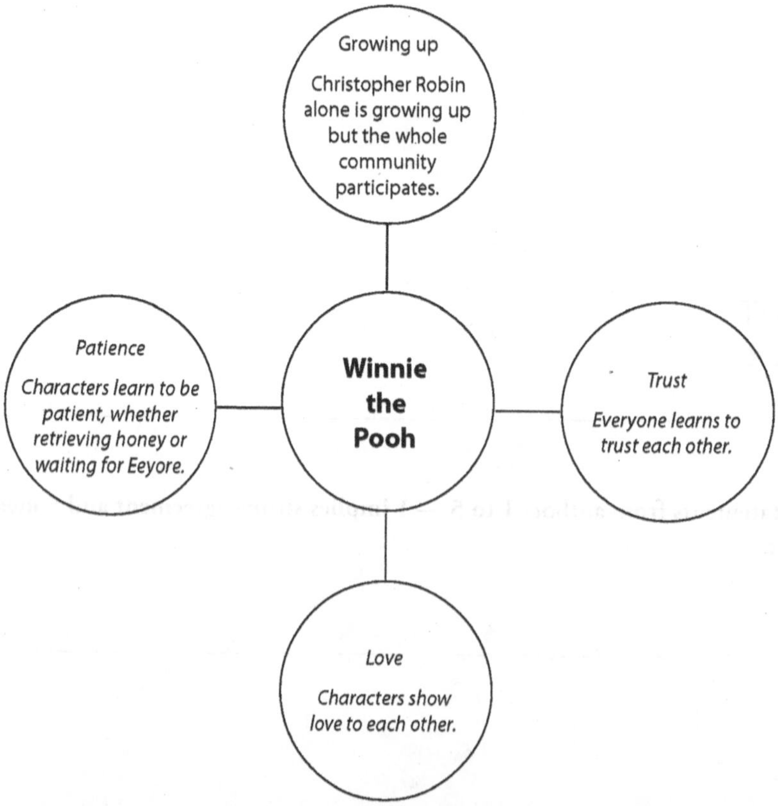

Growing up
Christopher Robin alone is growing up but the whole community participates.
Patience
Characters learn to be patient, whether retrieving honey or waiting for Eeyore.
Winnie the Pooh
Trust
Everyone learns to trust each other.
Love
Characters show love to each other.

Chapter 11 Review Questions

Writing a Novella

Write another chapter in your novella. By this point, you should know what theme(s) you are highlighting in your novella.

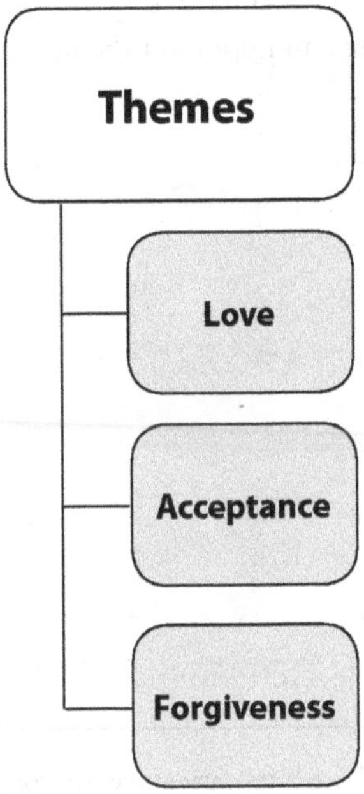

Literary Analysis

What are some themes in *Winnie the Pooh*? How does Milne develop these themes?

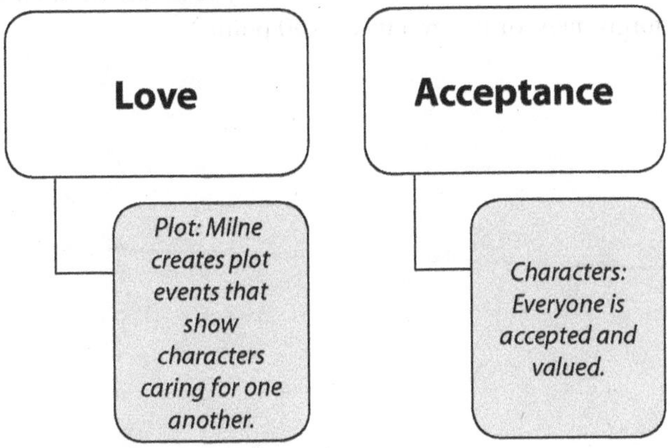

Biblical Application

Bruno Bettelheim's *The Uses of Enchantment: The Meaning and Importance of Fairy Tales* stresses the poignant and symbolic value of fairy tales and pretending in general. He argues that traditional fairy tales, with the themes of rejection, death, and injuries, allow us to grapple with our fears in remote, symbolic terms and thereby experience emotional growth — which make us stronger. Does this describe *Winnie the Pooh*?

In a way, yes. Readers observe good friends having a good time and celebrating wholesome community. Fear is dissipated by promises; evil is overcome by good. "The secret things belong to the LORD our God, but the things revealed belong to us and to our children forever" (Deuteronomy 29:29).

Chapter 11 Test

Write a fantasy story for your younger brother/sister or a friend. In your story illustrate through the plot, dialogue, etc., an important theme, such as love, forgiveness, or perseverance. (100 points)

Chapter 11 Test Answer Sample

Write a fantasy story for your younger brother/sister or a friend. In your story illustrate through the plot, dialogue, etc., an important theme, such as love, forgiveness, or perseverance. (100 points)

Answers will vary.

Reading 1

Song of Hiawatha by Henry David Longfellow

Chapter 12

First Thoughts

Henry David Longfellow met his first Native American in the 1830s when Chief Blackhawk visited Boston. Longfellow, like James Fennimore Cooper, was an "American Romantic." He saw Native Americans as "noble savages." He wrote in his diary, "I have at length hit upon a plan for a poem on the American Indians, which seems to me the right one and the only. It is to weave together their beautiful traditions into a whole. I have hit upon a measure, too, which I think the right and only one for such a theme."[1] In fact, the Finnish epic *Kalevala* inspired Longfellow to write this Native American epic.

1 www.Barclay.com.

Chapter Learning Objectives

In chapter 12 we will . . .

1. Understand multiculturalism, parody, rhyme, meter, narrative history, and strategic reading.
2. Analyze a comparison and contrast chart.

Look Ahead for Friday

- Turn in all assignments.
- Continue to work on your novella.

Active Reading: "The Peace Pipe" (Part one, continued in concept builder 12-A)

Compare this to other epic poems.
Like the gods descending from Mount Olympus, Gitche Manito descends. . . .

What is the central metaphor presented here?
A god smoking a peace pipe "as a signal to the nations."

Characterize Gitche Manito.
He is a compassionate, loving, all-powerful god.

Who does Gitche Manito promise to send?
I will send a Prophet to you,
A Deliverer of the nations,
Who shall guide you and shall teach you,
Who shall toil and suffer with you.
If you listen to his counsels,
You will multiply and prosper;
If his warnings pass unheeded,
You will fade away and perish!

Daily Assignment

- Warm-up: How effective is the beginning of this epic poem?
- In your essay, use the words who and whom.
- Students will complete Concept Builder 12-A.
- Prayer journal: students are encouraged to write in their prayer journal every day.
- Finish the next book you have been assigned.
- Students should systematically review their vocabulary words daily.

CONCEPT BUILDER 12-A

Active Reading (Part Two)

Read this portion of the poem, and answer the question that follows.

Predict the ending of this epic poem.

Answers will vary.

Reading Well

Daily Assignment

- Warm-up: Write a poem about your favorite hero.
- Students will complete Concept Builder 12-B.
- Prayer journal: students are encouraged to write in their prayer journal every day.
- Finish the next book you have been assigned.
- Students should systematically review their vocabulary words daily.

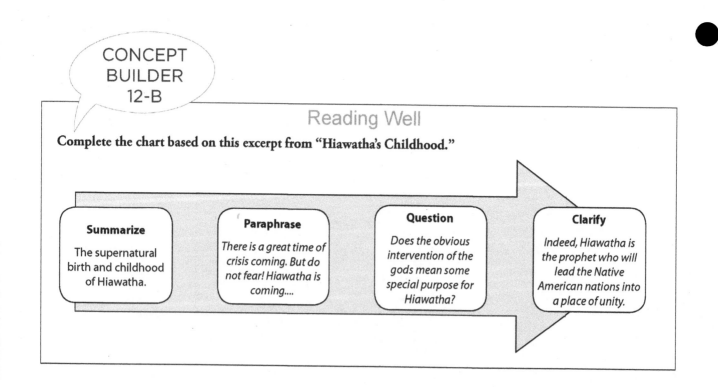

CONCEPT BUILDER 12-B

Reading Well

Complete the chart based on this excerpt from "Hiawatha's Childhood."

Summarize	Paraphrase	Question	Clarify
The supernatural birth and childhood of Hiawatha.	*There is a great time of crisis coming. But do not fear! Hiawatha is coming....*	*Does the obvious intervention of the gods mean some special purpose for Hiawatha?*	*Indeed, Hiawatha is the prophet who will lead the Native American nations into a place of unity.*

Lesson 3

Rhythm and Meter

Daily Assignment

- Warm-up: Consider contemporary songs that you know. What sort of meter, rhyme, and rhythm exist? Why does the songwriter choose those techniques?
- Students will complete Concept Builder 12-C.
- Prayer journal: students are encouraged to write in their prayer journal every day.
- Finish the next book you have been assigned.
- Students should systematically review their vocabulary words daily.

CONCEPT BUILDER 12-C

Rhythm and Meter

What is the rhyme scheme and meter of this passage?

Should you ask me, whence these stories? *a*
Whence these legends and traditions, *b*
With the odors of the forest *c* *(Notice the repetition of 'with")*
With the dew and damp of meadows, *d*
With the curling smoke of wigwams, *e*
With the rushing of great rivers, *f*
With their frequent repetitions, *g*
And their wild reverberations *h*
As of thunder in the mountains? *i*

Narrative Poetry

Daily Assignment

- Warm-up: The first stanza of the poem establishes the setting. Describe the setting, in a few sentences, paying attention to the time, place, and mood. What mood does Longfellow create by beginning the poem this way?
- Students will complete Concept Builder 12-D.
- Prayer journal: students are encouraged to write in their prayer journal every day.
- Finish the next book you have been assigned.
- Students should systematically review their vocabulary words daily.

CONCEPT BUILDER 12-D

Narrative Poetry: Inferno: Canto I

What is the storyline of this first canto of Longfellow's translation of Dante's *Inferno*?

Dante, like most epic heroes, is on a journey. He is in the "forest dark" but will eventually go to hell. Along the way, he will mature as a character as he overcomes many obstacles.

Reading: Comparison and Contrast

Daily Assignment

- Warm-up: Compare either two siblings, two parents, or two cousins in your family. Remember to compare their similarities.
- Students will complete Concept Builder 12-E.
- Prayer journal: students are encouraged to write in their prayer journal every day.
- Finish the next book you have been assigned.
- Students should systematically review their vocabulary words daily.

CONCEPT BUILDER 12-E

Comparison

Compare *The Kalevala* to *The Song of Hiawatha*.

	Kalevala	The Song of Hiawatha
Narrator	*The narrator connects with his reader.*	*The narrator connects with his reader.*
Metaphors	*Rich with metaphors from nature.*	*Rich with metaphors from nature.*

Chapter 12 Review Questions

Writing a Novella

Write another chapter in your novella.

Literary Analysis

Henry Wadsworth Longfellow was a professor at Harvard College. He created poems that are distinctly American. Many of his poems focused on people and events throughout American history. His romantic vision of the world made him the most popular American poet of his time. Analyze two of Longfellow's poems that fall into this category.

Both Song of Hiawatha *and* Paul Revere's Ride *fall into this category! Both are epic narratives based on American heroes.*

Biblical Application

As stated before, Longfellow was known as an "American Romantic." *Romanticism* is a complex artistic, literary, and intellectual movement that originated in the second half of the 18th century in Western Europe. It was also a very strong movement in the United States. Proponents included Ralph Waldo Emerson and Henry David Thoreau. It was a celebration of the subjective. Nature was a benevolent power. In part, it was a revolt against aristocratic social and political norms of the Age of Enlightenment and a reaction against the scientific rationalization of nature. Why would evangelical Christians have a problem with romanticism?

God is nature. Romanticism wandered into polytheism. It rejected both the notion of a benevolent God and the high view of Scripture.

Chapter 12 Test

I. Discussion Questions (60 points)

Why was *The Song of Hiawatha* so popular among Americans?

II. Write a six-line poem with rhythm and meter (40 points).

Chapter 12 Test Answer Sample

I. Discussion Questions (60 points)

Why was *The Song of Hiawatha* so popular among Americans?

What makes The Song of Hiawatha *a favorite of most Americans is that Longfellow captured the pathos of America. His rural settings are idyllic and familiar. Like the romantics, he celebrates nature and the "noble savage." His meter lends itself to a euphonic quality that creates music to the ears.*

II. Write a six-line poem with rhythm and meter (40 points).

The morning, the morning
Comes dancing and prancing,
Makes loving the day
So much nicer to say.
Night though to say.
Is even better than day.

Reading 2

Song of Hiawatha by Henry David Longfellow

Chapter 13

First Thoughts

The Song of Hiawatha, critically speaking, was not a "great" epic poem. None of Longfellow's poems were. However, Americans loved Longfellow. He was one of the earliest, most successful, and wealthiest American authors. Contrast his fame to Edgar Allan Poe, who made very little income on his critically acclaimed, well-written poetry and prose.

Chapter Learning Objectives

In chapter 13 we will . . .

1. Understand multiculturalism, parody, rhyme, meter, narrative history, and strategic reading
2. Analyze the concept parody and epic poem
3. Continue to work to your novella

Look Ahead for Friday

- Turn in all assignments.
- Continue to work on your novella.

Lesson 1

Longfellow and Multiculturalism

Daily Assignment

- Warm-up: Why should Americans take note of their multiculturalism?
- In your essay, use the words who and whom.
- Students will complete Concept Builder 13-A.
- Prayer journal: students are encouraged to write in their prayer journal every day.
- Finish the next book you have been assigned.
- Students should systematically review their vocabulary words daily.

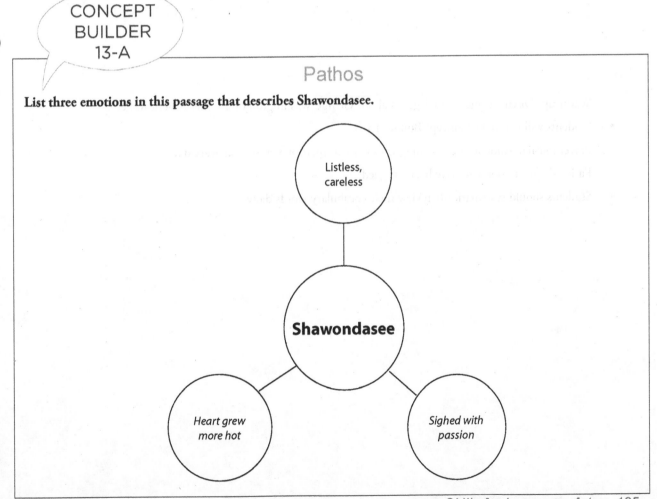

CONCEPT BUILDER 13-A

Pathos

List three emotions in this passage that describes Shawondasee.

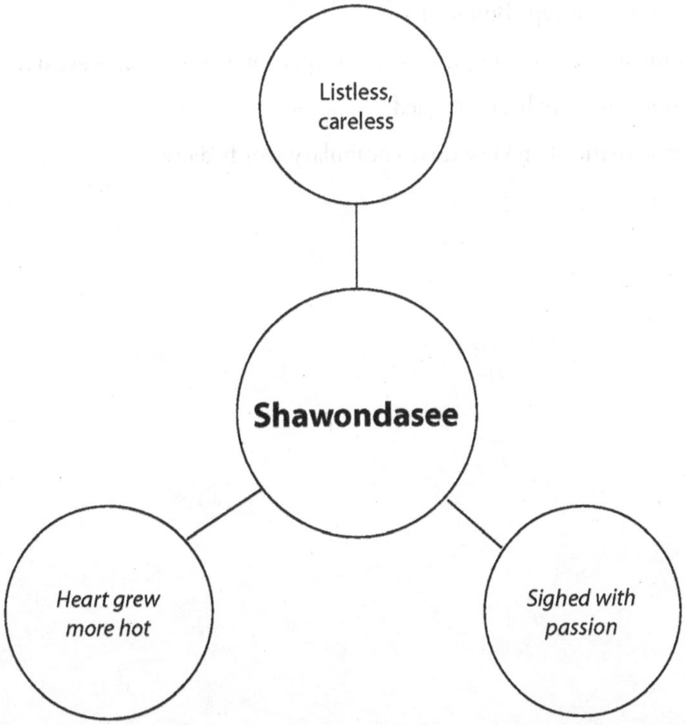

Lesson 2

The Historical Hiawatha

Daily Assignment

- Warm-up: Discuss some of the legends about George Washington or another American hero.
- Students will complete Concept Builder 13-B.
- Prayer journal: students are encouraged to write in their prayer journal every day.
- Finish the next book you have been assigned.
- Students should systematically review their vocabulary words daily.

CONCEPT BUILDER 13-B

Foreshadowing

Foreshadowing is a technique where the author gives a hint, in the text, of something that will happen later. Circle an example of foreshadowing in the end of XXI and XXII of *The Song of Hiawatha.*

"I beheld, too, in that vision
All the secrets of the future,
Of the distant days that shall be.
I beheld the westward marches
Of the unknown, crowded nations.
All the land was full of people,
Restless, struggling, toiling, striving,
Speaking many tongues, yet feeling
But one heart-beat in their bosoms.
In the woodlands rang their axes,
Smoked their towns in all the valleys,
Over all the lakes and rivers
Rushed their great canoes of thunder.

"Then a darker, drearier vision
Passed before me, vague and cloud-like;
I beheld our nation scattered,
All forgetful of my counsels,
Weakened, warring with each other:
Saw the remnants of our people
Sweeping westward, wild and woful,
Like the cloud-rack of a tempest,
Like the withered leaves of Autumn!"

Slowly o'er the simmering landscape
Fell the evening's dusk and coolness,
And the long and level sunbeams
Shot their spears into the forest,
Breaking through its shields of shadow,
Rushed into each secret ambush,
Searched each thicket, dingle, hollow;
Still the guests of Hiawatha
Slumbered in the silent wigwam.

Parody

Daily Assignment

- Warm-up: Write a short parody about some event you attend (e.g., church youth group).
- Students will complete Concept Builder 13-C.
- Prayer journal: students are encouraged to write in their prayer journal every day.
- Finish the next book you have been assigned.
- Students should systematically review their vocabulary words daily.

CONCEPT BUILDER 13-C

Parodies

Write a parody of Edgar Allan Poe's "The Raven."

Answers will vary.

Example:

Once upon a day so cheery, while I planted so strong and pearly,
Over many of ton of manure and peat moss,
While I shuddered, nearly fainting,
There came a cardinal flapping.

Critics' Corner

Daily Assignment

- Warm-up: Did you enjoy reading/studying *The Song of Hiawatha*? Why or why not?
- Students will complete Concept Builder 13-D.
- Prayer journal: students are encouraged to write in their prayer journal every day.
- Finish the next book you have been assigned.
- Students should systematically review their vocabulary words daily.

CONCEPT BUILDER 13-D

Inference

Most critics argue that the narrator in Edgar Allan Poe's "Tell-Tale Heart" is insane. Circle phrases/sentence/words that support that argument.

TRUE! — nervous — very, very dreadfully nervous I had been and am; but why will you say that I am mad? The disease had sharpened my senses — not destroyed — not dulled them. Above all was the sense of hearing acute. I heard all things in the heaven and in the earth. I heard many things in hell. How, then, am I mad? Hearken! and observe how healthily — how calmly I can tell you the whole story.

It is impossible to say how first the idea entered my brain; but once conceived, it haunted me day and night. Object there was none. Passion there was none. I loved the old man. He had never wronged me. He had never given me insult. For his gold I had no desire. I think it was his eye! yes, it was this! He had the eye of a vulture — a pale blue eye, with a film over it. Whenever it fell upon me, my blood ran cold; and so by degrees — very gradually — I made up my mind to take the life of the old man, and thus rid myself of the eye forever.

It was open — wide, wide open — and I grew

furious as I gazed upon it. I saw it with perfect distinctness — all a dull blue, with a hideous veil over it that chilled the very marrow in my bones; but I could see nothing else of the old man's face or person: for I had directed the ray as if by instinct, precisely upon the damned spot.

And have I not told you that what you mistake for madness is but over-acuteness of the sense? — now, I say, there came to my ears a low, dull, quick sound, such as a watch makes when enveloped in cotton. I knew that sound well, too. It was the beating of the old man's heart. It increased my fury, as the beating of a drum stimulates the soldier into courage.

No doubt I now grew very pale — but I talked more fluently, and with a heightened voice. Yet the sound increased — and what could I do? It was a low, dull, quick sound — much such a sound as a watch makes when enveloped in cotton. I gasped for breath — and yet the officers heard it not. I talked more quickly — more vehemently; but the noise steadily increased. I arose and argued about trifles, in a high key and with violent gesticulations; but the noise steadily increased. Why would they not be gone? I paced the floor to and fro with heavy strides, as if excited to fury by the observations of the men — but the noise steadily increased. Oh God! what could I do? I foamed — I raved — I swore! I swung the chair upon which I had been sitting, and grated it upon the boards, but the noise arose over all and continually increased. It grew louder — louder — louder! And still the men chatted pleasantly, and smiled. Was it possible they heard not? Almighty God! — no, no! They heard! — they suspected! — they knew! — they were making a mockery of my horror! — this I thought, and this I think. But anything was better than this agony! Anything was more tolerable than this derision! I could bear those hypocritical smiles no longer! I felt that I must scream or die! and now — again! — hark! louder! louder! louder! louder!

"Villains!" I shrieked, "dissemble no more! I admit the deed! — tear up the planks! here, here! — It is the beating of his hideous heart!"

Lesson 5

Epic Poem

Daily Assignment

- Warm-up: What was the flaw in Hiawatha's character?
- Students will complete Concept Builder 13-E.
- Prayer journal: students are encouraged to write in their prayer journal every day.
- Finish the next book you have been assigned.
- Students should systematically review their vocabulary words daily.

CONCEPT BUILDER 13-E

Women in Hiawatha

There are not a lot of women in *The Song of Hiawatha*. Read Hiawatha Wooing (X) and choose a representative woman from the list at the end.

C. *Laura Ingles*

Chapter 13 Review Questions

Writing a Novella

Write another chapter in your novella. What sort of hero(oine)(es) are you developing in your novella?

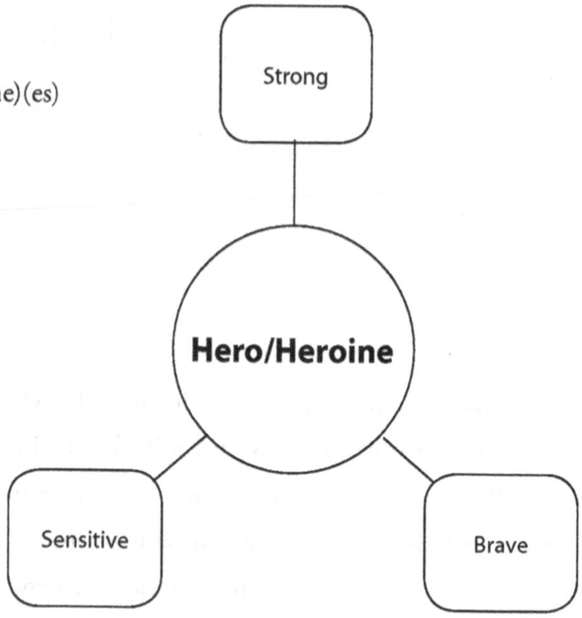

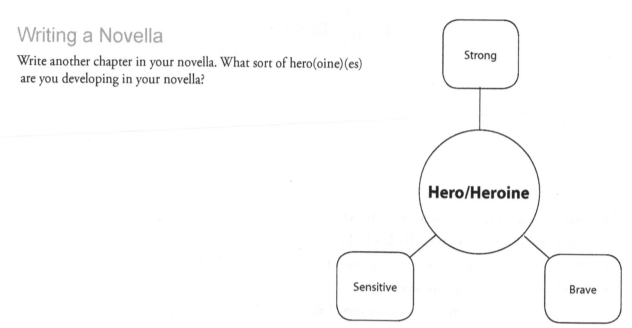

Literary Analysis

Compare Hiawatha to other epic heroes such as Achilleus, Aeneid, Beowulf, Roland, or a hero of your choice.

Epic heroes are strong — supernaturally strong. They are connected to the metaphysical through relationships, sometimes personal, even amorous relationships, with the gods and goddesses. In addition to the physical prowess demonstrated by Hiawatha and others, the tales emphasize how intelligence is highly valued among the American Indians. Hiawatha depends as much on his wit as does the Greek hero Odysseus. For example, he taunts Nahma the sturgeon into swallowing him so that he can kill the giant fish from the inside. When battling his father, Mudjekeewis, Hiawatha fools him into thinking that the bulrushes are his weakness.

Biblical Application

The Song of Hiawatha narrative begins when Gitche Manito, the Great Spirit, calls the warring tribes together, rebuking them for their immature behavior and informing them of a prophet who will come to guide and teach them. Hiawatha, the prophet mentioned by Gitche Manito, is born after Mudjekeewis, the West-Wind, seduces Wenonah, the daughter of Nokomis, and then leaves her to die heartbroken after giving birth to Hiawatha. Reared by Nokomis, Hiawatha grows to manhood and obtains magic gifts and powers that will enable him to perform his great deeds. Should Christians read books about pagan spirits and seduced maidens?

Certainly no one would consider The Song of Hiawatha *to be a "sacred" or religious book. Therefore, there should be no problem reading it.*

Chapter 13 Test

I. In a 300-word essay, describe Hiawatha as a peacemaker and a warrior. (100 points)

Your essay will be evaluated in these three areas:

Syntax and diction: grammar and style (20 points)

Organization: paragraphs, transitions, introduction, et al. (20 points)

Argument (60 points)

Chapter 13 Test Answer Sample

I. In a 300-word essay, describe Hiawatha as a peacemaker and a warrior. (50 points)

Your essay will be evaluated in these three areas:

Syntax and diction: grammar and style (20 points)

Organization: paragraphs, transitions, introduction, et al. (20 points)

Argument (60 points)

Longfellow himself was a pacifist. Hiawatha was a great warrior and he ruled from strength. But above all things he sought peace.

Reading 1

The Time Machine by H.G. Wells

Chapter 14

First Thoughts

The Time Machine (1895) was the first novel to deal with the futuristic subject of time travel, a topic that writers continue to explore. Yet *The Time Machine* also warns the Victorians, who first read it, about the effects of Victorian excesses. It also introduces readers to emerging scientific and social ideas (e.g., the excesses of naturalism).

Chapter Learning Objectives

In chapter 14 we will . . .

1. Review comma usage
2. Review narrative point of view
3. Explore better ways to read

Look Ahead for Friday

- Turn in all assignments.
- Continue to work on your novella.

Lesson 1

Grammar Review: Commas

Daily Assignment

- Warm-up: Write a paragraph listing your favorite five books.
- In your essay, use the words who and whom.
- Students will complete Concept Builder 14-A.
- Prayer journal: students are encouraged to write in their prayer journal every day.
- Finish the next book you have been assigned.
- Students should systematically review their vocabulary words daily.

CONCEPT BUILDER 14-A

Grammar Review: Commas

Put commas in these sentences.

1. Twenty years ago, when I moved to this farm, the yard and pasture were overrun with sharp briars and wiry thistle.
2. I declared war on both, and in a year or two, with sickle, bush hog, and Kaiser Blade, and the help of my children, I wrestled eight acres of rolling hills from my adversaries.
3. I left a couple of acres of trees and small bushes to sustain visiting deer and rabbits, hoping, I suppose, to divert these gluttonous carrot eaters from my one-acre vegetable garden.
4. It succeeded to a point, but briar and animal demanded more.

Lesson 2

Grammar: Capital Letters

Daily Assignment

- Warm-up: Describe the place you live, being sure to include street names and landmarks.
- Students will complete Concept Builder 14-B.
- Prayer journal: students are encouraged to write in their prayer journal every day.
- Finish the next book you have been assigned.
- Students should systematically review their vocabulary words daily.

CONCEPT BUILDER 14-B

Grammar Review: Capitalization

Punctuate these sentences.

1. Oh my! I have done it again.
2. His church is on Walnut Street.
3. Three lane highways in Boston, Massachusetts are dangerous.
4. Mexico City is the largest city in the world.
5. Nothing on earth is quite like it.

Lesson 3

Narrative Point of View

Daily Assignment

- Warm-up: In chapters 1-2 of *The Time Machine*, why did the author tell the story in first-person rather than omniscient or objective third-person point of view?
- Students will complete Concept Builder 14-C.
- Prayer journal: students are encouraged to write in their prayer journal every day.
- Finish the next book you have been assigned.
- Students should systematically review their vocabulary words daily.

CONCEPT BUILDER 14-C

Illustrated Book Review

Create an illustrated booklet of the most important scenes from the book. Skim through the novel to select the five most important scenes. Illustrate each by drawing, painting, or using magazine or computer pictures. On each page write a paragraph explaining why this is one of the five most significant scenes in the novel.

Answers will vary.

Book Study: *The Time Machine* (Book One)

H.G. Wells

Where, specifically, is the setting?

Be as exact as you can. The Time Traveler has returned from a trip. He is among friends, which gives the narrator a chance to tell his story to friends, and to the reader.

What is the Fourth Dimension?

"It is simply this. That Space, as our mathematicians have it, is spoken of as having three dimensions, which one may call Length, Breadth, and Thickness, and is always definable by reference to three planes, each at right angles to the others. But some philosophical people have been asking why three dimensions particularly — why not another direction at right angles to the other three? — and have even tried to construct a Four-Dimension geometry."

Daily Assignment

- Warm-up: What interests you about the possibility of time travel?
- Students will complete Concept Builder 14-D.
- Prayer journal: students are encouraged to write in their prayer journal every day.
- Finish the next book you have been assigned.
- Students should systematically review their vocabulary words daily.

CONCEPT BUILDER 14-D

Reading

Predict the ending of the book.

Answers will vary.

Lesson 5

Reading: Connecting to Self

Daily Assignment

- Warm-up: How do you connect with *The Time Machine*?
- Students will complete Concept Builder 14-E.
- Prayer journal: students are encouraged to write in their prayer journal every day.
- Finish the next book you have been assigned.
- Students should systematically review their vocabulary words daily.

CONCEPT BUILDER 14-E

Reading Skills: Connecting to Self

Connect the story to your own story.

Answers will vary.

Chapter 14 Review Questions

Writing a Novella

Write another chapter in your novella.

Literary Analysis

The narrative point of view shifts in chapter three of *The Time Machine* from the perspective of the guests to the time traveler himself. Why do you suppose Wells chose to make this transition?

Wells wants to build suspense. It is also easier for him to maintain the first person narration. He must do it later when the Time Traveler visits the future, so he maintains it through the first two chapters. Finally, dialogue is one of the most effective ways that an author can create credibility and evoke a response from readers — very necessary things in science fiction.

Biblical Application

What does the Time Traveler conclude about mankind's intellectual advancements? What does he feel caused the downfall of humanity?

Mankind, in fact, does not advance intellectually — which is interesting since Wells is a naturalist/social Darwinist/ evolutionist, and at the heart of this theory is natural selection.

Chapter 14 Test

I. Organize the events in the order in which they occur. (60 points)

________ Meanwhile, he saves Weena.

________ In the year A.D. 802,701, he finds himself in a paradisiacal world of small humanoid creatures called Eloi.

________ He then returns, exhausted, to the present time. The next day, he leaves again, but never returns.

________ Many Morlocks die in the fire, and Weena is killed too.

________ That night, retreating from the Morlocks through a giant wood, he accidentally starts a fire.

________ The next week, the guests return, and the Time Traveler begins his story.

________ The Time Traveler goes down into the world of Morlocks to try to retrieve his time machine.

________ The Time Traveler produces a miniature time machine and makes it disappear.

________ In the night, he sees white human-like creatures called the Morlocks take the Eloi.

________ He goes to what he calls the Palace of Green Porcelain, which turns out to be a museum.

________ The Time Traveler returns home.

II. Discussion Question (40 points)

Discuss what a frame story is and how it is used with effectiveness in this novella (short novel).

Chapter 14 Test Answer Sample

I. Organize the events in the order in which they occur. (60 points)

5 Meanwhile, he saves Weena.

3 In the year A.D. 802,701, he finds himself in a paradisiacal world of small humanoid creatures called Eloi.

11 He then returns, exhausted, to the present time. The next day, he leaves again, but never returns.

9 Many Morlocks die in the fire, and Weena is killed too.

8 That night, retreating from the Morlocks through a giant wood, he accidentally starts a fire.

2 The next week, the guests return, and the Time Traveler begins his story.

6 The Time Traveler goes down into the world of Morlocks to try to retrieve his time machine.

1 The Time Traveler produces a miniature time machine and makes it disappear.

4 In the night, he sees white human-like creatures called the Morlocks take the Eloi.

7 He goes to what he calls the Palace of Green Porcelain, which turns out to be a museum.

10 The Time Traveler returns home.

II. Discussion Question (40 points)

Discuss what a frame story is and how it is used with effectiveness in this novella (short novel).

A frame story is a story within a story — in this case there is a story about a time traveler and then a story about the Eloi and Morlocks. In both cases, the protagonist experiences different levels of internal and external conflict.

The Time Machine, by H.G. Wells

Chapter 15

First Thoughts

A dreamer passionate about traveling through time builds a time machine and travels over 800,000 years into the future. The world appeared to be a society living in apparent harmony and bliss, but as the Traveler stays in this world he discovers a depraved subterranean class. Wells' science-fiction bestseller launched the time-travel genre.

Chapter Learning Objectives

In chapter 15 we will . . .

1. Analyze Wells' use of figurative language
2. Grasp the concept of science fiction
3. Understand naturalism and grasp its inadequacies as a worldview
4. Review grammar

Look Ahead for Friday

- Turn in all assignments.
- Continue to work on your novella.

Lesson 1

Figurative Language
(From *The Time Machine*)

Daily Assignment

- Warm-up: What does the Time Traveler feel caused the downfall of humanity?
- In your essay, use the words who and whom.
- Students will complete Concept Builder 15-A.
- Prayer journal: students are encouraged to write in their prayer journal every day.
- Finish the next book you have been assigned.
- Students should systematically review their vocabulary words daily.

CONCEPT BUILDER 15-A

Connotation and Denotation

Names of characters reflect their characteristics. Give the denotation and connotation of each name.

Name	Connotation	Denotation
Morlocks	Life in the darkness	*Malevolent*
Eloi	Life in the light	*Helpless*
Weena	The Time Traveler's friend	*Good Natured and Innocent*

Lesson 2

Naturalism

Daily Assignment

- Warm-up: Why do you think that Wells doesn't tell the reader what happened to the Time Traveler at the end of the novel?
- Students will complete Concept Builder 15-B.
- Prayer journal: students are encouraged to write in their prayer journal every day.
- Finish the next book you have been assigned.
- Students should systematically review their vocabulary words daily.

CONCEPT BUILDER 15-B

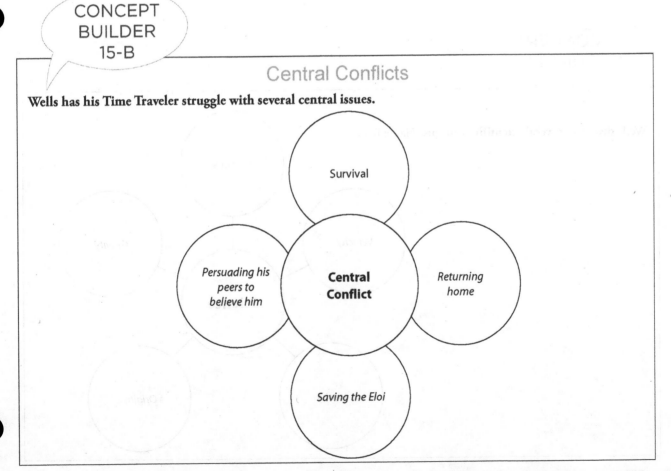

Central Conflicts

Wells has his Time Traveler struggle with several central issues.

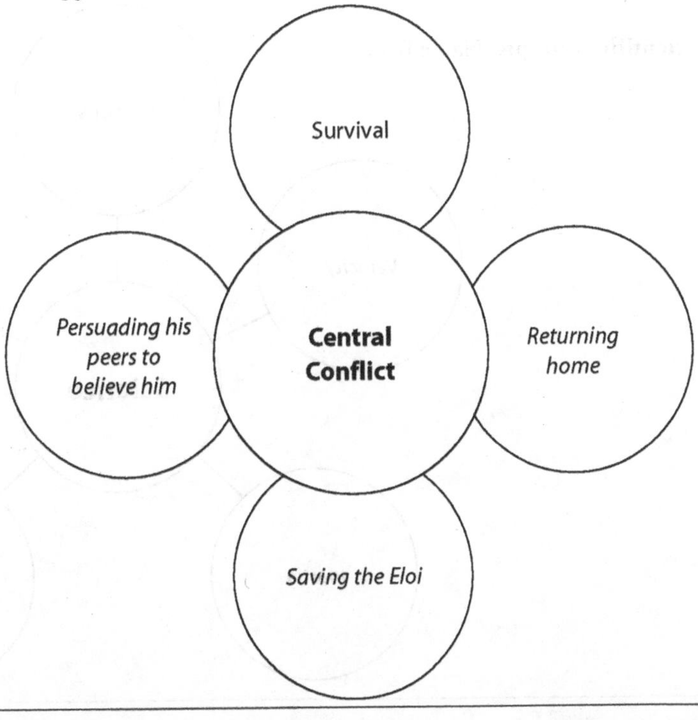

Lesson 3

Science Fiction

Daily Assignment

- Warm-up: How does the museum function symbolically in *The Time Machine*? What does a museum represent?
- Students will complete Concept Builder 15-C.
- Prayer journal: students are encouraged to write in their prayer journal every day.
- Finish the next book you have been assigned.
- Students should systematically review their vocabulary words daily.

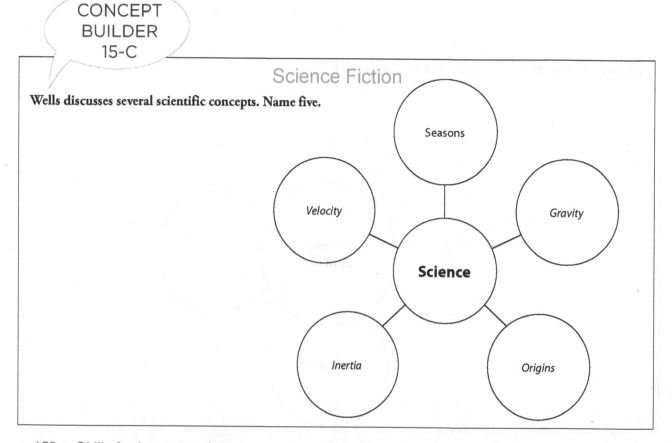

CONCEPT BUILDER 15-C

Science Fiction

Wells discusses several scientific concepts. Name five.

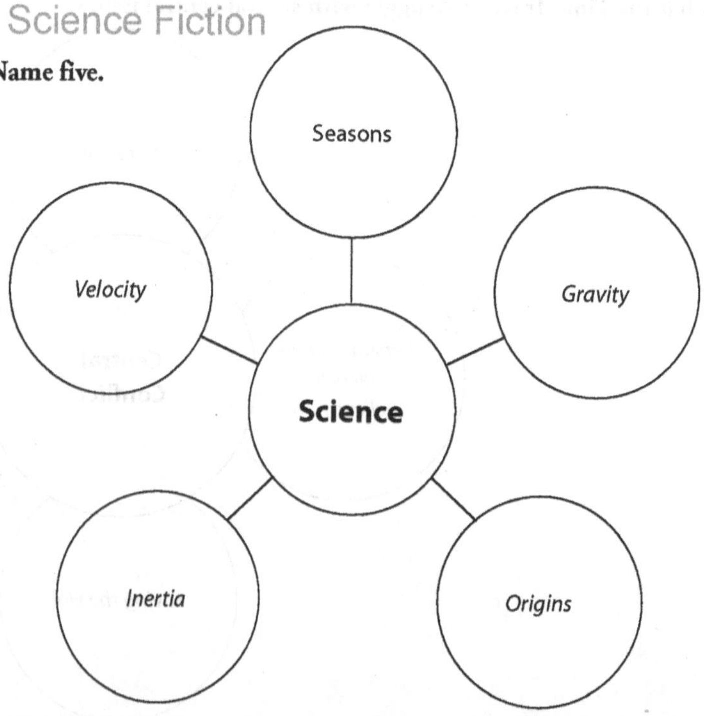

Lesson 4

Grammar Review: Semicolons and Colons

Daily Assignment

- Warm-up: If you were the Time Traveler, where would you go?
- Students will complete Concept Builder 15-D.
- Prayer journal: students are encouraged to write in their prayer journal every day.
- Finish the next book you have been assigned.
- Students should systematically review their vocabulary words daily.

CONCEPT BUILDER 15-D

Grammar Review: Semicolons & Colons

Punctuate these sentences properly.

1. There are two representatives from Chicago, Illinois; three from Scranton, Pennsylvania; and four from Dallas Texas.

2. I would like to go; however, I do not have the time.

3. The equipment you will need is as follows: a tent a sleeping bag and two stoves.

Lesson 5

Grammar Review: Quotation Marks

Daily Assignment

- Warm-up: What are three of your favorite quotes from books or movies?
- Students will complete Concept Builder 15-E.
- Prayer journal: students are encouraged to write in their prayer journal every day.
- Finish the next book you have been assigned.
- Students should systematically review their vocabulary words daily.

CONCEPT BUILDER 15-E

Quotation Marks

Punctuate these sentences properly.

1. "Happy birthday, Jacob," Anna smiled, as she entered the kitchen.

2. "Good morning, Anna," he responded.

3. He placed one Earl Gray, three PG Tip tea bags in the teapot, and wrapped it in a tea cozy. As Anna, whose parents were from Raasy, Skye, Scotland, were fond of saying, "The tea is stewing."

Chapter 15 Review Questions

Writing a Novella

Write another chapter in your novella. How do you use time in your novella? Does your novel move back and forth in time? Does your novel have flashbacks? Frame story?

Literary Analysis

Add an invented character to chapter two of *The Time Machine*. Add someone representing a different profession. (For example, add a clergyperson, a lawyer, or a housewife.) What questions might this person ask the Time Traveler?

No one seems to be worried about the moral implications of visiting the future. Mary Shelley, in her book Frankenstein, *shows the danger of tinkering with science!*

Biblical Application

Why would a Christian reject naturalism, which states that God is either neutral or removed from His Creation?

God so loved the world that He sent his only Begotten Son (John 3:16). God is very much involved in all aspects of human affairs and He is involved in a very positive way.

Chapter 15 Test

I. Matching (60 points)

A. "The fire burned brightly, and the soft radiance of the incandescent lights in the lilies of silver caught the bubbles that flashed and passed in our glasses" (p. 1).

B. ". . . his lips moving as one who repeats mystic words" (p. 3).

C. "At once, like a lash across the face, came the possibility of losing my own age, of being left helpless in this strange new world" (p. 39).

D. "I felt as if I was in a monstrous spider's web" (p. 86)

E. "That is the germ of my great discovery" (p. 5). ". . . almost see through it the Morlocks on their anthill going hither and thither . . ." (p. 69).

F. "There was a breath of wind . . ." (p. 8).
". . . with the big open portals that yawned before me shadowy and mysterious" (p. 28).
"The red tongues that went licking up my heap of wood . . ." (p. 83).

_______ Personification

_______ Metaphor

_______ Simile

_______ Imagery

II. Write an essay predicting what the world will be like in 150 years (40 points).

Your essay will be evaluated in these three areas:

Syntax and diction: grammar and style (10 points)

Organization: paragraphs, transitions, introduction, et al. (10 points)

Argument (20 points)

Chapter 15 Test Answer Sample

I. Matching (60 points)

A.	"The fire burned brightly, and the soft radiance of the incandescent lights in the lilies of silver caught the bubbles that flashed and passed in our glasses" (p. 1).	*F*	Personification
B.	". . . his lips moving as one who repeats mystic words" (p. 3).	*E*	Metaphor
C.	"At once, like a lash across the face, came the possibility of losing my own age, of being left helpless in this strange new world" (p. 39).	*C, D, B*	Simile
D.	"I felt as if I was in a monstrous spider's web" (p. 86)	*A*	Imagery
E.	"That is the germ of my great discovery" (p. 5). ". . . almost see through it the Morlocks on their anthill going hither and thither . . ." (p. 69).		
F.	"There was a breath of wind . . ." (p. 8). ". . . with the big open portals that yawned before me shadowy and mysterious" (p. 28). "The red tongues that went licking up my heap of wood . . ." (p. 83).		

II. Write an essay predicting what the world will be like in 150 years (40 points).

Your essay will be evaluated in these three areas:

Syntax and diction: grammar and style (10 points)

Organization: paragraphs, transitions, introduction, et al. (10 points)

Argument (20 points)

Answers will vary.

Reading 1

Moses Confronts Pharaoh (Exodus 5–12)

Chapter 16

First Thoughts

The meeting between Pharaoh and Moses and their subsequent confrontation is one of the most dramatic scenes in Western literature. At the end of the fight, God's people are released from bondage and they journey to the Promised Land. The way Moses develops his plot, rising action, climax, and denouement is masterfully done.

Chapter Learning Objectives

In chapter 16 we will . . .

1. Analyze the concept of a dramatic question and discern its presence in your novella.
2. Compare round and flat characters.
3. Discern internal and external conflicts in characters.
4. Continue to work on your novella.

Look Ahead for Friday

- Turn in all assignments.
- Continue to work on your novella.

Active Reading: Moses Confronts Pharaoh (Exodus 5–12)

Daily Assignment

- Warm-up: Pretend you are an advisor to Pharaoh. What would you say to him?
- In your essay, use the words who and whom.
- Students will complete Concept Builder 16-A.
- Prayer journal: students are encouraged to write in their prayer journal every day.
- Finish the next book you have been assigned.
- Students should systematically review their vocabulary words daily.

CONCEPT BUILDER 16-A

Suspense

How does Moses build suspense in this narrative?

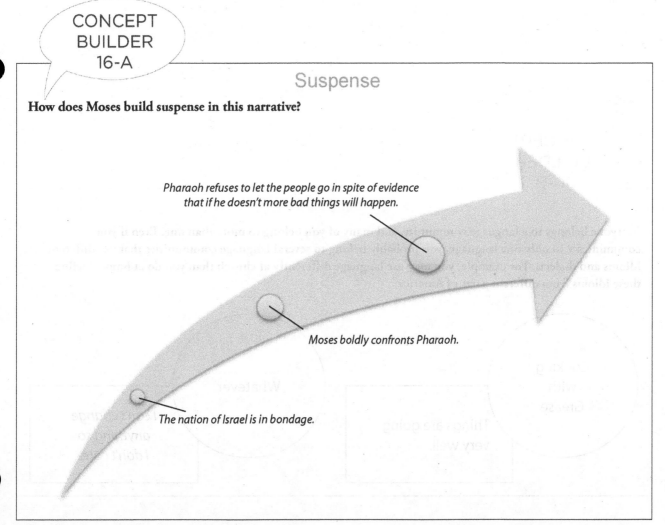

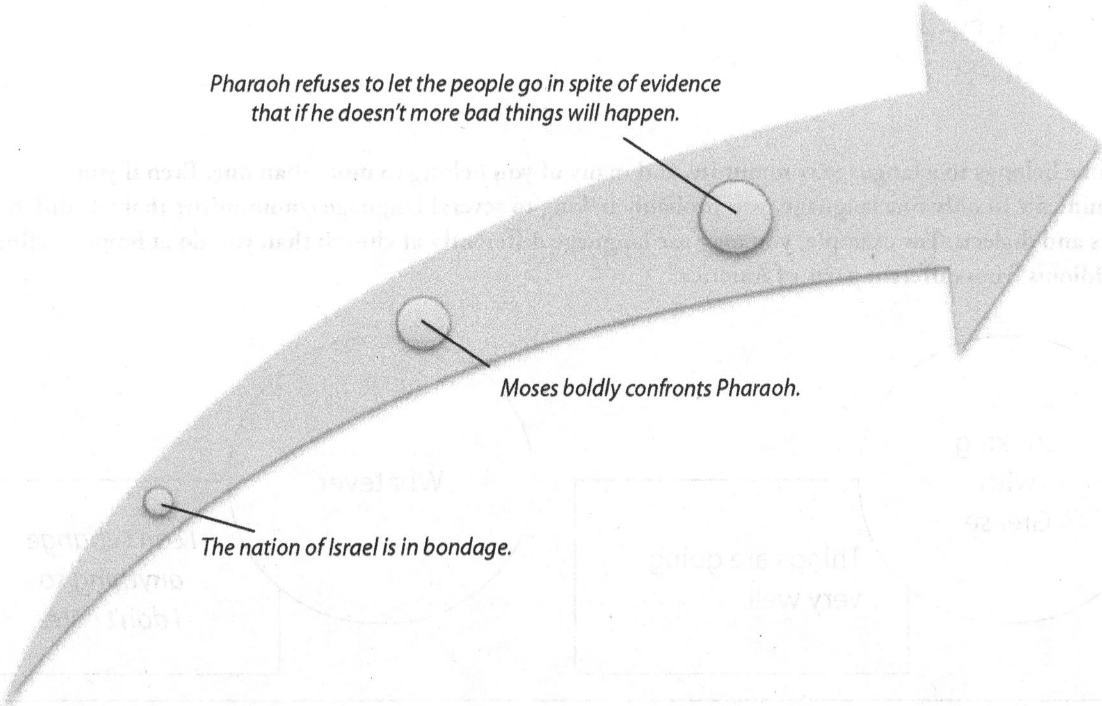

Pharaoh refuses to let the people go in spite of evidence that if he doesn't more bad things will happen.
Moses boldly confronts Pharaoh.
The nation of Israel is in bondage.

Rising Action: Dramatic Question

Daily Assignment

- Warm-up: In your novella, what dramatic question(s) does your protagonist face?
- Students will complete Concept Builder 16-B.
- Prayer journal: students are encouraged to write in their prayer journal every day.
- Finish the next book you have been assigned.
- Students should systematically review their vocabulary words daily.

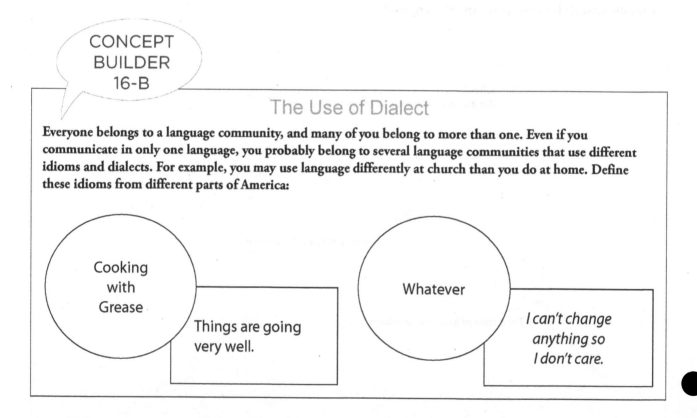

CONCEPT BUILDER 16-B

The Use of Dialect

Everyone belongs to a language community, and many of you belong to more than one. Even if you communicate in only one language, you probably belong to several language communities that use different idioms and dialects. For example, you may use language differently at church than you do at home. Define these idioms from different parts of America:

Cooking with Grease

Things are going very well.

Whatever

I can't change anything so I don't care.

Conflict

Daily Assignment

- What sort of conflicts are your characters facing in your novella?
- Students will complete Concept Builder 16-C.
- Prayer journal: students are encouraged to write in their prayer journal every day.
- Finish the next book you have been assigned.
- Students should systematically review their vocabulary words daily.

CONCEPT BUILDER 16-C

The Plot

Identify different components of the plot.

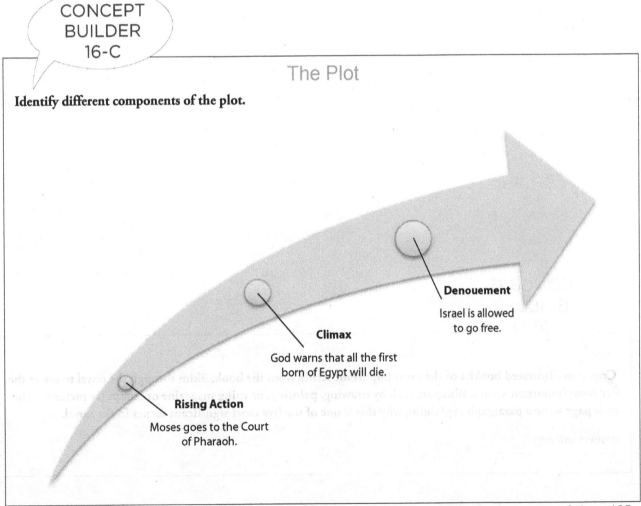

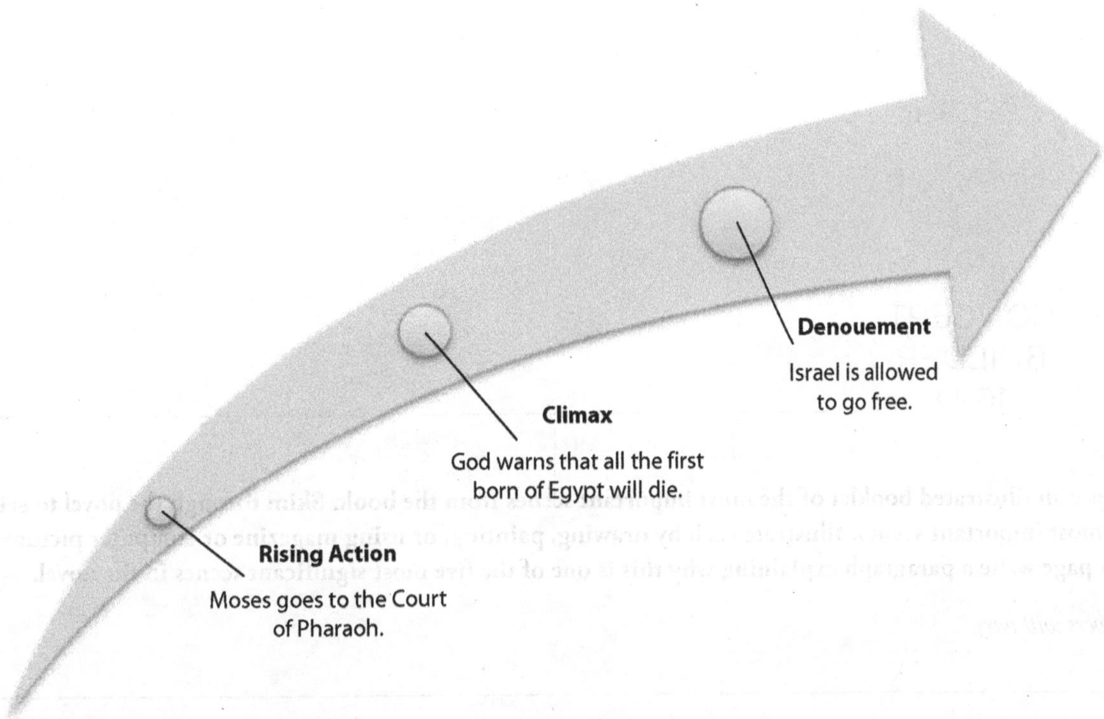

Rising Action
Moses goes to the Court of Pharaoh.
Climax
God warns that all the first born of Egypt will die.
Denouement
Israel is allowed to go free.

Lesson 4

Ancient Greek Tragic Hero versus Modern Tragic Hero

Daily Assignment

- Warm-up: Do you have a tragic hero in your novella? Describe him/her.
- Students will complete Concept Builder 16-D.
- Prayer journal: students are encouraged to write in their prayer journal every day.
- Finish the next book you have been assigned.
- Students should systematically review their vocabulary words daily.

CONCEPT BUILDER 16-D

Illustrated Book Review

Create an illustrated booklet of the most important scenes from the book. Skim through the novel to select the five most important scenes. Illustrate each by drawing, painting, or using magazine or computer pictures. On each page write a paragraph explaining why this is one of the five most significant scenes in the novel.

Answers will vary.

Round and Flat Characters

Daily Assignment

- Warm-up: Discuss a round and flat character in your novella.
- Students will complete Concept Builder 16-E.
- Prayer journal: students are encouraged to write in their prayer journal every day.
- Finish the next book you have been assigned.
- Students should systematically review their vocabulary words daily.

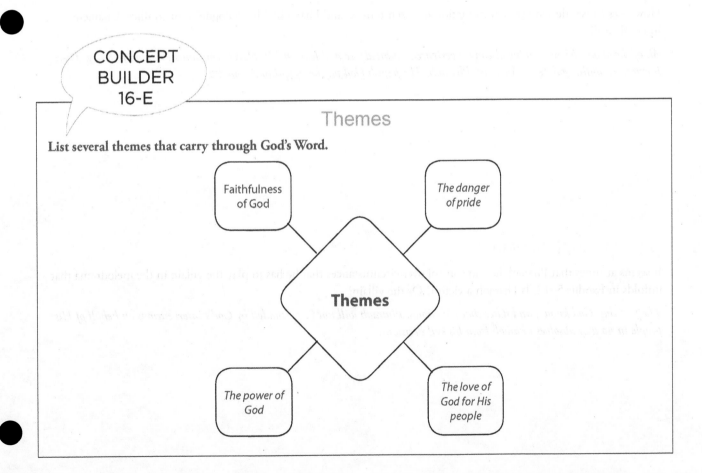

CONCEPT BUILDER 16-E

Themes

List several themes that carry through God's Word.

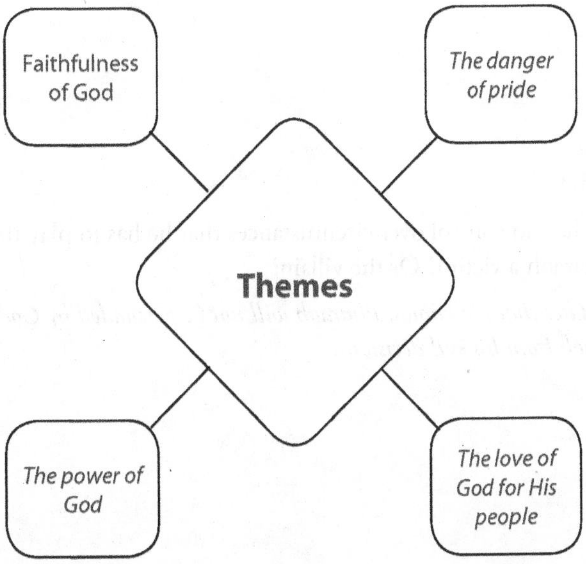

Chapter 16 Review Questions

Writing a Novella

Write another chapter in your novella. Who is your protagonist? Antagonist? What is the dramatic question(s) that must be answered?

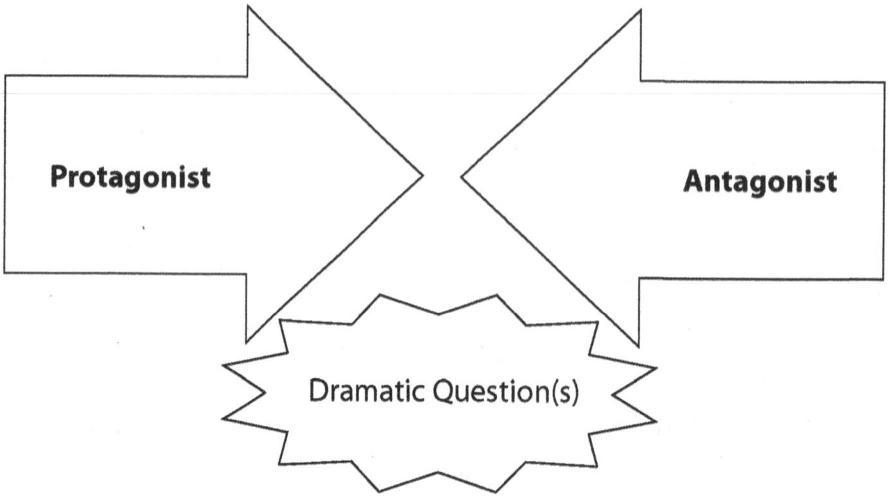

Literary Analysis

How does Moses develop the confrontation between himself and Pharaoh? The dialogue? Plot conflict? Character internal conflict?

All of the above. Moses, having already experienced ambivalence and fear on Mt. Horeb, confronts Pharaoh publicly. There is external conflict galore — Moses vs. Pharaoh. The Jewish God vs. the Egyptian Amon-Ra.

Biblical Application

It seems at times that Pharaoh has no control over circumstances that he has to play the villain in the melodrama that unfolds in Exodus 5–12. Is Pharaoh a victim? Or the villain?

The fact that God knows, and states that He knows, Pharaoh will not be persuaded by God's interventions on behalf of His people in no way absolves Pharaoh from his evil decisions.

Chapter 16 Test

I. Conflicts in characters: Matching (50 points)

______ Person versus fate	A. Samson
______ Person versus oneself	B. David and Goliath
______ Person versus person	C. Job
______ Person versus culture	D. Lot
______ Person versus nature	E. Joshua

II. Identify the following characters as round (A) or flat (B). (50 points)

______ Lot

______ Miriam

______ Abraham

______ Moses

______ Elizabeth

______ Joseph

______ Pharaoh

______ Daniel

______ Jacob

______ Obadiah

Chapter 16 Test Answer Sample

I. Conflicts in characters: Matching (50 points)

C	Person versus fate	A. Samson
A	Person versus oneself	B. David and Goliath
B	Person versus person	C. Job
D	Person versus culture	D. Lot
E	Person versus nature	E. Joshua

II. Identify the following characters as round (A) or flat (B). (50 points)

B	Lot
B	Miriam
A	Abraham
A	Moses
B	Elizabeth
A	Joseph
B	Pharaoh
A	Daniel
A	Jacob
B	Obadiah

Reading 2

Moses Confronts Pharaoh (Exodus 5–12)

Chapter 17

First Thoughts

Exodus 5–12 is written by Moses, led by the Holy Spirit. But it is also literature. It has all the elements that one would expect in good literature: plot, theme, setting, etc. There is real value in studying these different elements.

Chapter Learning Objectives

In chapter 17 we will . . .

1. Understand irony, setting, and motif
2. Analyze and learn spelling rules
3. Learn how to elaborate

Look Ahead for Friday

- Turn in all assignments.
- Continue to work on your novella.

Lesson 1

Active Reading: Moses Confronts Pharaoh (Exodus 5–12)

Daily Assignment

- Warm-up: What is an example of irony from the story of Moses confronting Pharaoh (Exodus 5–12)?
- In your essay, use the words who and whom.
- Students will complete Concept Builder 17-A.
- Prayer journal: students are encouraged to write in their prayer journal every day.
- Finish the next book you have been assigned.
- Students should systematically review their vocabulary words daily.

CONCEPT BUILDER 17-A

Irony

Match

A. Verbal Irony	1. *B* The Wizard of Oz
B. Situational Irony	2. *A* The Adventures of Huckleberry Finn
C. Dramatic Irony	3. *C* Moses confronts Pharaoh

Lesson 2

Settings in the Bible

Daily Assignment

- Warm-up: In your novella, how critical is the setting? Could the story happen anywhere?
- Students will complete Concept Builder 17-B.
- Prayer journal: students are encouraged to write in their prayer journal every day.
- Finish the next book you have been assigned.
- Students should systematically review their vocabulary words daily.

CONCEPT BUILDER 17-B

Setting

Match

A. Esther 4:9–16	1. *D* Island of Malta
B. Genesis 8:1–14	2. *E* The empty tomb
C. 1 Kings 18:16–39	3. *A* Babylon
D. Acts 27:1–28:10	4. *C* Mt. Carmel
E. Luke 24:1–12	5. *F* Prison
F. Philemon	6. *B* Mt. Arafat

Lesson 3

Motif

Daily Assignment

- Warm-up: What is the difference between a theme and a motif?
- Students will complete Concept Builder 17-C.
- Prayer journal: students are encouraged to write in their prayer journal every day.
- Finish the next book you have been assigned.
- Students should systematically review their vocabulary words daily.

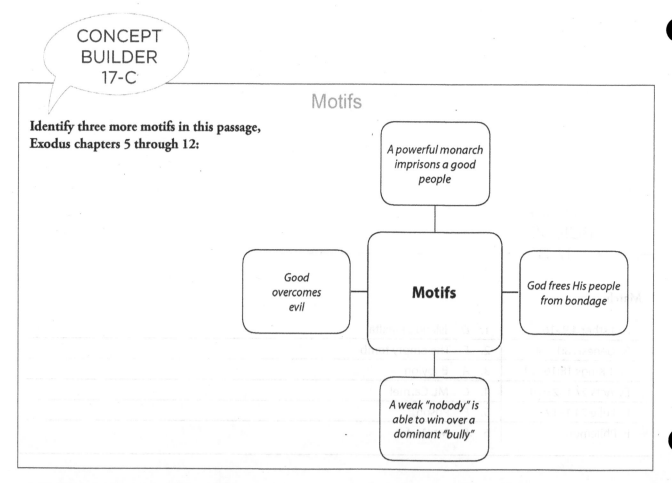

CONCEPT BUILDER 17-C

Motifs

Identify three more motifs in this passage, Exodus chapters 5 through 12:

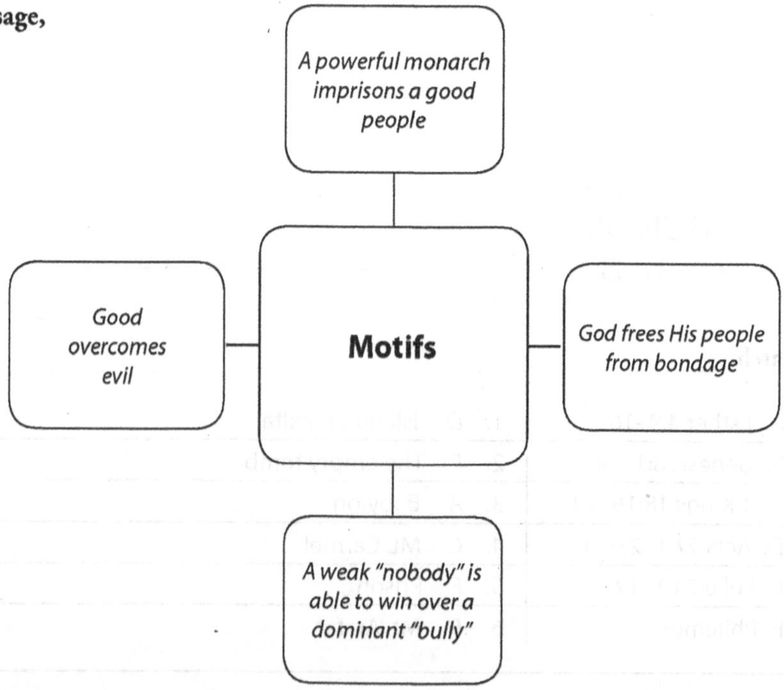

Motifs
A powerful monarch imprisons a good people
Good overcomes evil
God frees His people from bondage
A weak "nobody" is able to win over a dominant "bully"

Lesson 4

Rules for Spelling

Daily Assignment

- Warm-up: List the ten most common words that you misspell.
- Students will complete Concept Builder 17-D.
- Prayer journal: students are encouraged to write in their prayer journal every day.
- Finish the next book you have been assigned.
- Students should systematically review their vocabulary words daily.

CONCEPT BUILDER 17-D

Rules for Spelling

Write the correct spelling of these words:

Receive	*Illiterate*	*Usage*
Neighbor	*Judgment*	

Lesson 5

Writing: Elaboration

Daily Assignment

- Warm-up: Elaborate on this topic: Where is the best place to go on vacation?
- Students will complete Concept Builder 17-E.
- Prayer journal: students are encouraged to write in their prayer journal every day.
- Finish the next book you have been assigned.
- Students should systematically review their vocabulary words daily.

CONCEPT BUILDER 17-E

External and Internal Conflicts

Moses struggles with several conflicts. He struggled with Pharaoh but he also struggled with his calling (e.g., at the burning bush). Outline some of these.

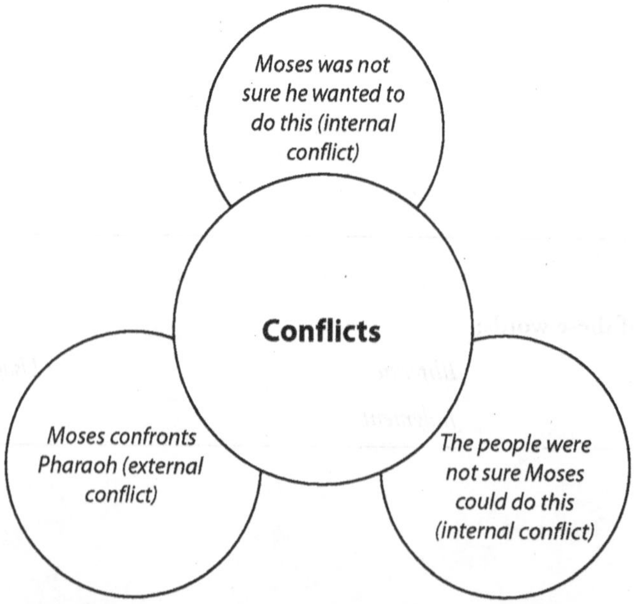

Chapter 17 Review Questions

Writing a Novella

Write another chapter in your novella.

Literary Analysis

Tell the story of the Exodus from the perspective of Pharaoh's wife.

Answers will vary.

Biblical Application

Write a sermon based on Exodus 5–12.

Answers will vary.

Chapter 17 Test

I. Spell the following words correctly: (60 points)

Ocasionally

Accomodation

Recieve

Murmer

Judgement

Monkay

Surgury

Confiscat

panorima

partality

Dandalion

pasttime

II. Match (40 points)

A. Interrogate	_____	Find connections between information
B. Discover	_____	Collect data; interview
C. Research	_____	Brainstorm: What if?
D. Cluster	_____	Who? What? When? How?

Chapter 17 Test Answer Sample

I. Spell the following words correctly: (60 points)

Occasionally

Accommodation

Receive

Murmur

Judgment

Monkey

Surgery

Confiscate

Panorama

Partiality

Dandelion

Pastime

II. Match (40 points)

A. Interrogate	*D*	Find connections between information
B. Discover	*C*	Collect data; interview
C. Research	*B*	Brainstorm: What if?
D. Cluster	*A*	Who? What? When? How?

Reading 1

John Brown's Body by Stephen Vincent Benet

Chapter 18

First Thoughts

John Brown's Body is a 1928 Pulitzer Prize-winning epic poem, in eight sections, about the American Civil War. The poem, like the war itself, begins just before John Brown's raid on Harpers Ferry, and ends after the assassination of Abraham Lincoln. Benet is not the least bit partisan. Benet's tone is one of reconciliation. From his viewpoint, there are few villains and many heroes.

Chapter Learning Objectives

In chapter 18 we will . . .

1. Understand the concept: epic
2. Review foreshadowing

Look Ahead for Friday

- Turn in all assignments.
- Continue to work on your novella.

Lesson 1

Epic

Daily Assignment

- Warm-up: Write a one-page epic of an incident your family faced.
- In your essay, use the words who and whom.
- Students will complete Concept Builder 18-A.
- Prayer journal: students are encouraged to write in their prayer journal every day.
- Finish the next book you have been assigned.
- Students should systematically review their vocabulary words daily.

CONCEPT BUILDER 18-A

Epic

What are the characteristics of an epic?

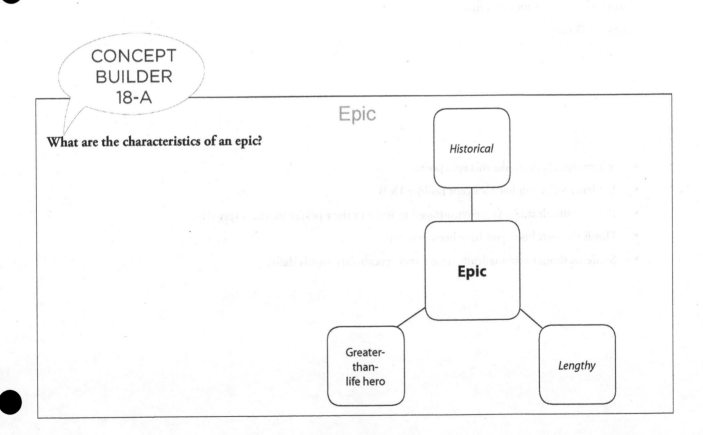

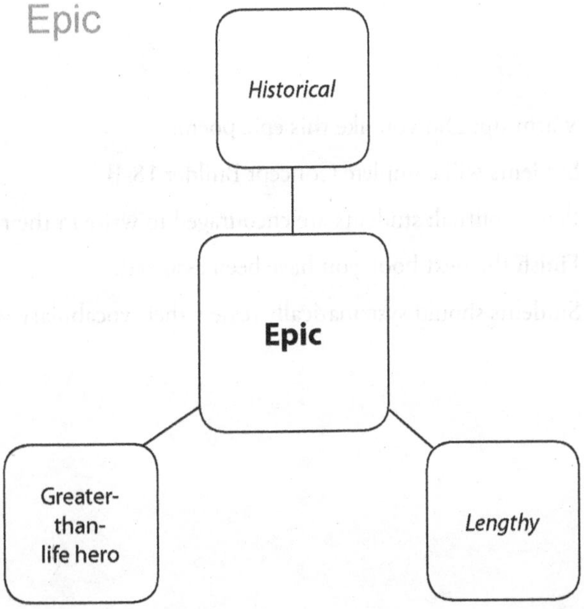

Active Reading: "John Brown's Body" Stephen Vincent Benet (Book One)

Benet begins with the introduction of a character. Why?

Benet begins his long narrative poem with a person so that the reader can identify with him. He has the character in nature, which, again, draws the reader into the plot. The reader, in effect, walks with Ellyat in the forest. The reader must see Ellyat in his normal routine in order to grasp the effect of the Civil War on his life.

Give an example of foreshadowing.

Then something broke the peace.
Like wind it was, the flutter of rising wind,
But then it grew until it was the rushing
Of winged stallions, distant and terrible,
Trampling beyond the sky.

Predict what will happen to Ellyat.

Answers will vary.

Daily Assignment

- Warm-up: Did you like this epic poem?
- Students will complete Concept Builder 18-B.
- Prayer journal: students are encouraged to write in their prayer journal every day.
- Finish the next book you have been assigned.
- Students should systematically review their vocabulary words daily.

CONCEPT BUILDER 18-B

Themes

List three themes in *John Brown's Body*.

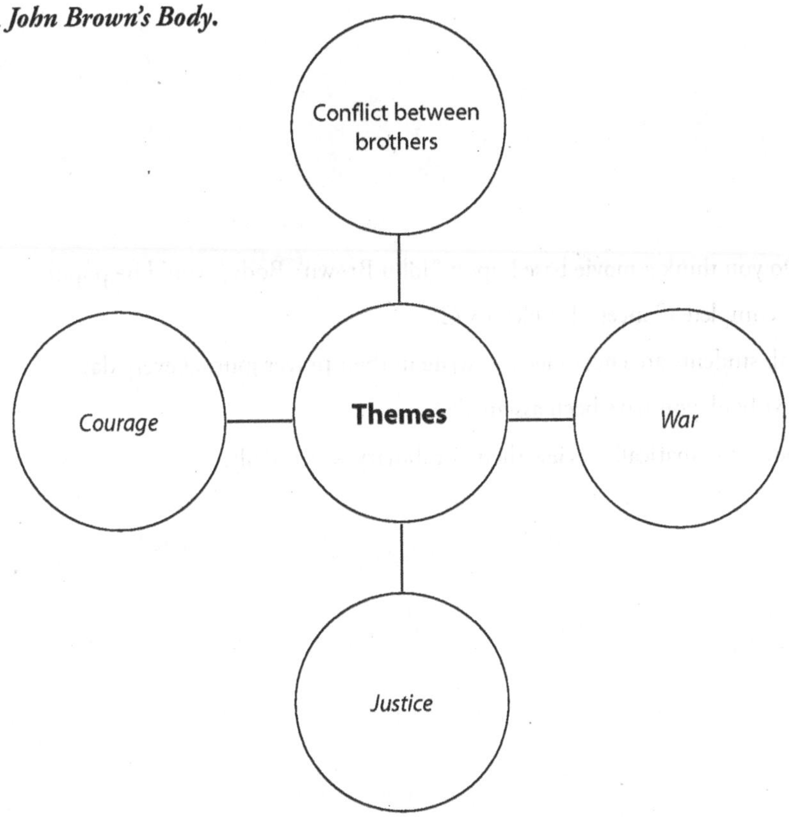

Lesson 3

A Forgotten Work

Daily Assignment

- Warm-up: Do you think a movie based upon "John Brown's Body" would be popular?
- Students will complete Concept Builder 18-C.
- Prayer journal: students are encouraged to write in their prayer journal every day.
- Finish the next book you have been assigned.
- Students should systematically review their vocabulary words daily.

CONCEPT BUILDER 18-C

Choreographing

Pretend that you are a producer of a movie version of *John Brown's Body*. The narrative poem is too long, so you are required to pick the five best scenes.

Answers will vary.

Fact vs. Fiction

Daily Assignment

- Warm-up: Compare the actual John Brown raid to Benet's version.
- Students will complete Concept Builder 18-D.
- Prayer journal: students are encouraged to write in their prayer journal every day.
- Finish the next book you have been assigned.
- Students should systematically review their vocabulary words daily.

CONCEPT BUILDER 18-D

Metaphors

Find three metaphors in the play.

White cotton, blowing like a fallen cloud, And foxhounds belling the Virginia hills . . .
While the painted Death went whooping by *— To die at last as she wished to die*
John Brown was none of these, *He was a stone,* *A stone eroded to a cutting edge* *By obstinacy, failure and cold prayers.*

Lesson 5

Foreshadowing

Daily Assignment

- Warm-up: Include at least one foreshadowing incident in your novella.
- Students will complete Concept Builder 18-E.
- Prayer journal: students are encouraged to write in their prayer journal every day.
- Finish the next book you have been assigned.
- Students should systematically review their vocabulary words daily.

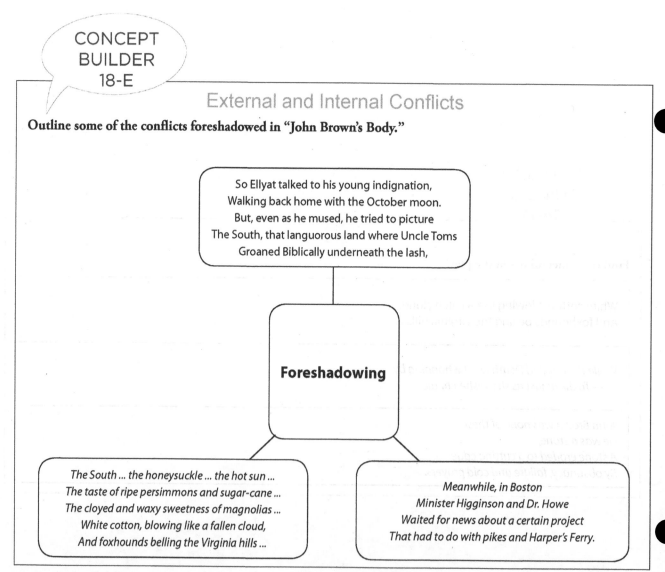

CONCEPT BUILDER 18-E

External and Internal Conflicts

Outline some of the conflicts foreshadowed in "John Brown's Body."

So Ellyat talked to his young indignation,
Walking back home with the October moon.
But, even as he mused, he tried to picture
The South, that languorous land where Uncle Toms
Groaned Biblically underneath the lash,

Foreshadowing

The South ... the honeysuckle ... the hot sun ...
The taste of ripe persimmons and sugar-cane ...
The cloyed and waxy sweetness of magnolias ...
White cotton, blowing like a fallen cloud,
And foxhounds belling the Virginia hills ...

Meanwhile, in Boston
Minister Higginson and Dr. Howe
Waited for news about a certain project
That had to do with pikes and Harper's Ferry.

Chapter 18 Review Questions

Writing a Novella

Write another chapter in your novella. Most authors base their fictional works on real-life situations, often autobiographical events in their own lives. Is your novella autobiographical? Or is it based on a historical fact?

Literary Analysis

Imagine an epic written as a novel. In what ways might it be different?

For one thing, it would have to be a lot longer. The plot would take more prose than poetry to develop. The advantages of meter and rhythm would be lost but could be compensated by solid prose.

Biblical Application

Christian killed Christian in the American Civil War. Was this war justified?

Answers will vary.

Chapter 18 Test

Essay (100 points)

Benet's classic is historical fiction — he admits that he is not writing an accurate, historical novel. Still, most readers consider it to be fact. Where does Benet get it right and get it wrong in his epic story of the American Civil War?

Your essay will be evaluated in these three areas:

Syntax and diction: grammar and style (25 points)

Organization: paragraphs, transitions, introduction, et al. (25 points)

Argument (50 points)

Chapter 18 Test Answer Sample

Essay (100 points)

Benet's classic is historical fiction — he admits that he is not writing an accurate, historical novel. Still, most readers consider it to be fact. Where does Benet get it right and get it wrong in his epic story of the American Civil War?

Your essay will be evaluated in these three areas:

Syntax and diction: grammar and style (25 points)

Organization: paragraphs, transitions, introduction, et al. (25 points)

Argument (50 points)

He is too easy on John Brown, who, by all estimations, was a murderer and psychotic. In general, too, he is too easy on the South, which, while it does present a historical front, was fighting to preserve an immoral institution: slavery.

Reading 2

John Brown's Body by Stephen Vincent Benet

Chapter 19

First Thoughts

Throughout history, societies have produced literary works like *The Iliad* or *The Aeneid* that define a nation's character and its people. In 1928, the end of a decade where patriotism was losing steam, Stephen Vincent Benet published *John Brown's Body*. It was 15,000 lines of blank verse celebrating the spirit of the American people as seen through the prism of its defining moment — the Civil War. Like Homer and Virgil before him, Benet used poetry to give moral significance to a time of seminal change and profound tragedy.

Chapter Learning Objectives

In chapter 19 we will . . .

1. Identify imagery in this epic poem
2. Work on character descriptions
3. Analyze archetypes in this epic poem and your novella
4. Analyze form and structure in this epic poem and your novella

Look Ahead for Friday

- Turn in all assignments.
- Continue to work on your novella.

Lesson 1

Song Lyrics

Daily Assignment

- Warm-up: Write a song about your favorite hero(oine).
- In your essay, use the words who and whom.
- Students will complete Concept Builder 19-A.
- Prayer journal: students are encouraged to write in their prayer journal every day.
- Finish the next book you have been assigned.
- Students should systematically review their vocabulary words daily.

CONCEPT BUILDER 19-A

Writing a Song

Write a song based on this passage.

A century before Columbus sailed, Europeans were probing the coast of Africa and eventually reached the East Indies, going east to China long before Columbus departed, sure that he could do the same thing going west. Europe was suited to lead the world into the modern age. It alone possessed the navigational expertise, the compass, the astrolabe, and mapmaking skills to launch the great nautical explorations, which resulted in the colonization of the Western Hemisphere and the development of the world economy. There were other exploration attempts. The Chinese, for instance, a century before Columbus, had sent out a very successful, and much more elaborate, exploratory voyage into the Indian Ocean. But it was to be the Europeans who initiated the modern era with their age of exploration.

Before Columbus
Other comrades probed the coast of dark Africa
The Ocean Blue would be yours when you had the right tools
The right Ship
Others had come and gone
The Chinese and the Vikings
But it was to be you, Christopher
And the Europeans
Who would initiate the age of exploration

Lesson 2

Imagery

Daily Assignment

- Warm-up: Add some rich descriptions full of imagery to your novella.
- Students will complete Concept Builder 19-B.
- Prayer journal: students are encouraged to write in their prayer journal every day.
- Finish the next book you have been assigned.
- Students should systematically review their vocabulary words daily.

CONCEPT BUILDER 19-B

Themes

Give examples of imagery in *John Brown's Body*.

John Brown's body lies a-mouldering in the grave.
He will not come again with foolish pikes
And a pack of desperate boys to shadow the sun.
He has gone back North.
The slaves have forgotten his eyes.
John Brown's body lies a-mouldering in the grave.

Themes

"Bind my white bones together — hollow them
To skeleton pipes of music. When the wind
Blows from the budded Spring, the song will blow."

I hear no song. I hear
Only the blunt seeds growing secretly
In the dark entrails of the preparate earth,
The rustle of the cricket under the leaf,
The creaking of the cold wheel of the stars.

Not the silk flag and the shouts, the catchword patrioteers,
The screaming noise of the press, the preachers who howled for blood,
But a certain and stubborn pith in the hearts of the cannoneers
Who hardly knew their guns before they died in the mud.

A Forgotten Work

Daily Assignment

- Warm-up: Add at least one rich character description to your novella.
- Students will complete Concept Builder 19-C.
- Prayer journal: students are encouraged to write in their prayer journal every day.
- Finish the next book you have been assigned.
- Students should systematically review their vocabulary words daily.

CONCEPT BUILDER 19-C

Character Descriptions

Benet offers several memorable character descriptions. Offer three of them.

Character Descriptions

Lincoln, six feet one in his stocking feet,
The lank man, knotty and tough as a hickory rail,
Whose hands were always too big for white-kid gloves,
Whose wit was a coonskin sack of dry, tall tales,
Whose weathered face was homely as a plowed field--

Cudjo watched and measured and knew them,
Seeing behind and around and through them
With the shrewd, dispassionate, smiling eye
Of the old-time servant in days gone by.
He couldn't read and he couldn't write.

John Brown was none of these,
He was a stone,
A stone eroded to a cutting edge
By obstinacy, failure, and cold prayers.

Lesson 4

Archetypes: Christlike Characters

Daily Assignment

- Warm-up: What archetype would represent you?
- Students will complete Concept Builder 19-D.
- Prayer journal: students are encouraged to write in their prayer journal every day.
- Finish the next book you have been assigned.
- Students should systematically review their vocabulary words daily.

CONCEPT BUILDER 19-D

Christlike Characters

Both Abraham Lincoln and John Brown are Christlike characters. Explain.

Christ	John Brown	Abraham Lincoln
Sacrificed His life for a cause	*John Brown died to set the slaves free.*	*Lincoln was martyred for his desire to set the slaves free.*
Was larger than life	*John Brown, a flawed instrument, still assumed larger than life influence.*	*Lincoln, with his rhetoric and mercy, became an epic hero.*

Lesson 5

Form and Structure

Daily Assignment

- Warm-up: What is the form and the structure of your novella? How many chapters do you have so far?
- Students will complete Concept Builder 19-E.
- Prayer journal: students are encouraged to write in their prayer journal every day.
- Finish the next book you have been assigned.
- Students should systematically review their vocabulary words daily.

CONCEPT BUILDER 19-E

Form and Structure

Use the following diagram to show the structure of your novella (so far):

Answers will vary.

Chapter 19 Review Questions

Writing a Novella

Write another chapter in your novella. What is the form and structure of your novella? How is it organized? Chronologically? By settings? By crises? By characters?

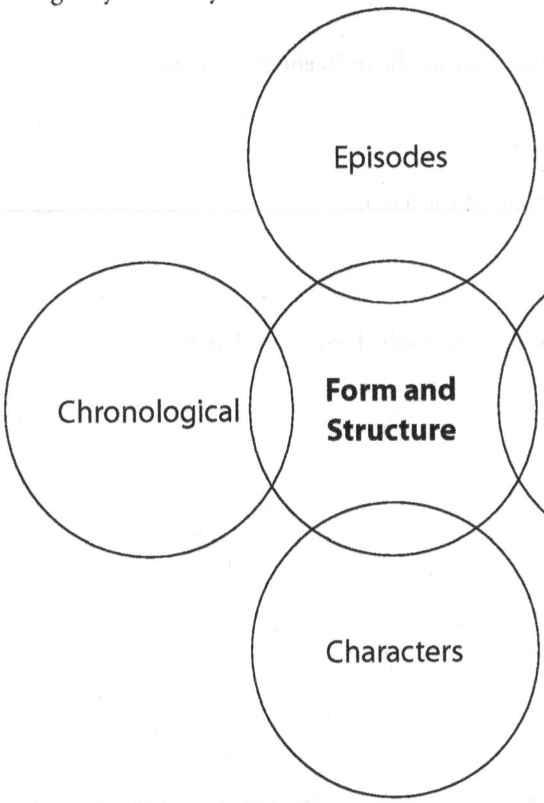

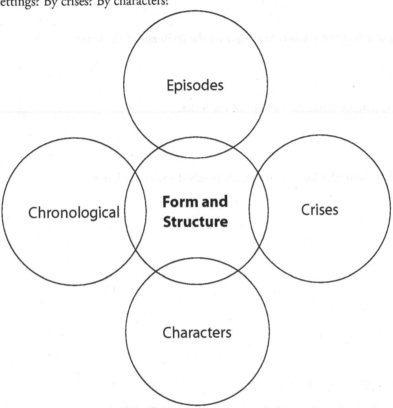

Literary Analysis

Critics have debated the book's literary merits ever since it won the Pulitzer Prize in 1929. Some consider Benet's portrayal of historical personages like Lincoln, Lee, Grant, Beauregard, Judah Benjamin, Jefferson Davis, and others to be flat and uninspiring. What do you think?

Answers will vary.

Biblical Application

Pretend that you were John Brown's pastor and you are meeting with him the night before he is executed. What will you say to him?

Answers will vary.

Chapter 19 Test

Write a letter to John Brown a few weeks before he leads his revolt. Support him or persuade him to change his mind. You decide! Follow the following format: (100 points)

1. Greeting

   The greeting or salutation is where you identify the recipient of the letter.

2. Body

   The body is where you write the content of the letter.

3. Closing

   The closing lets the reader know that you are finished with your letter.

Chapter 19 Test Answer Sample

Write a letter to John Brown a few weeks before he leads his revolt. Support him or persuade him to change his mind. You decide! Follow the following format: (100 points)

1. Greeting

   The greeting or salutation is where you identify the recipient of the letter.

2. Body

   The body is where you write the content of the letter.

3. Closing

   The closing lets the reader know that you are finished with your letter.

Answers will vary.

Reading 1

The Legend of Sleepy Hollow, Washington Irving

Chapter 20

First Thoughts

Most people are probably familiar with the story of *The Legend of Sleepy Hollow* through the movie and television renditions. The earliest was a movie in 1922: a version called *The Headless Horseman* starring Will Rogers as the main character — Ichabod Crane. In 1949, Disney created its own version, *The Adventures of Ichabod and Mr. Toad,* with Bing Crosby narrating. In 1999, Tim Burton's account of *Sleepy Hollow*, starring Johnny Depp, takes a darker approach and it misses the mark, really, since Irving was writing a romantic, whimsical piece — not a horror story. Even some TV shows, like Nickelodeon's *Are You Afraid of the Dark, Wishbone,* and *Charmed* have taken the basics of the story and adapted it for their own purposes.

Chapter Learning Objectives

In chapter 20 we will . . .

1. Learn how to determine the subject in a composition.
2. Understand what local color writing means.
3. Learn how to construct an outline.

Look Ahead for Friday

- Turn in all assignments.
- Continue to work on your novella.

Lesson 1

The Author and His Times

Daily Assignment

- Warm-up: Who is the headless horseman? How did he lose his head?
- In your essay, use the words who and whom.
- Students will complete Concept Builder 20-A.
- Prayer journal: students are encouraged to write in their prayer journal every day.
- Finish the next book you have been assigned.
- Students should systematically review their vocabulary words daily.

CONCEPT BUILDER 20-A

Illustrated Book Review

Create an illustrated booklet of the most important scenes from the book. Skim through the novel to select the five most important scenes. Illustrate each by either drawing, painting, or using magazine or computer pictures. On each page write a paragraph explaining why this is one of the five most significant scenes in the novel.

Answers will vary.

Lesson 2

Local Color Writings

Daily Assignment

- Warm-up: What does Ichabod like to read? Do you see how this is foreshadowing?
- Students will complete Concept Builder 20-B.
- Prayer journal: students are encouraged to write in their prayer journal every day.
- Finish the next book you have been assigned.
- Students should systematically review their vocabulary words daily.

CONCEPT BUILDER 20-B

Local Color Writings

Identify the part of the country this passage is from:

D. The Rural South

Lesson 3

Active Reading: *The Legend of Sleepy Hollow* Washington Irving

The short story begins with a frame story. What is that?

A story surrounding a story. In this case, the storyteller is recapitulating an event about a headless horseman that occurred in Upstate New York.

How does the setting add to suspense?

Foreshadowing. The eerie setting.

Predict what will happen next.

Answers will vary.

Daily Assignment

- Warm-up: Add another colorful character description to your novella.
- Students will complete Concept Builder 20-C.
- Prayer journal: students are encouraged to write in their prayer journal every day.
- Finish the next book you have been assigned.
- Students should systematically review their vocabulary words daily.

CONCEPT BUILDER 20-C

Mood

How does Irving create the mood/tone of his short story?

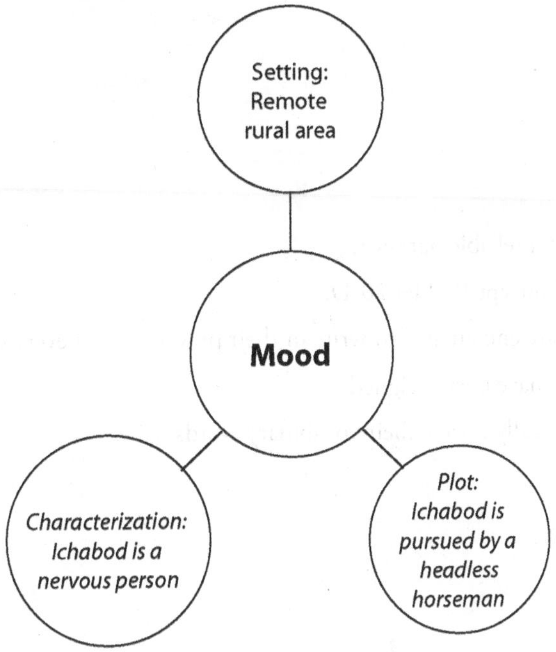
Setting:
Remote
rural area
Mood
Characterization:
Ichabod is a
nervous person
Plot:
Ichabod is
pursued by a
headless
horseman

Lesson 4

Writing Compositions: Narrowing the Subject

Daily Assignment

- Warm-up: Is the narrator a reliable narrator?
- Students will complete Concept Builder 20-D.
- Prayer journal: students are encouraged to write in their prayer journal every day.
- Finish the next book you have been assigned.
- Students should systematically review their vocabulary words daily.

CONCEPT BUILDER 20-D

Writing Compositions: Narrowing the Subject

Complete the following charts:

Subject: Businesses in the United States

More Focused Subject: *Fortune 500 Companies*

Even More Focused Subject: *Retailers*

Thesis Statement: Walmart is the most successful retailer in America because it controls inventory well and uses innovating marketing strategies.

Subject: *Living Things*

More Focused Subject: *Animals*

Even More Focused Subject: Mammals

Thesis Statement: Rabbits

Lesson 5

Writing Composition: Creating an Outline

Daily Assignment

- Warm-up: Create an outline for an essay you are writing or your novella.
- Students will complete Concept Builder 20-E.
- Prayer journal: students are encouraged to write in their prayer journal every day.
- Finish the next book you have been assigned.
- Students should systematically review their vocabulary words daily.

CONCEPT BUILDER 20-E

Writing Composition: Creating an Outline

Create an outline for this essay:

I. The Delta runs from Eudora north to Blytheville and as far west as Little Rock. It is in every way the creation of one phenomenon: the mighty Mississippi River.

A. The Mississippi River encompasses everything that is American. With its many tributaries, the Mississippi's watershed drains all or parts of 31 U.S. states and 2 Canadian provinces between the Rocky and Appalachian Mountains.

B. The Mississippi River begins as a 20-foot tributary in Lake Itasca and ends as a mile-wide juggernaut flowing through 10 states into the Gulf of Mexico. It is the epicenter of the nation, indeed, most think of the world. Some historians and theologians argue that the world began at the Tigris and the Euphrates or the Nile or the Indus, but they are wrong. The world began somewhere between Lake Itasca and New Orleans along the 2,530 miles of the Mississippi River.

i. Native Americans long lived along the Mississippi in the Arkansas Delta. Most were hunter-gatherers or goat herders, but some, such as the Mound builders, formed productive agricultural societies. Europeans in the 1500s brought horses, cattle, and smallpox. Life was never static along the river. Annual flooding and spotty drought constantly transformed the land.

ii. The river was at first a boundary, a limit to what was and a start of what would be. Its frothy water formed borders for New Spain, New France, and the early United States — then became a vital transportation artery and communications link between them all. In the 19th century, the Mississippi and its diminutive cousin, the Missouri, formed pathways for the western expansion of the United States.

II. Conclusion

Chapter 20 Review Questions

Writing a Novella

Write another chapter in your novella.

Literary Analysis

How do women function in *The Legend of Sleepy Hollow*?

Women are important foils. Ichabod is not exactly Tom Cruise with the ladies, but schoolmasters were thought to be superior in their tastes and habits and it was considered a privilege to associate with such a learned person. The mothers, therefore, treated him to their finest food and nicest china in an attempt to show him their own refinement. Ichabod spent a great deal of time with the girls, impressing them (and making the boys jealous) with his "superior elegance."

Biblical Application

Irving, in a rather playful way, discusses the supernatural in *The Legend of Sleepy Hollow*. Many people, including this author, struggle with literary works that trivialize the supernatural. Does Irving trivialize the supernatural? Can you think of a literary work that does?

Irving in good humor explores the folklore and romanticism of a section of the country, but he does not trivialize the supernatural. In this author's opinion, the Harry Potter books do indeed trivialize the supernatural by romanticism and fanaticizing something — the supernatural — that is very real to the author.

Chapter 20 Test

I. Discussion Question (75 points)

Discuss the importance of the setting to "The Legend of Sleepy Hollow."

Your essay will be evaluated in these three areas:

Syntax and diction: grammar and style (15 points)

Organization: paragraphs, transitions, introduction, et al. (15 points)

Argument (45 points)

II. Fill in the following components of the setting in Irving's short novel: (25 points)

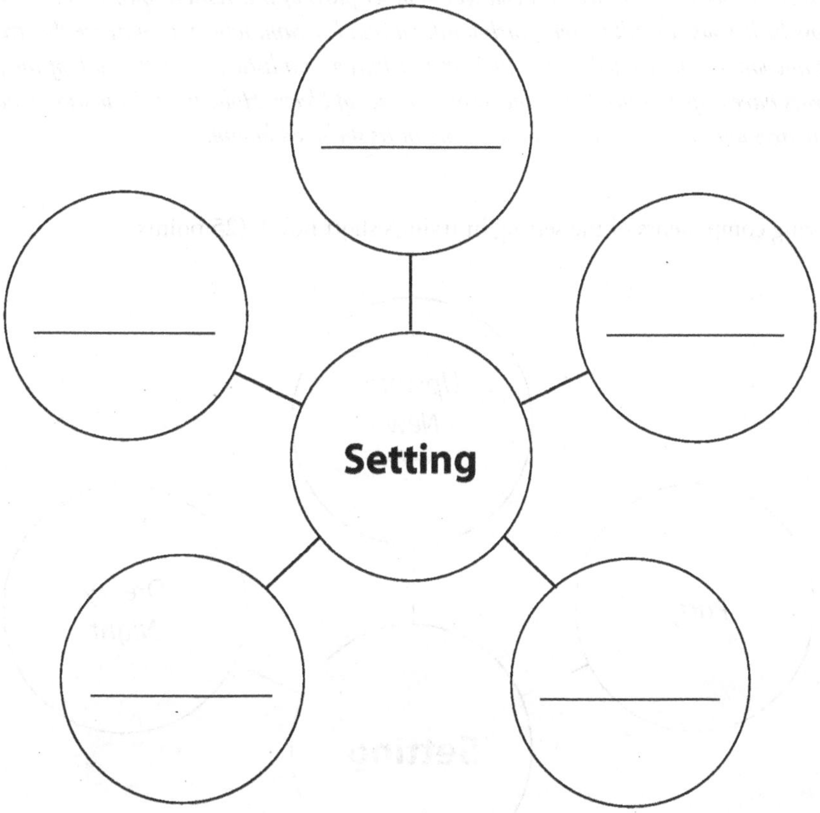

Chapter 20 Test Answer Sample

I. Discussion Question (75 points)

Discuss the importance of the setting to "The Legend of Sleepy Hollow."

Your essay will be evaluated in these three areas:

Syntax and diction: grammar and style (15 points)

Organization: paragraphs, transitions, introduction, et al. (15 points)

Argument (45 points)

The setting sets the tone and direction for the novel. It adds a mysterious, rural touch to the plot that is critical to the outcome. Superstition and innocence exist in almost equal quantities in this quaint place. "I mention this peaceful spot with all possible laud; for it is in such little retired Dutch valleys, found here and there embosomed in the great State of New York, that population, manners, and customs, remain fixed; while the great torrent of migration and improvement, which is making such incessant changes in other parts of this restless country, sweeps by them unobserved. They are like those little nooks of still water which border a rapid stream; where we may see the straw and bubble riding quietly at anchor, or slowly revolving in their mimic harbor, undisturbed by the rush of the passing current. Though many years have elapsed since I trod the drowsy shades of Sleepy Hollow, yet I question whether I should not still find the same trees and the same families vegetating in its sheltered bosom."

II. Fill in the following components of the setting in Irving's short novel: (25 points)

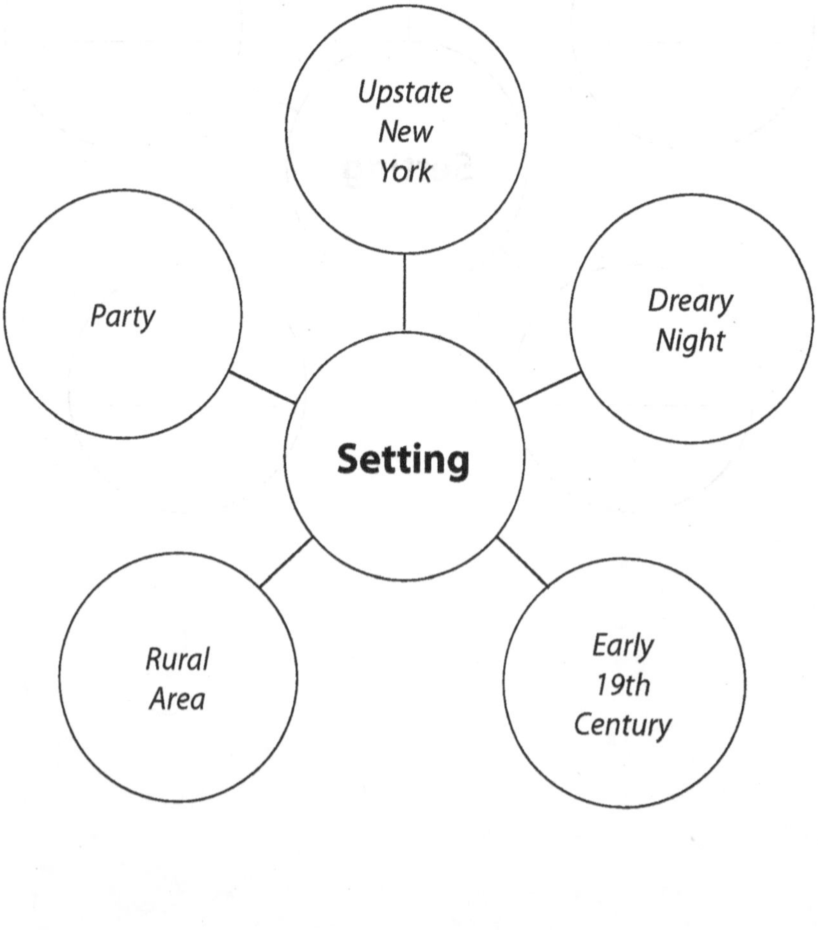

Reading 2

The Legend of Sleepy Hollow, Washington Irving

Chapter 21

First Thoughts

Born on April 3, 1783, Washington Irving was a member of the first generation who were natives to the newly created United States of America; therefore, it is fitting that he became known as the first writer to see the potential for a native literature in the "New World" that could rival that of the "Old World." The decade-long struggle for liberty, which finally resulted in a new nation in 1783, was echoed in the struggle that ensued over the next century to develop a national literature worthy of the new land. The flowering of Irving's talent made him the first to gain the respect of the literary community in Europe while still being faithful to the seeds he found in his native soil.

Chapter Learning Objectives

In chapter 21 we will . . .

1. Understand frame story, style, romanticism, and characterization.
2. Discern the limitations of romanticism as a world view.

Look Ahead for Friday

- Turn in all assignments.
- Continue to work on your novella.

Lesson 1

Style

Daily Assignment

- Warm-up: What style does Irving employ?
- In your essay, use the words who and whom.
- Students will complete Concept Builder 21-A.
- Prayer journal: students are encouraged to write in their prayer journal every day.
- Finish the next book you have been assigned.
- Students should systematically review their vocabulary words daily.

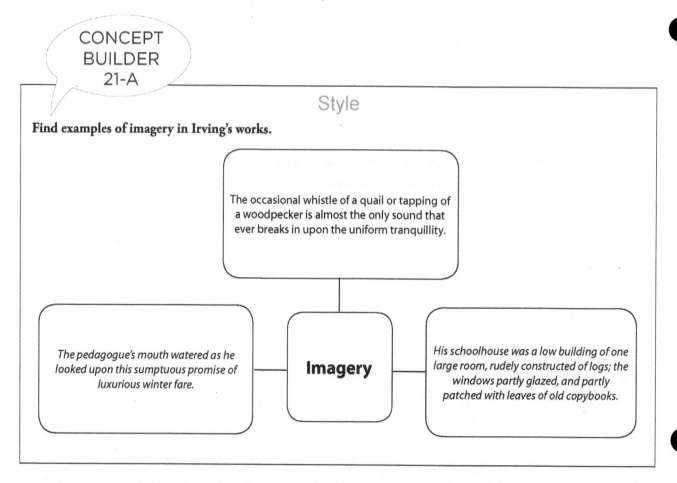

CONCEPT BUILDER 21-A

Style

Find examples of imagery in Irving's works.

The occasional whistle of a quail or tapping of a woodpecker is almost the only sound that ever breaks in upon the uniform tranquillity.

The pedagogue's mouth watered as he looked upon this sumptuous promise of luxurious winter fare.

Imagery

His schoolhouse was a low building of one large room, rudely constructed of logs; the windows partly glazed, and partly patched with leaves of old copybooks.

Lesson 2

Frame Story

Daily Assignment

- Warm-up: What is the purpose of the Postscript?
- Students will complete Concept Builder 21-B.
- Prayer journal: students are encouraged to write in their prayer journal every day.
- Finish the next book you have been assigned.
- Students should systematically review their vocabulary words daily.

CONCEPT BUILDER 21-B

Suspense

List elements of suspense from *The Legend of Sleepy Hollow*.

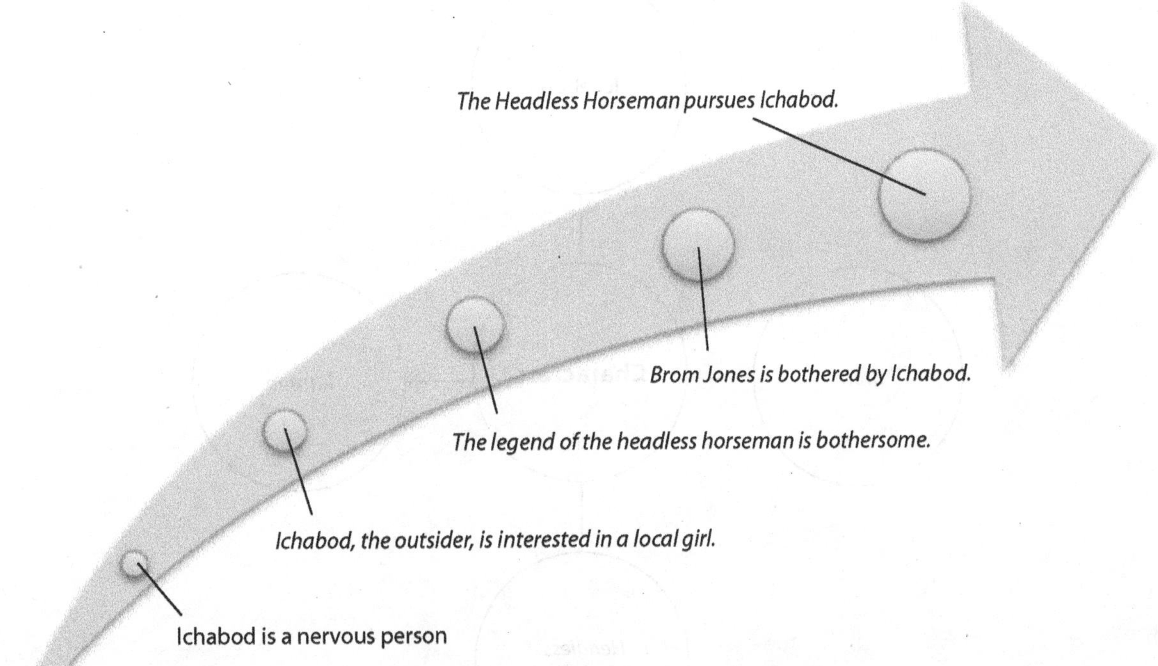

The Headless Horseman pursues Ichabod.
Brom Jones is bothered by Ichabod.
The legend of the headless horseman is bothersome.
Ichabod, the outsider, is interested in a local girl.
Ichabod is a nervous person

Lesson 3

Active Reading: *The Legend of Sleepy Hollow* Washington Irving

Daily Assignment

- Warm-up: Besides Ichabod, who is your favorite character?
- Students will complete Concept Builder 21-C.
- Prayer journal: students are encouraged to write in their prayer journal every day.
- Finish the next book you have been assigned.
- Students should systematically review their vocabulary words daily.

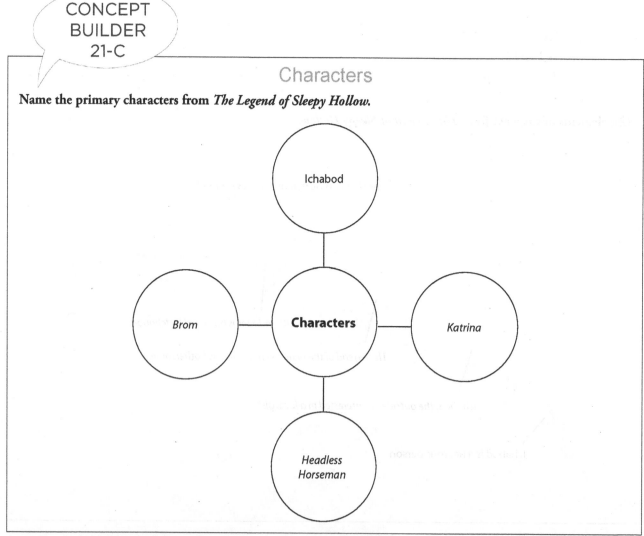

CONCEPT BUILDER 21-C

Characters

Name the primary characters from *The Legend of Sleepy Hollow.*

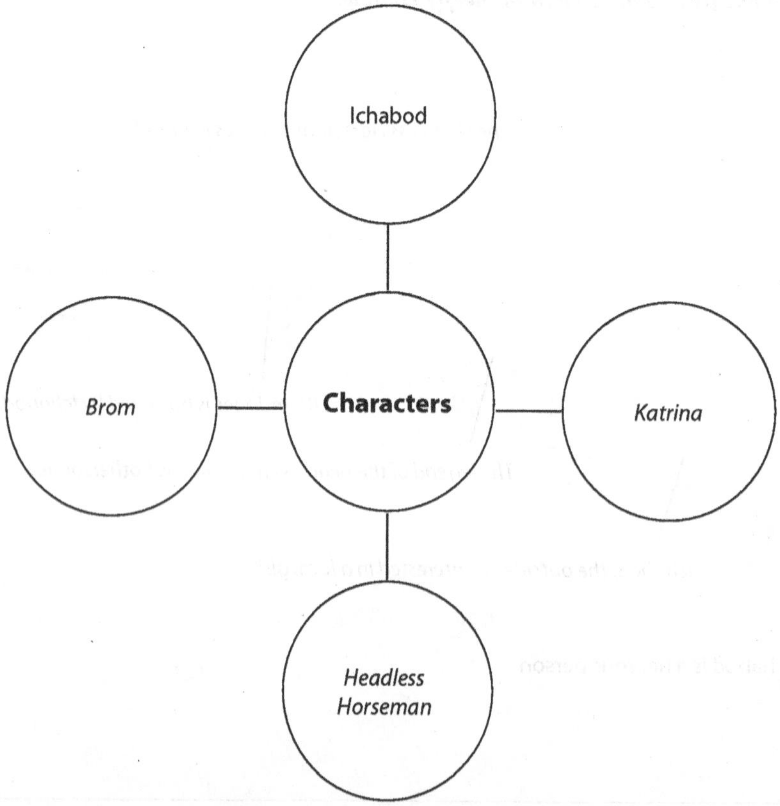

Lesson 4

Romanticism

Daily Assignment

- Warm-up: Did you enjoy this short story/novella? Why or why not?
- Students will complete Concept Builder 21-D.
- Prayer journal: students are encouraged to write in their prayer journal every day.
- Finish the next book you have been assigned.
- Students should systematically review their vocabulary words daily.

CONCEPT BUILDER 21-D

Romantic Characteristics

Name some characteristics of romantic characteristics from the story.

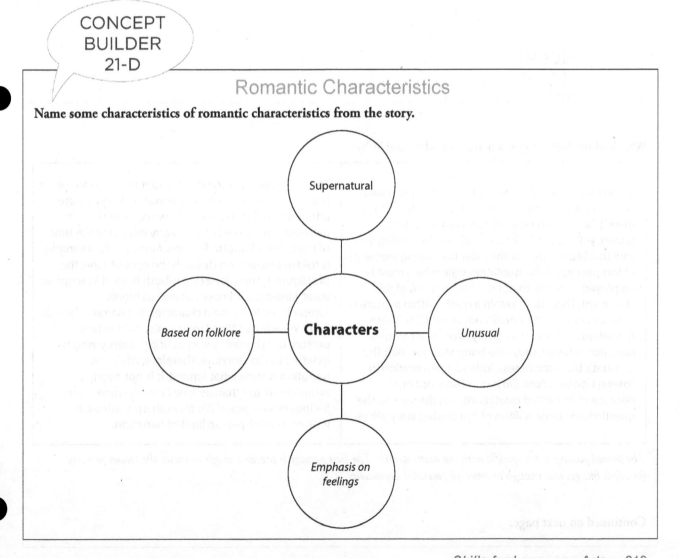

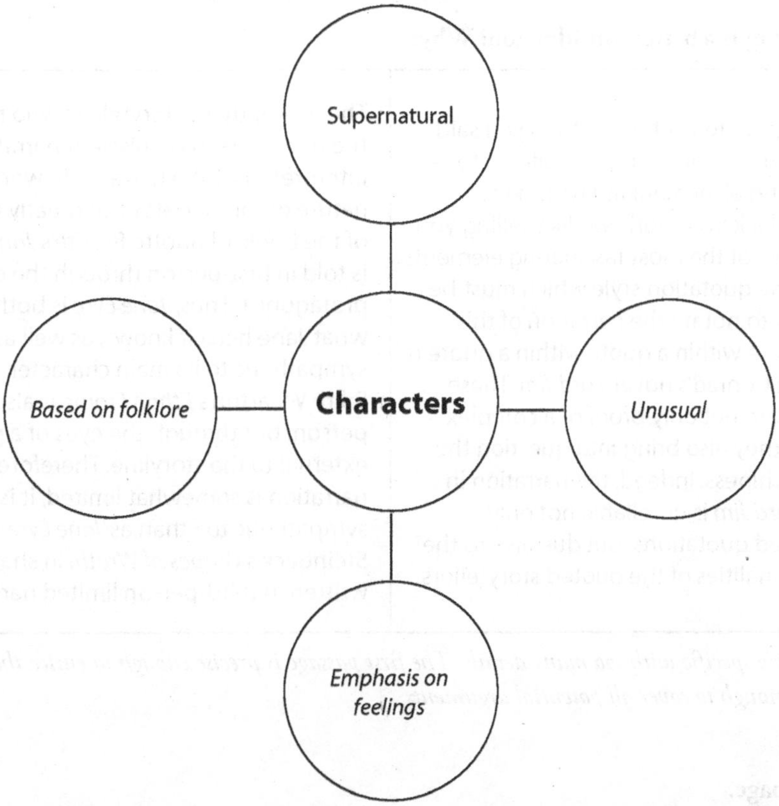

Lesson 5

Writing the Composition: Introduction

Daily Assignment

- Warm-up: Examine an introduction you wrote in another essay. Was it an effective introduction?
- Students will complete Concept Builder 21-E.
- Prayer journal: students are encouraged to write in their prayer journal every day.
- Finish the next book you have been assigned.
- Students should systematically review their vocabulary words daily.
- Turn in the final copy of the essay assignment(s) for the week and then rewrite if necessary.

CONCEPT BUILDER 21-E

Writing the Composition: Introduction

Which of the following is a better introduction? Why?

"I don't suppose you've forgotten . . . (that) you said also — I call to mind — that 'giving your life up to them' (them meaning all of mankind with skins brown, yellow, or black in colour) 'was like selling your soul to a brute.' " One of the most fascinating elements of this passage is the quotation style which must be employed properly to notate the narration of this statement. This quote within a quote within a quote is common in Joseph Conrad's novel, *Lord Jim*. These nested quotations are not only proof of a complex narration scheme, they also bring into question the account's trustworthiness. Indeed, the narration in Joseph Conrad's *Lord Jim* is unreliable not only because of its nested quotations, but due also to the questionable personalities of the quoted storytellers.	The first of these storytellers who must be examined is the third-person omniscient narrator. All books are interpreted by the narrator. In works of fiction, the nature of this narrator can greatly influence the tone of the book. Charlotte Bronte's *Jane Eyre*, for example, is told in first-person through the eyes of Jane, the protagonist. Thus, *Jane Eyre* is both limited in scope to what Jane herself knows, as well as highly sympathetic to its main character, the narrator herself. Edith Wharton's *Ethan Frome* is also told in first-person, but through the eyes of a passerby who is external to the storyline. Therefore, while the narration is somewhat limited, it is not nearly as sympathetic to Ethan as *Jane Eyre* is to Jane. John Steinbeck's *Grapes of Wrath*, in sharp contrast, is written in third-person limited narration.

The second passage is too specific with too many details. The first passage is precise enough to entice the reader to move forward, but general enough to cover all potential arguments.

Continued on next page.

Rewrite this introduction and make it better.

The most prevalent theme in George Eliot's *Silas Marner* is redemption. But truthfully, the setting is important too. This theme is cemented into the story through important foils, develops over the course of the plot, and has universal application no matter the setting. So I guess the setting might not be that important. Marner's road toward redemption weaves its way through the plot. In the exposition he is lost to society and is in obvious need of a savior. "So had his way of life — he invited no comer to step across his door-sill, and he never strolled into the village to drink a pint at the Rainbow, or to gossip at the wheelwright's: he sought no man or woman, save for the purposes of his calling, or in order to supply himself with necessaries." The events that occur in the rising action begin to prepare him for redemptive love. But don't worry! The book has a happy ending. One such event is the theft of his much beloved gold. "Robbed!" said Silas, gaspingly. "I've been robbed!" "And the little one, rising on its legs, toddled through the snow, the old grimy shawl in which it was wrapped trailing behind it, and the queer little bonnet dangling at its back — toddled on to the open door of Silas Marner's cottage, and right up to the warm hearth."	*The most prevalent theme in George Eliot's* Silas Marner *is redemption. This theme is cemented into the story through important foils, develops over the course of the plot, and has universal application no matter the setting. Marner's road toward redemption weaves its way through the plot. In the exposition he is lost to society and is in obvious need of a Savior. "So had his way of life — he invited no comer to step across his door-sill, and he never strolled into the village to drink a pint at the Rainbow, or to gossip at the wheelwright's: he sought no man or woman, save for the purposes of his calling, or in order to supply himself with necessaries." The events that occur in the rising action begin to prepare him for redemptive love. One such event is the theft of his much beloved gold. "'Robbed!' said Silas, gaspingly. 'I've been robbed!' And the little one, rising on its legs, toddled through the snow, the old grimy shawl in which it was wrapped trailing behind it, and the queer little bonnet dangling at its back — toddled on to the open door of Silas Marner's cottage, and right up to the warm hearth."*

Chapter 21 Review Questions

Writing a Novella

Write a chapter in your novella.

Literary Analysis

What advantages and disadvantages do frame stories offer an author?

The frame story allows the author to manipulate narration and offers some credibility to his story. The problem is that the frame story may become more interesting than the main plot. In some ways, that nearly occurs in the "Custom House" chapter of Nathaniel Hawthorne's Scarlet Letter.

Biblical Application

Why should Christians fear no man or demon?

Christians are more than conquerors in Christ Jesus (Romans 8). Christ conquered heaven and hell on the Cross.

Chapter 21 Test

I. True or False. (50 points)

_____ Romanticism is just another form of Christianity.

_____ Romanticism, and its American version, transcendentalism, posits that God is nature and that "It" is good. The more natural things are, the better.

_____ Nature is inherently good. Nature alone is the ultimate reality. In other words, nature is the romantic god.

_____ Man is essentially a simple, stupid animal, too stupid to be controlled by absolute, codified truth (as one would find in the Bible).

_____ Human intuition replaces the Holy Spirit. Depending upon the demands on individual lives, truth and good are relative and changing.

II. Discussion Question (50 points)

Irving describes Ichabod Crane: "He was, in fact, an odd mixture of small shrewdness and simple credulity. His appetite for the marvelous, and his powers of digesting it, were equally extraordinary; and both had been increased by his residence in this spellbound region." Explain.

Your essay will be evaluated in these three areas.

Syntax and diction: grammar and style (15 points)

Organization: paragraphs, transitions, introduction, et al. (15 points)

Argument (20 points)

Chapter 21 Test Answer Sample

I. True or False. (50 points)

T Romanticism is just another form of Christianity.

T Romanticism, and its American version, transcendentalism, posits that God is nature and that "It" is good. The more natural things are, the better.

F Nature is inherently good. Nature alone is the ultimate reality. In other words, nature is the romantic god.

F Man is essentially a simple, stupid animal, too stupid to be controlled by absolute, codified truth (as one would find in the Bible).

F Human intuition replaces the Holy Spirit. Depending upon the demands on individual lives, truth and good are relative and changing.

II. Discussion Question (50 points)

Irving describes Ichabod Crane: "He was, in fact, an odd mixture of small shrewdness and simple credulity. His appetite for the marvelous, and his powers of digesting it, were equally extraordinary; and both had been increased by his residence in this spellbound region." Explain.

Your essay will be evaluated in these three areas.

Syntax and diction: grammar and style (15 points)

Organization: paragraphs, transitions, introduction, et al. (15 points)

Argument (20 points)

Answers will vary.

Reading 1

Life with Father by Clarence Day

Chapter 22

First Thoughts

Life with Father is a collection of stories by Clarence Day Jr., mostly having to do with his childhood and primarily involving his father. Clarence Day, Sr. is one of the most interesting protagonists in literature. He is tyrannical, yet is also, in his own way, loving and kind. His interactions with his wife are particularly interesting.

Chapter Learning Objectives

In chapter 22 we will . . .

1. Explore the way Day uses narration as remembrances
2. Analyze the mother character as a foil
3. Evaluate Day's use of religion
4. Review use of dialogue

Look Ahead for Friday

- Turn in all assignments.
- Continue to work on your novella.

Lesson 1

Active Reading: *Life with Father* (Chapter 1) "A Holiday with Father" by Clarence Day

Why does Day begin this way?

The narrator is interacting with the main character, Father.

What do we learn about Father?

He can be a little grumpy, but he is really soft and gentle. He is respected by his staff.

The narrator becomes the center of attention now. How?

Through dialogue and stream of consciousness.

Daily Assignment

- Warm-up: What funny thing does your dad/guardian do?
- In your essay, use the words who and whom.
- Students will complete Concept Builder 22-A.
- Prayer journal: students are encouraged to write in their prayer journal every day.
- Finish the next book you have been assigned.
- Students should systematically review their vocabulary words daily.

CONCEPT BUILDER 22-A

Illustrated Book Review

Create an illustrated booklet of the most important scenes from the book. Skim through the novel to select the five most important scenes. Illustrate each by either drawing, painting, or using magazine or computer pictures. On each page write a paragraph explaining why this is one of the five most significant scenes in the novel.

Answers will vary.

Narration: Remembrances

Daily Assignment

- Warm-up: How reliable is the narrator?
- Students will complete Concept Builder 22-B.
- Prayer journal: students are encouraged to write in their prayer journal every day.
- Finish the next book you have been assigned.
- Students should systematically review their vocabulary words daily.

CONCEPT BUILDER 22-B

The Plot

The plot is more or less disconnected. Even the narrator's age is not consistent. He follows no discernable pattern. The net result is that there is no climax. List elements of this plot from *Life with Father*.

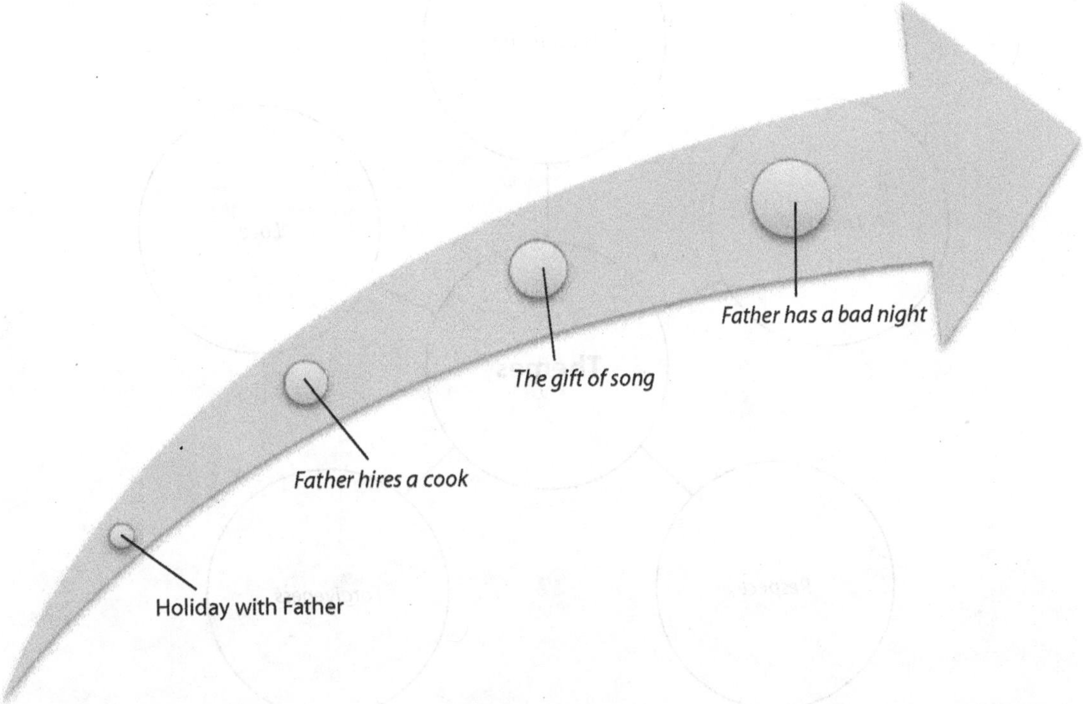

Lesson 3

Mother: A Foil

Daily Assignment

- Warm-up: What does Day reveal about Father by having him interact with Mother?
- Students will complete Concept Builder 22-C.
- Prayer journal: students are encouraged to write in their prayer journal every day.
- Finish the next book you have been assigned.
- Students should systematically review their vocabulary words daily.

CONCEPT BUILDER 22-C

Themes

List various themes from *Life with Father*.

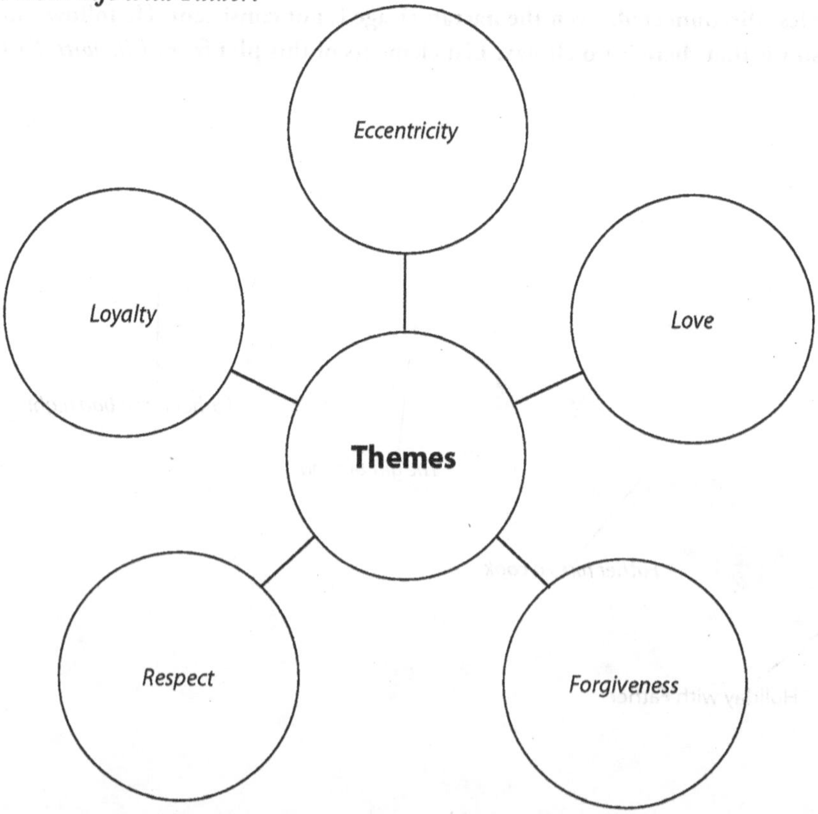

Lesson 4

Use of Dialogue

Daily Assignment

- Warm-up: Reveal the character of a sibling or friend by the use of dialogue. You cannot tell the reader; use dialogue to reveal the character.
- Students will complete Concept Builder 22-D.
- Prayer journal: students are encouraged to write in their prayer journal every day.
- Finish the next book you have been assigned.
- Students should systematically review their vocabulary words daily.

CONCEPT BUILDER 22-D

Characters

List various characters from *Life with Father*.

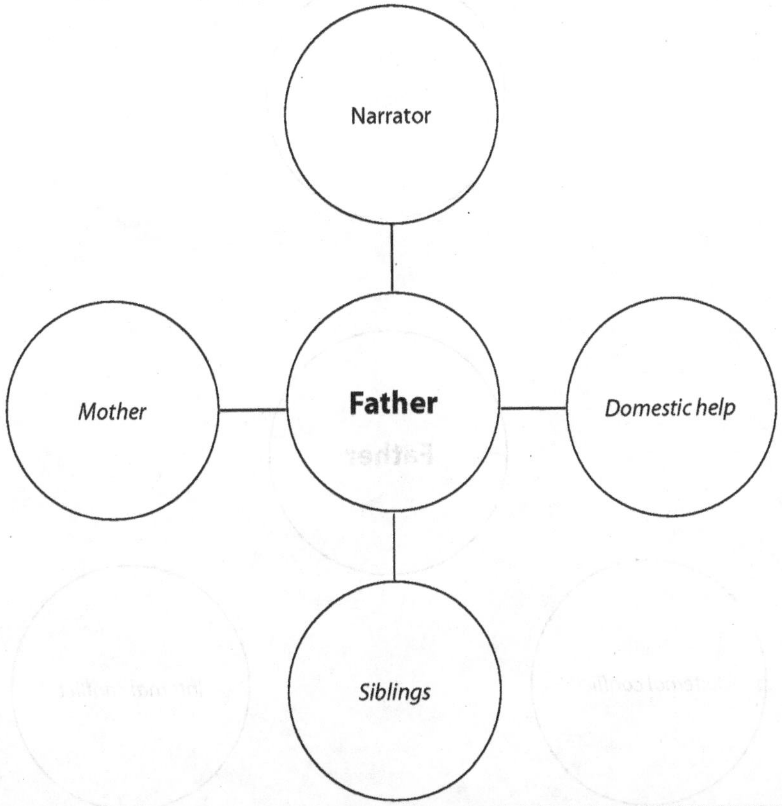

Lesson 5

Clarence Day and Religion

Daily Assignment

- Warm-up: In *Life with Father*, is Father a born-again Christian?
- Students will complete Concept Builder 22-E.
- Prayer journal: students are encouraged to write in their prayer journal every day.
- Finish the next book you have been assigned.
- Students should systematically review their vocabulary words daily.

CONCEPT BUILDER 22-E

Character Formation

Father is not an easy character to develop. The author works hard and uses many different literary elements to create this profound, complicated character. Name three. There are more than three ways, so answers will vary.

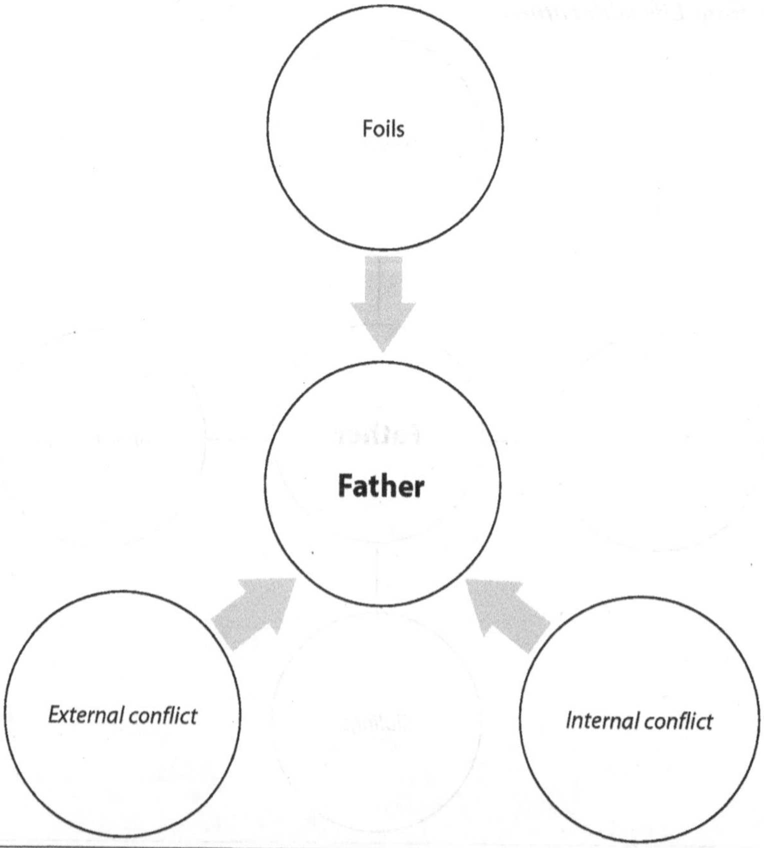

Chapter 22 Review Questions

Writing a Novella

Write a chapter in your novella. Work hard to add some humor without moving to sarcasm or cynicism.

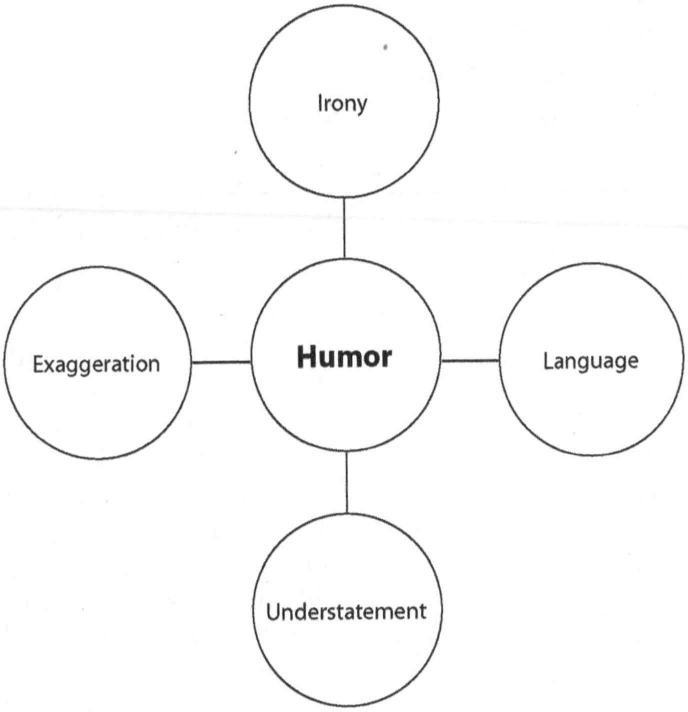

Literary Analysis

The point of view, of course, is from young Clarence Day. Is he a reliable narrator? Why or why not?

While the narrator admires, even loves his dad, he also presents unflattering details about him. Because of this, and his exhaustive details, he is a reliable narrator.

Biblical Application

Literature, especially American literature, is practically devoid of positive father figures. Why?

The notion of a sacrificial, godly father is alien to a Modern and Post-modern world.

Chapter 22 Test

Discussion Question (100 points)

Life with Father, at its most basic level, is a memoir full of disparate stories only connected by the same characters and the same narrator. Along the way readers learn a lot about both. What can readers discern about the characters and narrator in this passage?

Your essay will be evaluated in these three areas:

Syntax and diction: grammar and style (25 points)

Organization: paragraphs, transitions, introduction, et al. (25 points)

Argument (50 points)

"Dad, where are we?"

I was nine years old and with my dad in Southeast Arkansas' Devil's Den Swamp hunting whitetail deer, and as usual, we arrived way too early.

"Nice night, dad," I sarcastically quipped. Perhaps it was an insight to my dad's personality that his nine-year-old son was already a cynic.

Nothing about this morning resembled its raison d'être. I stared into the heavens and contemplated the absurdity of our situation.

The Devil's Den Swamp was a thousand acre quagmire. It was the last wheeze of antediluvian mayhem in the wild Mississippi River Delta before pilgrims entered the subdued lowland piedmont.

Other little boys, waiting for trophy bucks, were relaxing in comfortable shelters on the edge of Milo maze fields. But no, not me. I was sloshing around in the Devil Den's Swamp.

With no hint of dawn, Dad and I languished in a slough of despair.

"We are right where we should be, Jacob." Dad smiled. "If we follow the North Star we shall surely be near the deer stand before dawn."

"Okay, Dad," I muttered deferentially.

We were doing no such thing. We were following Venus. Venus, squatting on the right of the first quarter moon, had been in the same place for millennium. Nowhere near the North Star.

We were following Venus, not the North Star, but I discerned that it was not propitious to challenge Dad's misapprehension of the universe.

My dad was 28-year-old dad Martin Stevens. Dad, five feet eight inches tall, wore heavy canvas camouflage pants and a grey flannel shirt. He wore his favorite green knee high rubber boots with tiny brand name red balls peering over the top of murky swamp water. In truth, he looked more like my older brother than my dad.

"Dad, where are we?"

"I don't know, but we are following the North Star so we are fine."

There was quicksand in the Devil's Den. I wondered if Dad remembered that. I knew a lot about quicksand—it regularly gobbled up unwary travelers in Saturday morning Tarzan movies.

Three years ago, while duck hunting, Jedidiah Morris walked into the Devil's Den and never returned. Old-timers claimed he fell into quicksand and disappeared forever. I was certain, this morning, that I would step on old, slimy, Jedidiah's head.

We were headed to the "deer stand" which was a euphemism for a rickety wooden structure strapped to an ancient Pin Oak Tree. Earlier that spring, fighting bloodthirsty mosquitoes and angry water moccasins, we built our deer stand on an obscure Indian mound in the middle of the Devil's Den.

Remote and unapproachable by man and deer alike, on this early November, the deer stand awaited our arrival and the debut of the first deer-hunting trip of the season.

I, Jacob Stevens, too wore camouflage attire, although I had pinned captain bars to my authentic Marine fatigue camouflage shirt. I was a captain in the Corps but I expected to be promoted any day, like my cousin Major Eddy Jones, a U. S. Marine Phantom II jet pilot who flew beer between Manila and Saigon. Even at age nine I knew it was a terrible waste to use a genuine American hero like Uncle Eddy and his superior flying machine the Phantom II to transport Budweiser when both hero and machine could be more profitably used to bomb the Charley.[1]

1 James P. Stobaugh, *Growing Up White* (New York: Harvard Square Editions, 2014), p. 9–10.

Chapter 22 Test Answer Sample

Discussion Question (100 points)

Life with Father, at its most basic level, is a memoir full of disparate stories only connected by the same characters and the same narrator. Along the way readers learn a lot about both. What can readers discern about the characters and narrator in this passage?

Your essay will be evaluated in these three areas:

Syntax and diction: grammar and style (25 points)

Organization: paragraphs, transitions, introduction, et al. (25 points)

Argument (50 points)

The narrator is an older adult who is remembering when he was younger. The protagonist in the narrative is a precocious nine-year-old boy who is enjoying a hunting trip with his youthful father.

Reading 2

Life With Father by Clarence Day

Chapter 23

First Thoughts

Life with Father struck a cord in modern America, which at the time so desperately wanted to have the sort of family presented in this memoir.

Chapter Learning Objectives

In chapter 23 we will . . .

1. Understand narration strategies
2. Analyze the use of humor in *Life with Father*
3. Review the parts of a composition

Look Ahead for Friday

- Turn in all assignments.
- Continue to work on your novella.

Lesson 1

Narration Strategies

Daily Assignment

- Warm-up: What narrative strategies do you employ in your novella?
- In your essay, use the words who and whom.
- Students will complete Concept Builder 23-A.
- Prayer journal: students are encouraged to write in their prayer journal every day.
- Finish the next book you have been assigned.
- Students should systematically review their vocabulary words daily.

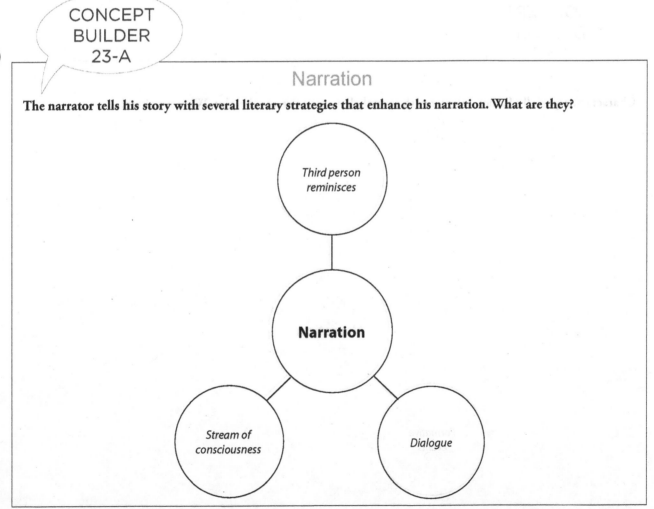

CONCEPT BUILDER 23-A

Narration

The narrator tells his story with several literary strategies that enhance his narration. What are they?

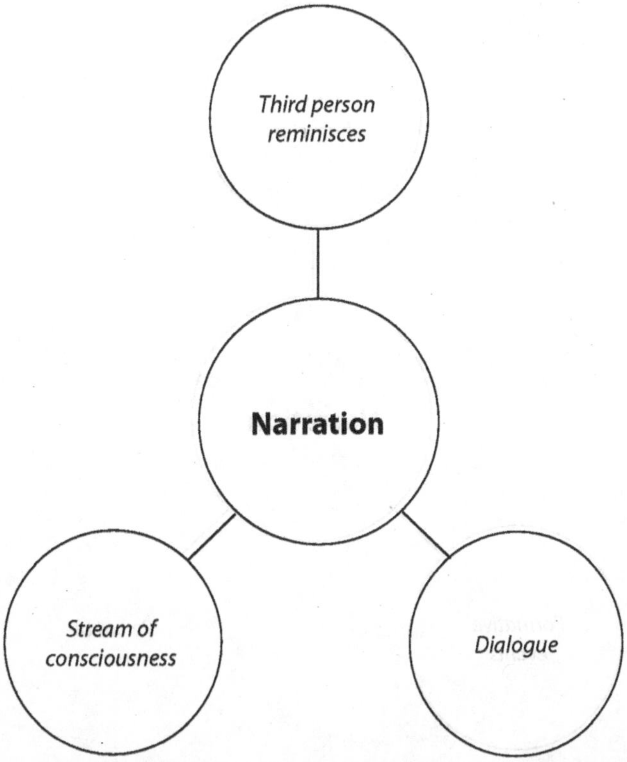

Lesson 2

The Gift of Song: Characterization

Daily Assignment

- Warm-up: Did you enjoy this *Life with Father*? Why or why not?
- Students will complete Concept Builder 23-B.
- Prayer journal: students are encouraged to write in their prayer journal every day.
- Finish the next book you have been assigned.
- Students should systematically review their vocabulary words daily.

CONCEPT BUILDER 23-B

Character Interactions

Characters, especially Father, interact with several elements to create the plot. What are these?

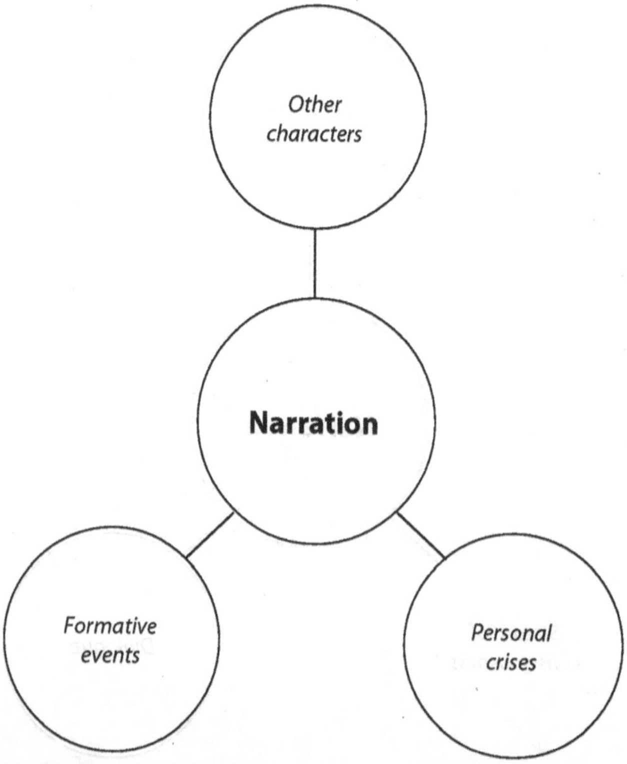

Lesson 3

Humor

Daily Assignment

- Warm-up: Write at least one humorous scene in your novella.
- Students will complete Concept Builder 23-C.
- Prayer journal: students are encouraged to write in their prayer journal every day.
- Finish the next book you have been assigned.
- Students should systematically review their vocabulary words daily.

CONCEPT BUILDER 23-C

Humor

List excerpts from the text that demonstrate humor in dialogue, irony, and exaggeration.

Dialogue

The manager was flustered, but still she kept trying to enforce her authority. She protested she didn't yet know the position....

"Cook," Father said, "cook."

"But Margaret doesn't wish to be a cook, she wants—"

"You can cook, can't you?" Father demanded.

Irony

From Father's point of view, Mother didn't know how to handle an ailment. He admired her most of the time and thought there was nobody like her; he often said to us boys, "Your mother is a wonderful woman"; but he always seemed to disapprove of her when she was ill.

Exaggeration

I watched them. Margaret was baking a cake. She screwed up her face, raised her arms, and brought them down with hands clenched.

"I don't know what we shall do, Margaret."

"The poor little feller," Margaret whispered. "He can't make the thing go."

This made me indignant. They were making me look like a lubber. I wished to feel always that I could make anything go....

Humor

Lesson 4

Writing the Composition: The Body

Daily Assignment

- Warm-up: Examine a conclusion you wrote in another essay. Was it an effective conclusion — did you finish your essay effectively? Is the reader satisfied? Did you summarize the arguments?
- Students will complete Concept Builder 23-D.
- Prayer journal: students are encouraged to write in their prayer journal every day.
- Finish the next book you have been assigned.
- Students should systematically review their vocabulary words daily.

CONCEPT BUILDER 23-D

Writing the Composition: The Body

Place the parts of the following essay about Jack London's *Call of the Wild* in the right order.

4 With regard to the reliability of the narration/narrator, I am quite disappointed. He takes an innocent character and uses his confused thoughts to promote beliefs. This makes the narrator unreliable because he took the confusion of a dog and makes the world seem to be in fact very pointless. Everything is tied to nature and nature controls everything. The narrator is only reliable when it comes to the basic facts of the story.

2 Of course it is almost unavoidable for an author to portray his worldview through his works but this was a very interesting way to do it. I do not agree with the beliefs that London portrayed, but the way he did it was commendable and should be noted.

1 "Buck did not read the newspapers, or he would have known that trouble was brewing, not alone for himself, but for every tidewater dog, strong of muscle and with warm, long hair, from Puget Sound to Sand Diego." The author of *The Call of the Wild*, Jack London, uses an unusual form of Limited Omniscient narration. What makes it unusual is that the one mind the author/narrator has access to is the mind of Buck, a dog. The idea is brilliant and makes this book stand out in the world of literature. However, through using this method, the narrator portrays his naturalistic worldview very convincingly.

3 ". . . he was aware of wild yearnings and stirrings for he knew not what. Sometimes he pursued the call into the forest, looking for it as though it were a tangible thing. . . ." Through the whole book, the narrator is able to convey a sense of life that is meaningless, through the misunderstanding and the easily manipulated opinions of a dog. A dog who discovers that men are brutal and cannot be trusted. Nor can any other thing existing. A dog who is thrown into a world he does not know. A dog whose whole life has been turned upside-down. Buck sees a sad world of mistrust, death, and hopelessness.

Lesson 5

Writing the Composition: Conclusion

Daily Assignment

- Warm-up: What book do you believe has a powerful conclusion, and why?
- Students will complete Concept Builder 23-E.
- Prayer journal: students are encouraged to write in their prayer journal every day.
- Finish the next book you have been assigned.
- Students should systematically review their vocabulary words daily.

CONCEPT BUILDER 23-E

Writing the Composition: The Conclusion

Place the parts of the following essay about Jack London's *Call of the Wild* in the right order.

4 After much time of a continued change into a wilder creature, Buck's loyalty also undergoes a transformation. It changes from loyalty to a group and the loyalty of a working partnership with the sled drivers into a fierce loyalty of love. Previous to John Thornton saving his life, Buck would have never been loyal to anyone in such a capacity. This all changes with his new loyalty to Thornton. Buck truly changes into a loving, loyal dog.

2 The transformation starts immediately, just a few pages into the first chapter. Buck experiences a transformation of environment. He is taken from warm, sunny California to harsh northern Alaska. This first transformation leads to many more.

3 Next, he experiences a transformation of character. As he is adapting to his new environment, Buck begins to change. "He swiftly lost the fastidiousness that characterized his old life. . . . It marked his adaptability, his capacity to adjust himself to changing conditions. . . . It marked, further, the decay or going to pieces of his moral nature."

1 In *The Call of the Wild*, by Jack London, there is a theme of transformation. He develops this theme in several ways throughout the book.

5 John Thornton's death marks Buck's last transformation. "John Thornton was dead. The last tie was broken. Man and the claims of man no longer bound him." He was free to finally answer the "call of the wild." Buck was completely transformed from the dog he used to be.

Chapter 23 Review Questions

Writing a Novella

Write a chapter in your novella.

Literary Analysis

Some reviewers argue that *Silas Marner* is mostly about the rest of the family, and how they manipulated the autocratic "Father" into leaving them to their own lives while appearing to let him have his way. Agree or disagree with this and offer evidence from the text.

Answers will vary.

Biblical Application

God, religion, and the Church are all more or less absent from this book. Yet the characters manifest biblical values. How?

Clearly they live in an era when the biblical witness is still appreciated and followed by most Americans.

Chapter 23 Test

I. Narration Strategies: Matching (30 points)

A. Third Person Reminiscences: The narrator remembers important events in his life as they relate to his father and his family. Of course, readers must judge if these are reliable. That can be ascertained by the amount of details offered and of objectivity employed.	______ The dancers were whirling in David's head as they whirled on the dance floor
B. Stream of Consciousness: This is a literary technique that authors use to let the reader see into the mind of the narrator. This is a favorite strategy for first person narrators. Sometimes the narrator will even speak to himself and thereby reveal important details.	______ The weary pilgrim remembered the first time God delivered him, and he gave thanks.
C. Dialogue: As the characters speak to one another we learn a lot about the story and the characters in it.	______ "I will never forgive him!" Mary cried. "Never!"

II. Matching. Identify the types of humor in this passage. Answers may be used more than once. (70 points)

A. When Jake and Anna first arrived, Davy phoned and asked to speak to Jake.
Anna answered. "Hi Davy. Pastor Jake is not home. May I help you?"
Davy was reticent, maybe even a little insulted, to speak to what he thought was the B team.

B. "I am going to kill myself. Right now!"
"No wait, Davy. Let's talk!" Anna pleaded.
"Ok," Davy, in obvious stress, responded.
Anna, meanwhile, was motioning to Grace to come to her.

C. She wrote on a piece of paper, "See if Dad is outside. Bring him. Hurry!"
"Davy, can you tell me why you are so upset?"
"No one likes me, Anna. No one likes me."
"I like you, Davy, and so does Pastor Jake."
"You don't count. You have to like me because you are my pastor."

D. Anna was growing more concerned.
"What can I do to save his life?" She thought.
"Davy, how are you feeling, right now?" Anna asked.
"Depressed. Oh Anna! I am going to hurt myself right now!"
And then Davy screamed into the telephone.
"No! Don't," Anna cried. "Stop!"
By this time Anna was crying. Nathan and Emily were crying too. Everyone was crying!
"Davy, please! Let's pray!"
Only silence was on the other end of the phone line.

______ Irony

______ Exaggeration

______ Dialogue

E. Anna was sure Davy was dead. The police would come and find him lying in a pool of blood and it would be her fault. She did it. She pushed him over the edge.
"Davy?" Anna tried one last time before she called the police.
Nathan and Emily were alternately crying loudly and praying in their small voices.
Only silence.
Then Anna heard a sound. It sounding like keys jingling.
"Davy?"
"Oh yes, sorry, Anna. What did you say?"
Anna sighed. "Now Davy, wait where you are. I want to pray with you and then I will phone the police."

F. "I would like to, Anna. Thanks. But I have no time. I have to go to the bank. Will miss the bus if I talk any longer. Thanks for the offer though. Bye."
Davy hung up.

G. Anna held the phone in disbelief.
Suddenly Grace and Jake burst into the room.
Anna looked up and hit Jake hard on the arm.
"What? What?" Jake asked in consternation.
"Your stupid, crazy congregation!" was all that Anna could say.

_____ Irony

_____ Exaggeration

_____ Dialogue

Chapter 23 Test Answer Sample

I. Narration Strategies: Matching (30 points)

A. Third Person Reminiscences: The narrator remembers important events in his life as they relate to his father and his family. Of course, readers must judge if these are reliable. That can be ascertained by the amount of details offered and of objectivity employed.	*B*	The dancers were whirling in David's head as they whirled on the dance floor
B. Stream of Consciousness: This is a literary technique that authors use to let the reader see into the mind of the narrator. This is a favorite strategy for first person narrators. Sometimes the narrator will even speak to himself and thereby reveal important details.	*A*	The weary pilgrim remembered the first time God delivered him, and he gave thanks.
C. Dialogue: As the characters speak to one another we learn a lot about the story and the characters in it.	*C*	"I will never forgive him!" Mary cried. "Never!"

II. Matching. Identify the types of humor in this passage. Answers may be used more than once. (70 points)

A, E, F Irony

B, D Exaggeration

B, C, D, G Dialogue

Reading 1

The Old Man and the Sea by Ernest Hemingway

Chapter 24

First Thoughts

In the autumn of 1952, *The Old Man and the Sea* was first published in an issue of *Life Magazine*. Within 48 hours, 5.5 million copies were sold. Critics went wild. This small novel, a novella really, was incredibly successful. As you explore this novel, ask yourself, "Why is it successful?" and "How can I duplicate this success in my novella?"

Chapter Learning Objectives

In chapter 24 we will . . .

1. Understand the author's time
2. Analyze the setting, style, and point of view

Look Ahead for Friday

- Turn in all assignments.
- Continue to work on your novella.

Active Reading: *The Old Man and the Sea* (Chapter I) by Ernest Hemingway

What are the first images Hemingway presents to the reader and why?

Hemingway wants the reader to see the sense of despondency, old age, and struggle that is a part of the world in general, and the world of Santiago in particular.

The boy is a foil. What is Hemingway showing the reader about Santiago?

Santiago is a wise and compassionate man.

Predict how this book will end.

Answers will vary.

Daily Assignment

- Warm-up: Did you enjoy this book? Why or why not?
- In your essay, use the words who and whom.
- Students will complete Concept Builder 24-A.
- Prayer journal: students are encouraged to write in their prayer journal every day.
- Finish the next book you have been assigned.
- Students should systematically review their vocabulary words daily.

CONCEPT BUILDER 24-A

Illustrated Book Review

Create an illustrated booklet of three of the most important scenes from *The Old Man and the Sea*.

Answers will vary.

Lesson 2

The Author and His Times

Daily Assignment

- Warm-up: The author's generation is called the Baby Boomers. Hemingway was part of the "lost generation." How could a generation lose itself?
- Students will complete Concept Builder 24-B.
- Prayer journal: students are encouraged to write in their prayer journal every day.
- Finish the next book you have been assigned.
- Students should systematically review their vocabulary words daily.

CONCEPT BUILDER 24-B

The Plot

List elements of the plot from *The Old Man and the Sea.*

The Day Before

Santiago, the "old man," has gone 84 days without catching a fish. He's a widower and there's no mention of any children of his own. He has only "the boy," Manolin, as companion and genuine friend.

→

The First Day and Night

Santiago rows his skiff out from the Havana harbor far beyond normal fishing waters, hoping to end his string of bad luck with a really huge catch. He sets his lines and reads the signs of the sea, finding them favorable. He catches a huge marlin and struggles all night.

↓

The Second Day and Night

Santiago continues to struggle and is encouraged that the marlin is alive.

→

The Third Day and Night

The sharks attack and eat the entire marlin. Santiago returns home.

↓

The Day After

Santiago rests. Is he defeated or triumphant?

Lesson 3

Setting

Daily Assignment

- Warm-up: How important was the setting to *The Old Man and the Sea*?
- Students will complete Concept Builder 24-C.
- Prayer journal: students are encouraged to write in their prayer journal every day.
- Finish the next book you have been assigned.
- Students should systematically review their vocabulary words daily.

CONCEPT BUILDER 24-C

Setting

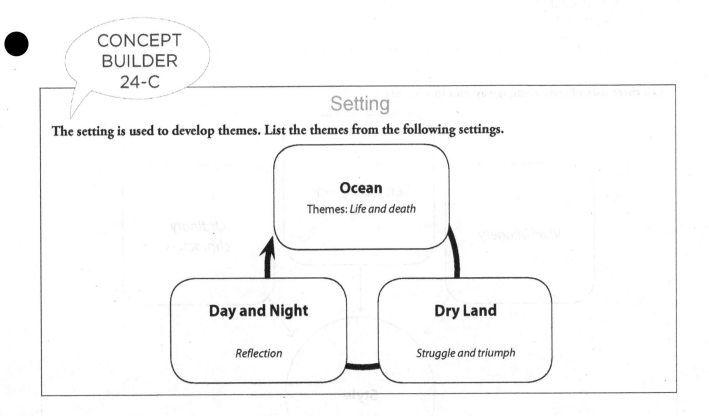

The setting is used to develop themes. List the themes from the following settings.

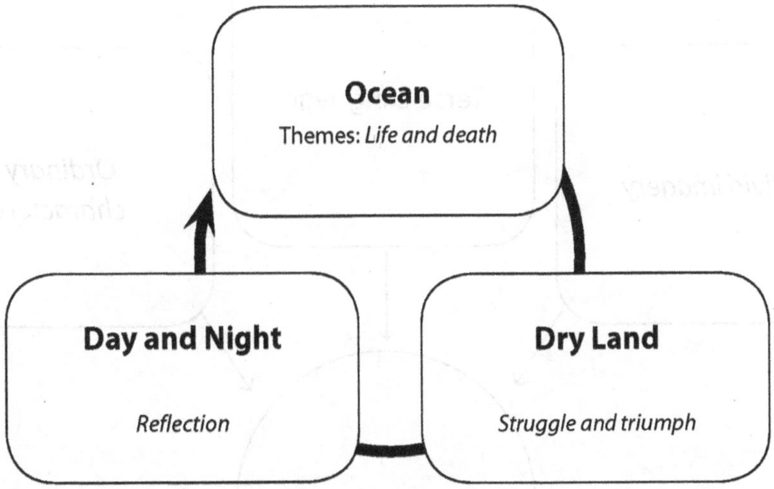

Lesson 4

Style

Daily Assignment

- Warm-up: Contrast the style of writing Hemingway employs with your style of writing. Talk about things like: length of sentences, types of vocabulary words, literary techniques (e.g., metaphors).
- Students will complete Concept Builder 24-D.
- Prayer journal: students are encouraged to write in their prayer journal every day.
- Finish the next book you have been assigned.
- Students should systematically review their vocabulary words daily.

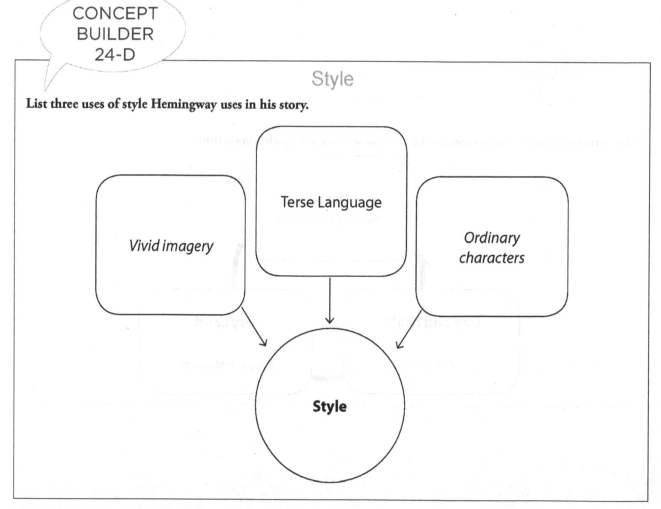

CONCEPT BUILDER 24-D

Style

List three uses of style Hemingway uses in his story.

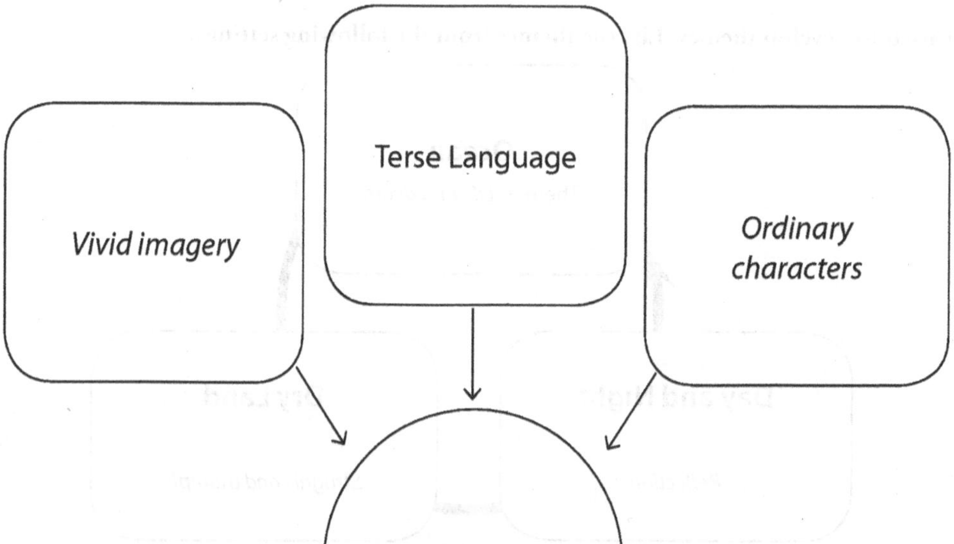

Lesson 5

Point of View

Daily Assignment

- Warm-up: Why would Hemingway choose to write in third-person narration rather than first-person, as he does in several of his other novels?
- Students will complete Concept Builder 24-E.
- Prayer journal: students are encouraged to write in their prayer journal every day.
- Finish the next book you have been assigned.
- Students should systematically review their vocabulary words daily.

CONCEPT BUILDER 24-E

Point of View

How does Hemingway develop his omniscient narration?

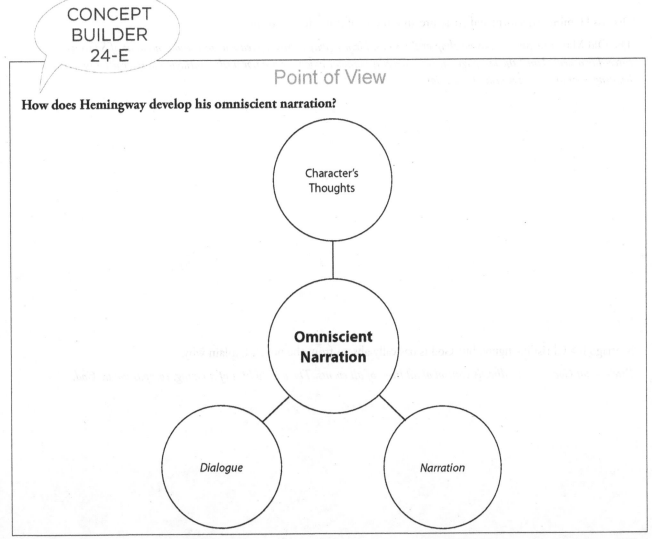

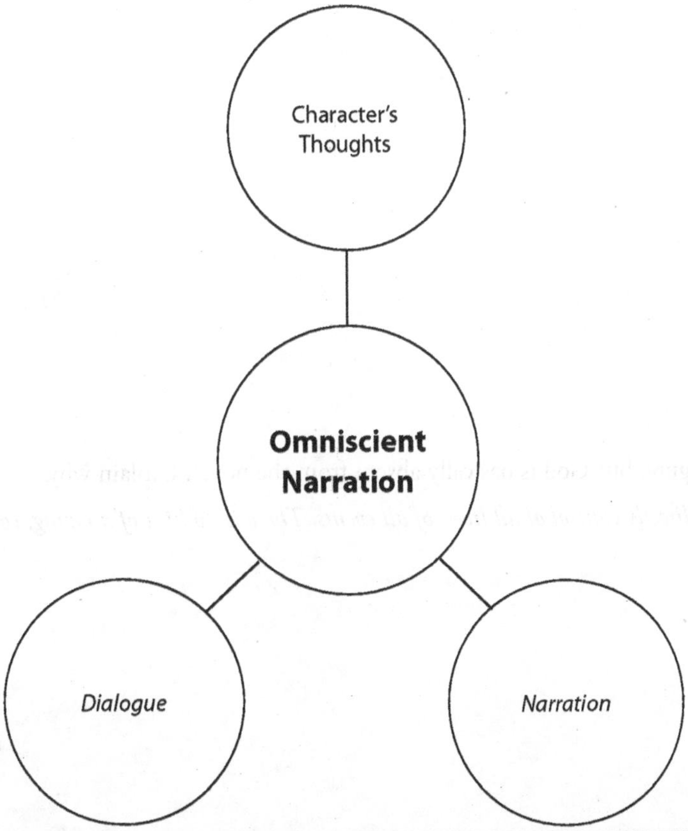

Chapter 24 Review Questions

Writing a Novella

Write a chapter in your novella. These two authors write in entirely different style. How does your writing style compare?

The old man was thin and gaunt with deep wrinkles in the back of his neck. The brown blotches of the benevolent skin cancer the sun brings from its reflection on the tropic sea were on his cheeks. (E. Hemingway, *The Old Man and the Sea*, chapter 1)

There are some things which happen to us which the intelligence and the senses refuse just as the stomach sometimes refuses what the palate has accepted but which digestion cannot compass — occurrences which stop us dead as though by some impalpable intervention, like a sheet of glass through which we watch all subsequent events transpire as though in a soundless vacuum, and fade, vanish; are gone, leaving us immobile, impotent, helpless; fixed, until we can die. (W. Faulkner, Absalom, Absalom, chapter 5)

Literary Analysis

Discuss Hemingway's form and structure and discuss if it is effective or not.

The Old Man and the Sea *has no chapter divisions. Hemingway wants to create a continuous account of Santiago's three-day ordeal. Until the last pages, there is never a moment when we are not with Santiago. Chapter divisions or headings would be an unnatural intrusion.*

Biblical Application

Santiago is a Christlike figure, but God is basically absent from the novel. Explain why.

Fate — not God — is in directly control of all lives, of all events. There is no hint of a loving, compassionate God.

Chapter 24 Test

I. Place these events in the order in which they occur: (75 points)

_____ The fish pulls Santiago's skiff out to sea like a child pulling a toy wagon.

_____ Santiago rows his boat far beyond normal fishing waters, hoping to end his string of bad luck with a really huge catch.

_____ Santiago begins to see the reflected glare of Havana lights. But the sharks now come in a pack. He fights them with a club and even with the skiff's tiller, but they strip the remaining flesh from the marlin.

_____ His deepest line shows signs of a fish nibbling at the bait, and he catches a huge fish.

_____ Santiago, the "old man," has gone 84 days without catching a fish.

_____ Santiago increases tension on the line to the breaking point, attempting to make the fish jump. The line has been stretched over his back for hours now.

_____ Manolin had been Santiago's apprentice, but the boy's parents have made him work on another fishing boat because Santiago has "bad luck." But he's still loyal to Santiago and helps the old man prepare for an attempt to catch "the big one."

_____ The fish surfaces for the first time. Santiago sees he has hooked a marlin "longer than the skiff."

_____ The great marlin is jumping. This is good because its air sacs will fill and the fish won't sink to the bottom and die, unable to be pulled back up.

_____ The marlin begins to circle the boat rather than tow it. This is a major breakthrough in the struggle to bring in the fish.

_____ Tourists look with detached amusement at the skeletal remains of Santiago's three-day battle.

_____ Santiago kills it with his harpoon. Since the fish is much longer than the skiff, it must be lashed to the side rather than towed behind. Santiago puts up the mast and sets sail to the southwest, back toward Havana.

_____ Manolin tends to the spent, pain-ridden old man and vows to fish with him again.

_____ While killing a shark that is consuming his catch, he loses his harpoon. Now there is a massive trail of blood and scent in the water, which will inevitably attract other sharks.

_____ So now he pilots his small craft home, bringing only a huge skeleton.

II. Discussion Question (25 points)

Discuss the theme of suffering in this book.

Chapter 24 Test

I. Place these events in the order in which they occur: (75 points)

5 The fish pulls Santiago's skiff out to sea like a child pulling a toy wagon.

3 Santiago rows his boat far beyond normal fishing waters, hoping to end his string of bad luck with a really huge catch.

12 Santiago begins to see the reflected glare of Havana lights. But the sharks now come in a pack. He fights them with a club and even with the skiff's tiller, but they strip the remaining flesh from the marlin.

4 His deepest line shows signs of a fish nibbling at the bait, and he catches a huge fish.

1 Santiago, the "old man," has gone 84 days without catching a fish.

6 Santiago increases tension on the line to the breaking point, attempting to make the fish jump. The line has been stretched over his back for hours now.

2 Manolin had been Santiago's apprentice, but the boy's parents have made him work on another fishing boat because Santiago has "bad luck." But he's still loyal to Santiago and helps the old man prepare for an attempt to catch "the big one."

7 The fish surfaces for the first time. Santiago sees he has hooked a marlin "longer than the skiff."

8 The great marlin is jumping. This is good because its air sacs will fill and the fish won't sink to the bottom and die, unable to be pulled back up.

9 The marlin begins to circle the boat rather than tow it. This is a major breakthrough in the struggle to bring in the fish.

15 Tourists look with detached amusement at the skeletal remains of Santiago's three-day battle.

10 Santiago kills it with his harpoon. Since the fish is much longer than the skiff, it must be lashed to the side rather than towed behind. Santiago puts up the mast and sets sail to the southwest, back toward Havana.

14 Manolin tends to the spent, pain-ridden old man and vows to fish with him again.

11 While killing a shark that is consuming his catch, he loses his harpoon. Now there is a massive trail of blood and scent in the water, which will inevitably attract other sharks.

13 So now he pilots his small craft home, bringing only a huge skeleton.

II. Discussion Question (25 points)

Discuss the theme of suffering in this book.

Suffering is everywhere and unavoidable in this book. Santiago suffers from poverty, old age, and loneliness. His hands bear the scars of old wounds. The pain in his back is relentless. He nearly passes out several times. All of it is unavoidable because it results from his being what he was born to be: a fisherman and, in a sense, a man — any man. We all suffer. Hemingway argues that destiny will bring inevitable suffering.

Reading 2

The Old Man and the Sea by Ernest Hemingway

Chapter 25

First Thoughts

In 1945, Ernest Hemingway, with his personal life in a shambles, had more bad news on the horizon. The year 1950 brought professional disaster, at least in terms of critical opinion. His book, *Across the River and Into the Trees*, received biting, almost vicious, reviews. Then in 1952 came *The Old Man and the Sea*. And then the Pulitzer. And then the Nobel. It would be his last major work published while he was still alive.

Chapter Learning Objectives

In chapter 25 we will . . .

1. Review usage problems
2. Analyze the motif honor in the struggle
3. Review the concept of allusion and Santiago as a Christ figure
4. Learn how to do a book report

Look Ahead for Friday

- Turn in all assignments.
- Continue to work on your novella.

Lesson 1

Writing Problems: Usage

Daily Assignment

- Warm-up: Proofread your novella and make sure that you have used all of the above words correctly.
- In your essay, use the words who and whom.
- Students will complete Concept Builder 25-A.
- Prayer journal: students are encouraged to write in their prayer journal every day.
- Finish the next book you have been assigned.
- Students should systematically review their vocabulary words daily.

CONCEPT BUILDER 25-A

Writing Problem: Usage

Choose the right word:

1. I (**can**, may) do that.
2. (**May**, can) I do that?
3. I am different (**from**, than) most people.
4. What kind of (**effect**, affect) will that have on the game?
5. You really (**affected**, effected) the outcome?
6. (Will, **Shall**) I do it?
7. To (who, **whom**) am I speaking?

Lesson 2

Motif (often-repeated theme in one or more literary works): Honor in the Struggle

Daily Assignment

- Warm-up: Describe a contest or struggle that you lost, but yet you still felt like a winner.
- Students will complete Concept Builder 25-B.
- Prayer journal: students are encouraged to write in their prayer journal every day.
- Finish the next book you have been assigned.
- Students should systematically review their vocabulary words daily.

CONCEPT BUILDER 25-B

Themes

List themes from *The Old Man and the Sea*.

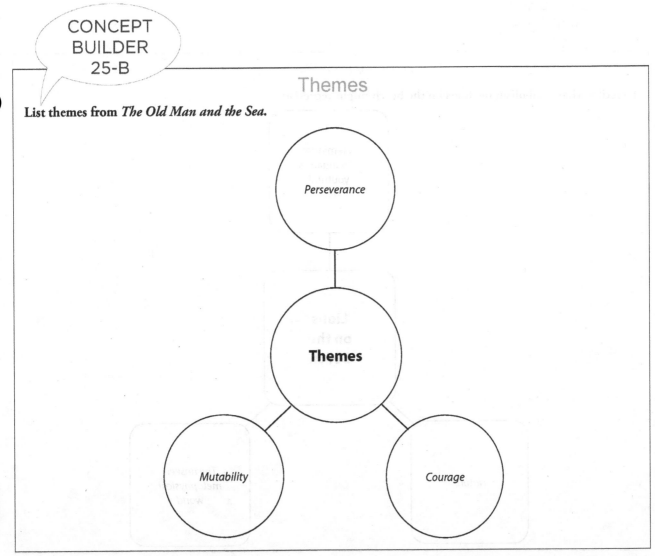

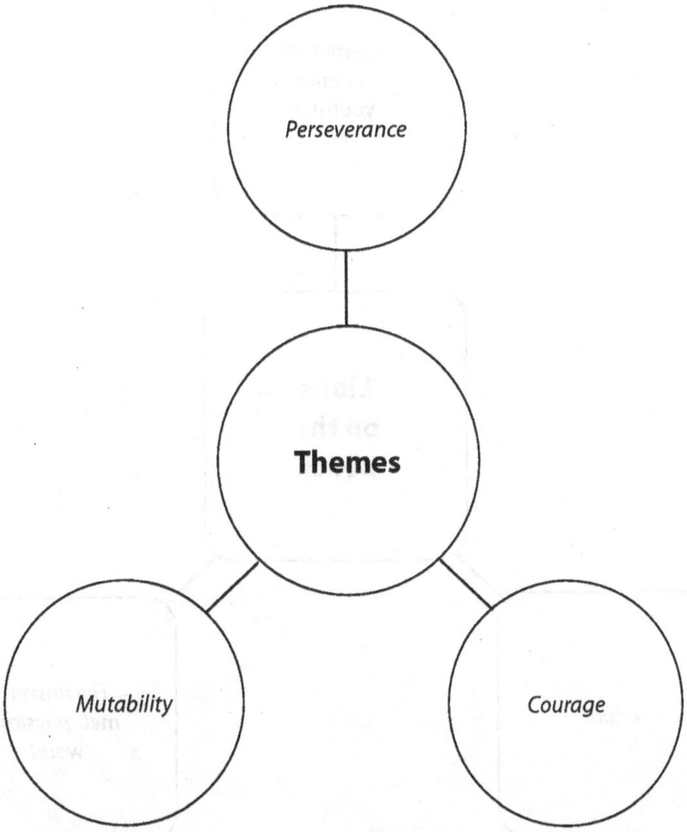

Lesson 3

Allegory

Daily Assignment

- Warm-up: What are two meaningful symbols in your life?
- Students will complete Concept Builder 25-C.
- Prayer journal: students are encouraged to write in their prayer journal every day.
- Finish the next book you have been assigned.
- Students should systematically review their vocabulary words daily.

CONCEPT BUILDER 25-C

Symbolism

Describe what symbolism the lions on the beach might represent.

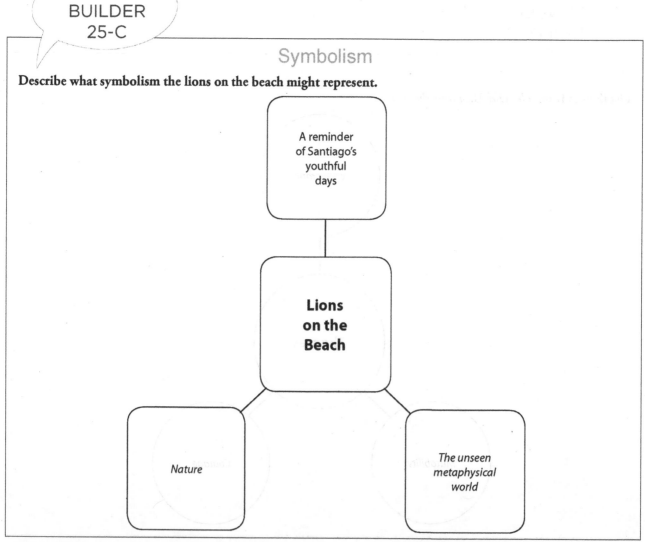

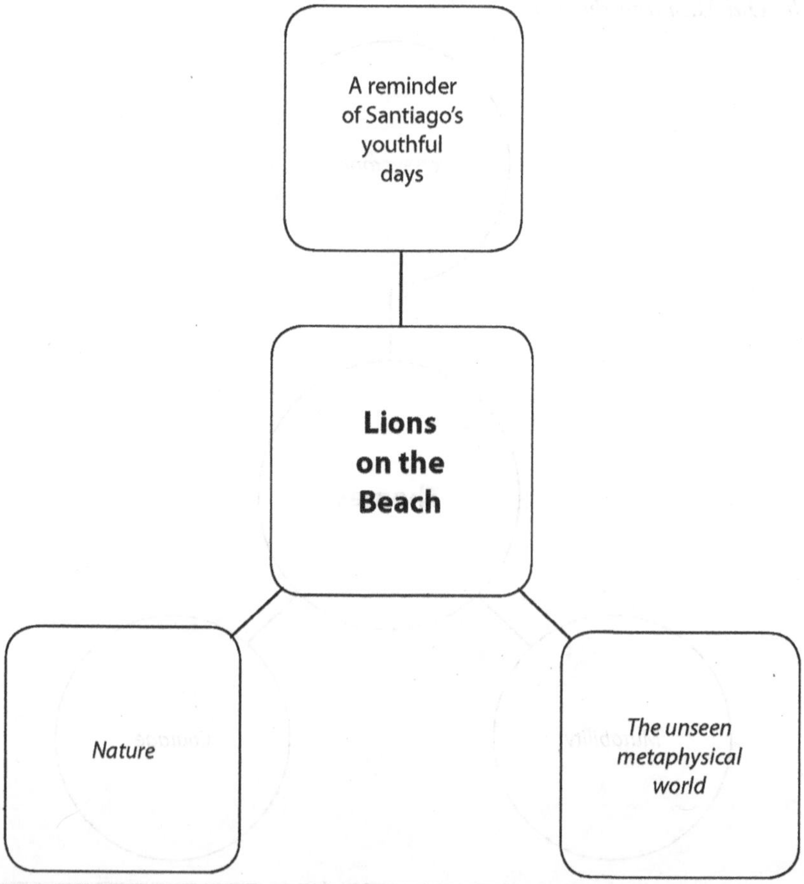

Lesson 4

Santiago, the old man, as Christlike Figure

Daily Assignment

- Warm-up: Describe another character from a movie or book who is also a Christlike figure.
- Students will complete Concept Builder 25-D.
- Prayer journal: students are encouraged to write in their prayer journal every day.
- Finish the next book you have been assigned.
- Students should systematically review their vocabulary words daily.

CONCEPT BUILDER 25-D

Main Characters

List the main characters from Hemingway's story.

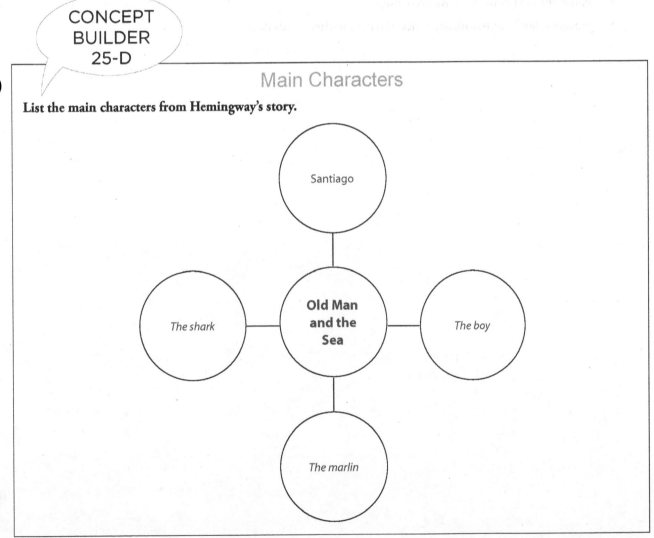

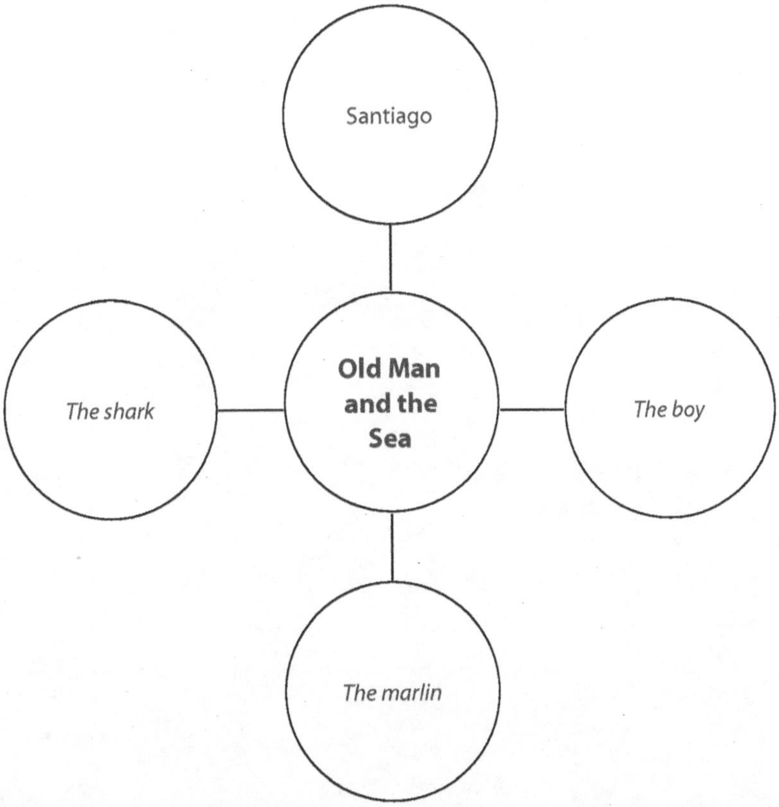

Lesson 5

Writing a Composition: A Book Report

Daily Assignment

- Warm-up: Write a short book report on a non-fiction book you read (perhaps biblical commentary).
- Students will complete Concept Builder 25-E.
- Prayer journal: students are encouraged to write in their prayer journal every day.
- Finish the next book you have been assigned.
- Students should systematically review their vocabulary words daily.

CONCEPT BUILDER 25-E

The Code Hero

"Code Hero" is a phrase used to describe the main character in many of Hemingway's novels. Some critics regard Santiago as the finest, most developed example of these code heroes. The code hero acts bravely in a losing battle.

In this phrase, "code" means a set of rules or guidelines for conduct. In Hemingway's code, the principal ideals are honor, courage, and endurance in a life of stress, misfortune, and pain. Often in Hemingway's stories, the hero's world is violent and disorderly; moreover, the violence and disorder seem to win.

The "code" dictates that the hero act honorably in the midst of what will be a losing battle. In doing so he finds fulfillment: he becomes a man or proves his manhood and his worth. The phrase "grace under pressure" is often used to describe the conduct of the code hero. List the characteristics of a code hero:

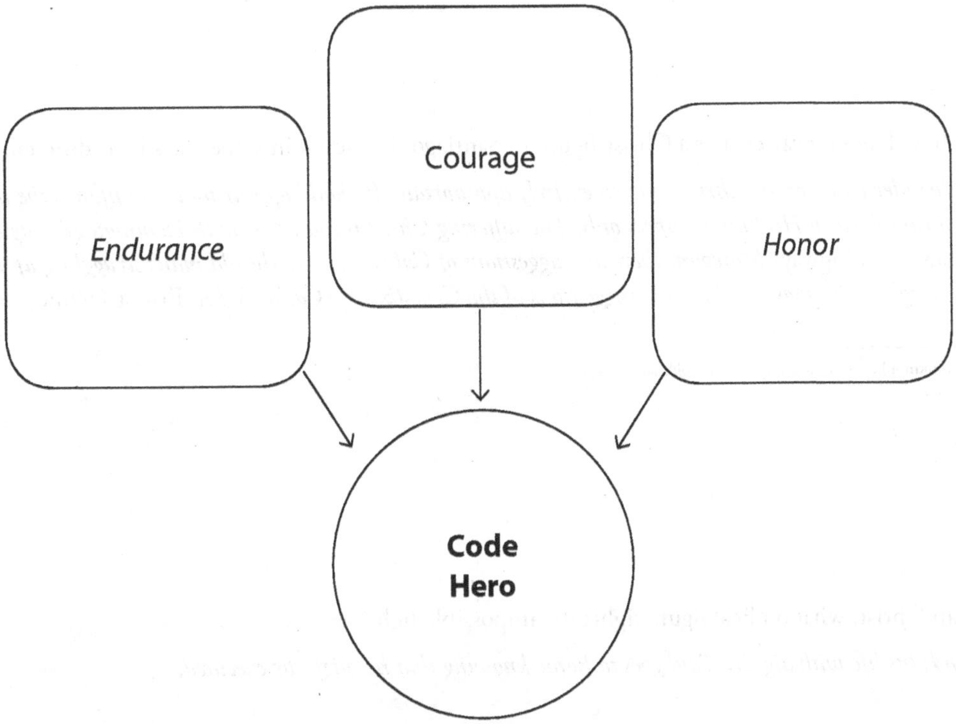

Chapter 25 Review Questions

Writing a Novella

Write a chapter in your novella. Do you have any symbols in your novella?

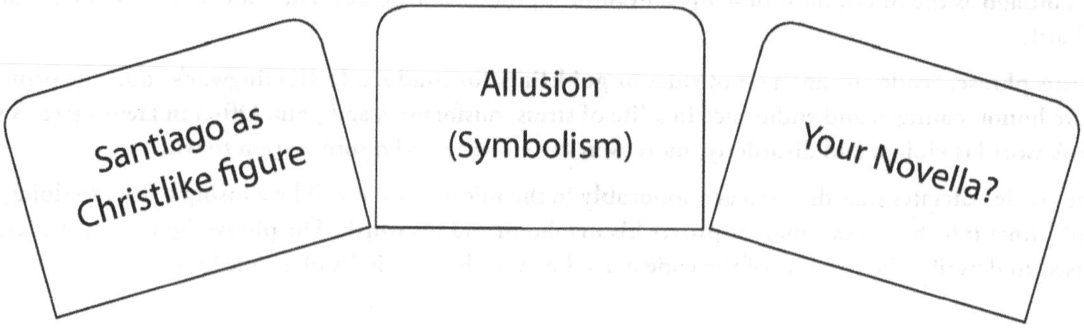

Literary Analysis

Describe how Hemingway creates a Christ-figure in Santiago. However, in some ways he is different. How is that?

One may wonder whether the Christ image is entirely appropriate. It would appear that it reinforces the thrust of the book, as Christ is conceived in His human aspect only. The suffering Christ is consistent with Hemingway's tragic vision. (Samuel Shaw, Ernest Hemingway) *Moreover, there are suggestions of Calvary . . . in the old man's struggling up the hill and falling under the weight of his mast, and further suggestions of the Crucifixion. (Carlos Baker,* Ernest Hemingway)[1]

1 http://pinkmonkey.com/booknotes/barrons/oldmans34.asp.

Biblical Application

Other than Christ, what biblical figure fights the impossible fight?

Samson ends his life with dignity. Paul goes to Rome knowing that he might be executed.

Chapter 25 Test

Create a short story of a similar situation that captures the theme of this short novel. (100 points)

Chapter 25 Test Answer Sample

Create a short story of a similar situation that captures the theme of this short novel. (100 points)

Answers will vary.

Reading 1

"The Cask of the Amontillado" by Edgar Allan Poe

Chapter 26

First Thoughts

Crumbling mansions, plague-ridden nightmares, and mysterious criminals are just a few of the ingredients in Edgar Allan Poe's short stories. Poe travels deep into unexplored territory. Poe's life itself was a dark and often haunting tale. But no one — no one — wrote short stories as well as Poe.

Chapter Learning Objectives

In chapter 26 we will . . .

1. Understand narration & plot development
2. Evaluate how the life of Poe affected his literary works

Look Ahead for Friday

- Turn in all assignments.
- Continue to work on your novella.

Active Reading: "The Cask of Amantillado" by Edgar Allen Poe (excerpt from Chapter I)

What is the narrative technique?

First person.

How would Fortunato tell this tale?

Answers will vary but certainly it would be different from the narrator!

What is the purpose of so much dialogue?

To build suspense.

"Enough," he said; "the cough is a mere nothing; it will not kill me. I shall not die of a cough." What is ironical about this statement?

The narrator will die but not of a cough.

Predict the end of the story.

Answers will vary.

Daily Assignment

- Warm-up: In what way did Poe's own life affect this story? Is your novella partly autobiographical?
- In your essay, use the words who and whom.
- Students will complete Concept Builder 26-A.
- Prayer journal: students are encouraged to write in their prayer journal every day.
- Finish the next book you have been assigned.
- Students should systematically review their vocabulary words daily.

CONCEPT BUILDER 26-A

The Plot

Identify different components of the plot.

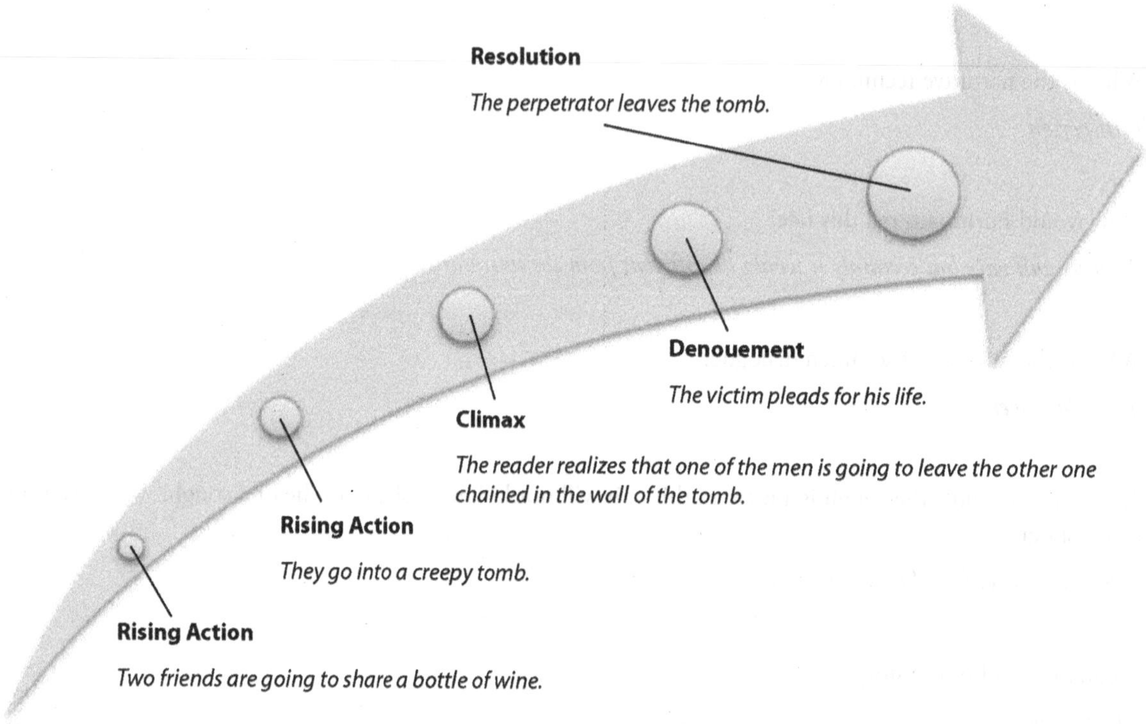

Resolution
The perpetrator leaves the tomb.
Denouement
The victim pleads for his life.
Climax
The reader realizes that one of the men is going to leave the other one chained in the wall of the tomb.
Rising Action
They go into a creepy tomb.
Rising Action
Two friends are going to share a bottle of wine.

Edgar Allan Poe: a Dark Journey

Daily Assignment

- Warm-up: Describe a frightening event in your life.
- Students will complete Concept Builder 26-B.
- Prayer journal: students are encouraged to write in their prayer journal every day.
- Finish the next book you have been assigned.
- Students should systematically review their vocabulary words daily.

CONCEPT BUILDER 26-B

Illustrated Book Review

Create an illustrated booklet of three of the most important scenes from this short story.

Answers will vary.

Lesson 3

Plot

Daily Assignment

- Warm-up: In this short story, the narrator waits 50 years to tell readers what happened. Why?
- Students will complete Concept Builder 26-C.
- Prayer journal: students are encouraged to write in their prayer journal every day.
- Finish the next book you have been assigned.
- Students should systematically review their vocabulary words daily.

CONCEPT BUILDER 26-C

Mood

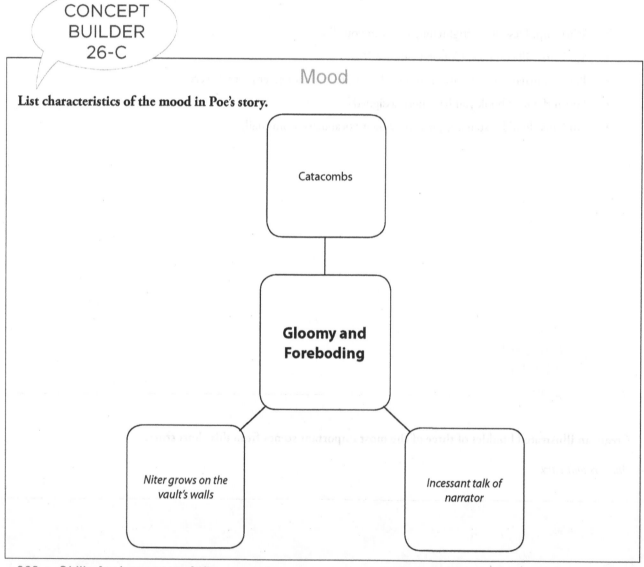

List characteristics of the mood in Poe's story.

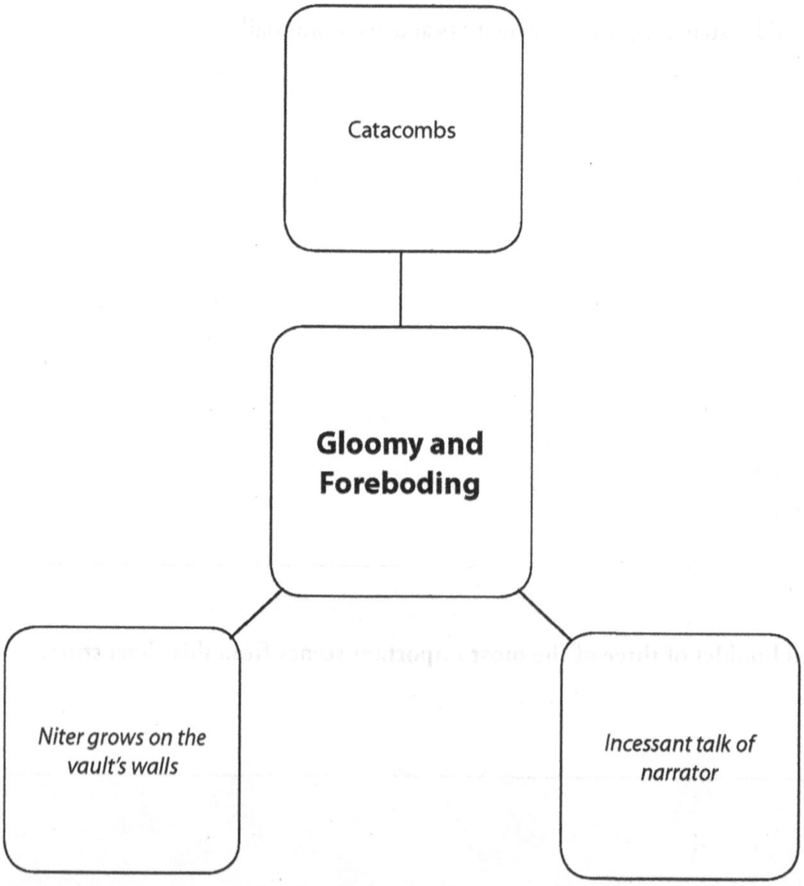

Lesson 4

Narrator

Daily Assignment

- Warm-up: How would the story of "The Cask of Amontillado" be different if the narrator was an objective third party?
- Students will complete Concept Builder 26-D.
- Prayer journal: students are encouraged to write in their prayer journal every day.
- Finish the next book you have been assigned.
- Students should systematically review their vocabulary words daily.

CONCEPT BUILDER 26-D

Themes

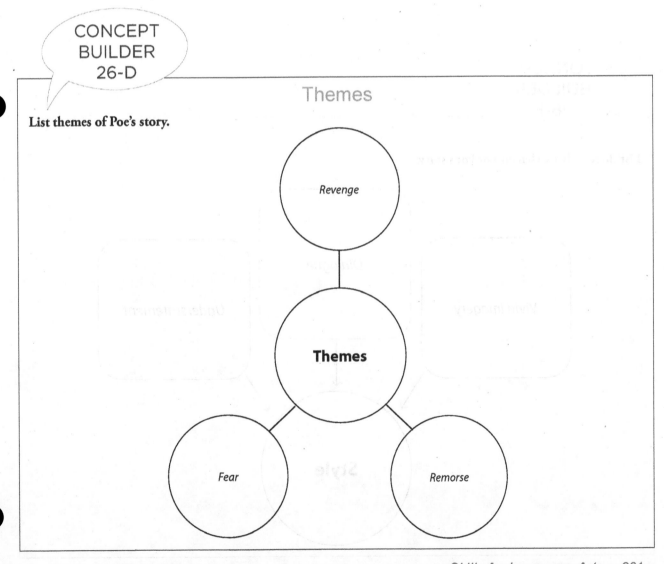

List themes of Poe's story.

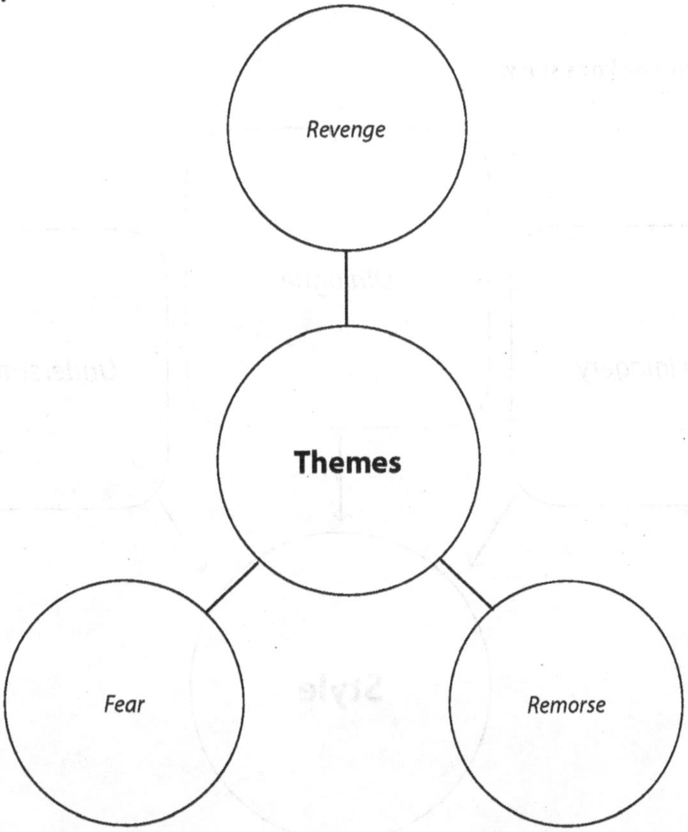

Student Essay
The Setting in "The Fall of the House of Usher" by Edgar Allan Poe

Daily Assignment

- Warm-up: This is a horror story of sorts. When does a horror story cross the line and become offensive?
- Students will complete Concept Builder 26-E.
- Prayer journal: students are encouraged to write in their prayer journal every day.
- Finish the next book you have been assigned.
- Students should systematically review their vocabulary words daily.

CONCEPT BUILDER 26-E

Style

List three stylistic elements of Poe's story.

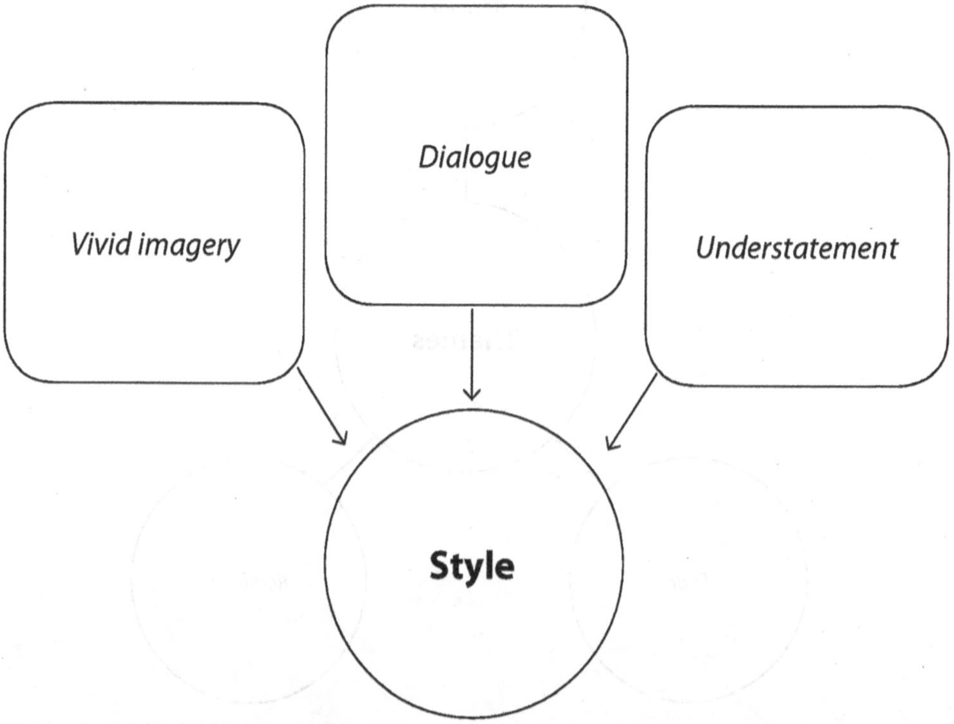

Chapter 26 Review Questions

Writing a Novella

Write a chapter in your novella. What is the tone/mood of your novella? The tone is created through plot incidences, character insights, and the language of the text (syntax) itself.

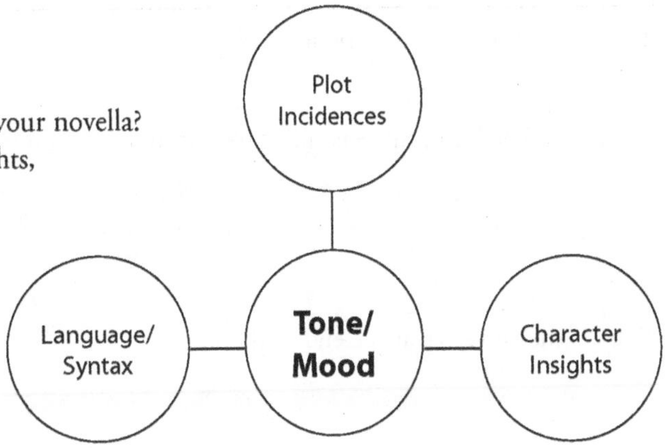

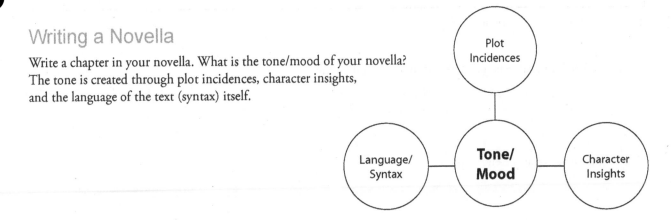

Literary Analysis

Mood is the emotional quality of a literary work. A writer's choice of language, subject matter, setting, and tone, as well as such sound devices as rhyme and rhythm, contribute to creating mood. What is the mood in this short story?

The bizarre short story begins at the carnival and ends in the catacombs. The sound of the carnival and the festive atmosphere creates a surreal atmosphere.

Biblical Application

What does the Bible say about revenge?

Revenge belongs to God and it is always wrong to overcome evil with evil.

Chapter 26 Test

Discussion Questions (50 points each)

How does Poe build suspense in "The Cast of the Amontillado"?

Who is the audience at the end of the story?

Chapter 26 Test Answer Sample

Discussion Questions (50 points each)

How does Poe build suspense in "The Cast of the Amontillado"?

Poe creates suspense through use of setting (dark, takes place during a carnival, description of the vaults they go into) as well as through foreshadowing. Later, the reader discovers that this whole story is a flashback!

Who is the audience at the end of the story?

The narrator is speaking to the reader. At the same time, Montresor challenges readers to try to catch him, to try to guess what will happen next.

Reading 2

"The Cask of the Amontillado" by Edgar Allan Poe

Chapter 27

First Thoughts

We will take a break in this chapter from writing to give you a chance to read ahead. The last three books we will study are really quite lengthy and will require a lot of time to read. We will review the writing process and hopefully be prepared to finish our novellas in a few weeks.

Chapter Learning Objectives

In chapter 27 we will . . .

1. Write better, using positive statements, concrete language, and precise language
2. End your writings
3. Edit your writings

Look Ahead for Friday

- Turn in all assignments.
- Continue to work on your novella.

Lesson 1

Writing: Positive Statements

Daily Assignment

- Warm-up: Examine your novella. Did you use "not" too often?
- In your essay, use the words who and whom.
- Students will complete Concept Builder 27-A.
- Prayer journal: students are encouraged to write in their prayer journal every day.
- Finish the next book you have been assigned.
- Students should systematically review their vocabulary words daily.

CONCEPT BUILDER 27-A

Writing: Positive Statements

Rewrite this essay in a more positive way:

Understanding Media: The Extension of Man, in 1964, Marshal McLuhan published it. No one thought that this little known academic who never saw that this book was academic would transform the way people viewed technology. This book was at heart a prophecy, and what it prophesied was the effect that technology would have upon the human mind, and upon our society. McLuhan declared that electronic devices of the 20th century — the telephone, radio, movies, etc. — were breaking our train of thought, they were harming our thoughts and senses, and rewiring our brains. McLuhan did not know that his predictions would come true.

In 1964, Marshal McLuhan published *Understanding Media: The Extension of Man*. This little-known academic never imagined that this book would transform the way people viewed technology. This book was at heart a prophecy, and what it prophesied was the effect that technology would have upon the human mind, and upon our society. McLuhan declared that electronic devices of the 20th century — the telephone, radio, movies, etc. — were breaking our train of thought, they were harming our thoughts and senses, and rewiring our brains. Little did McLuhan know that his predictions would come true.

Writing: Concrete Language

Daily Assignment

- Warm-up: Look closely at your novella and make sure that your descriptions are concrete.
- Students will complete Concept Builder 27-B.
- Prayer journal: students are encouraged to write in their prayer journal every day.
- Finish the next book you have been assigned.
- Students should systematically review their vocabulary words daily.

CONCEPT BUILDER 27-B

Writing: Concrete Language

Rewrite this essay so that it has more concrete language.

The old lady came again. Harbinger of hope and of continuity. She stood on the corner of a city street, and gently laid bread whose crust on the street corner sidewalk.

The old stooped lady came again. Harbinger of hope and of continuity. She stood on the corner of Friendship and Butler, in front of Friendship Church, and gently laid pieces of neatly cut squares of white bread whose crust had carefully been removed — very much like the communion bread Friendship congregants enjoyed in their Lord's Supper celebration — on the street corner sidewalk under the blue and white street sign that warned "neighborhood watch."

Lesson 3

Writing: Precise Language

Daily Assignment

- Warm-up: Look closely at your novella and make sure you are writing with precise language.
- Students will complete Concept Builder 27-C.
- Prayer journal: students are encouraged to write in their prayer journal every day.
- Finish the next book you have been assigned.
- Students should systematically review their vocabulary words daily.

CONCEPT BUILDER 27-C

Writing: Precise Language

Rewrite this essay so that it has more precise language.

The squirrel wanted to eat the bread. Did she not know that this could not happen.

She would not say. She did not contemplate such things.

She was not without means.

And they came. The birds came.

Answers will vary:

The old lady shook a crooked finger at a marauding gray squirrel that sought to abscond its breakfast from this foolish human who so gratuitously threw bread and anticipation on the warped sidewalks of the East End. Did she not know that there was nothing free in this part of time? Even happiness, normally free and abundant, was paid for with a price.

She would not say. She did not contemplate such things. She did not say who she was and what she did. She did not have to do that. She was the Goddess Athena who showered love on the sidewalks of the East End.

She was not without means. She was richer than the Queen of Sheba and she brought bread and eternal life to the East End. Her pockets were stuffed with free brochures from West Penn Hospital. "And you wonder what gall bladder surgery is. . . ." What were these brochures? Toilet paper? Sunday morning reading? Did they merely pad her pockets and hide priceless treasures like a bagel from the Hallelujah Kitchen or even a dollar bill or two? All wondered, but none knew, who this sidewalk princess was. Peeking from another pocket, like a wispy calico kitten was another brochure. The observer could only see "Cancer — you can survive." Did she have cancer? If so, how bad was it? No one knew. Everyone wondered as this lady laid sliced sacred cut bread for the birds of the East End of Pittsburgh.

And they came. Urban birds, like urban people, had to learn to take risks, to grab food unnaturally displayed on open, dangerous sidewalks. The wren and golden finch did not have the suburban bird feeder to satisfy hunger, nor the pristine bird feeder to luxuriate in and to satisfy thirst. Life was on the edge. They had to fight for survival, like all living things in the city. Life was niggardly dispensed to the smart, to the quick, to the resolute. All others merely died.

Lesson 4

Writing: How to End a Story

Daily Assignment

- Warm-up: Rewrite the ending of a story whose ending you did not like.
- Students will complete Concept Builder 27-D.
- Prayer journal: students are encouraged to write in their prayer journal every day.
- Finish the next book you have been assigned.
- Students should systematically review their vocabulary words daily.

CONCEPT BUILDER 27-D

Writing: How to End a Story

This is the ending of Charles Dickens' *A Tale of Two Cities.* What can you surmise about the story from the ending?

Answers will vary but clearly there is a great sacrifice being committed by one of the characters. "It is a far, far better thing that I do, than I have ever done; it is a far, far better rest that I go to than I have ever known."

Lesson 5

Writing: How to Edit Your Work

Daily Assignment

- Warm-up: Proofread your novella. Read it out loud.
- Students will complete Concept Builder 27-E.
- Prayer journal: students are encouraged to write in their prayer journal every day.
- Finish the next book you have been assigned.
- Students should systematically review their vocabulary words daily.

CONCEPT BUILDER 27-E

Writing: How to Edit Your Work

Edit this essay (student text).

King Arthur, from the Arthurian legends, and King David, from the Bible, though very different men, have some interesting similarities (You should not introduce characters, even familiar characters, without telling the reader who they are). They have many similar strengths, but the source of those strengths is different, as well as how they use them.

For example, King David and King Arthur are both great warriors and very courageous. David's courage and skill comes from God, whereas Arthur's comes from Excalibur and his knights. Also, both men work toward destroying evil and injustice. For Arthur, this is for his safety and his greatness. "Were all one will, and through that strength the King Drew in the petty princedoms under him, Fought, and in twelve great battles overcame."[1] For David, it is simply doing the will of God. "The Lord has sought out a man after his own heart and appointed him ruler of his people" (1 Samuel 13:14, speaking of David).

King Arthur's greatest weaknesses are pride and overconfidence. In much of *Idylls of the King*, Arthur does much of what he does to make his name greater. His great battles are to bring himself more fame. Though he does it with great chivalry, it is much for his own importance. David however struggled with the fact that though he had a great heart for God, he didn't always live it. He loved God he still committed murder and adultery.

Another contrast between the Kings is their leadership styles. Both King David and King Arthur are (consistent tense) strong leaders. Arthur exhibited chivalry, won great battles, and protected his land. His subjects, for the most part, respected his authority as final. In David's case, that meant showing the Israelites what God wanted for them, leading them in the Lord's battles and showing them that God is the final authority. Despite many differences, King David and King Arthur are similar men.

1 Alfred Lord Tennyson, *Idylls of the King*.

Chapter 27 Review Questions

Writing a Novella

Write a chapter in your novella.

Literary Analysis

Choose a literary work we have read this year and analyze its writing. Did you enjoy it? Why or why not? How could it be improved?

Answers will vary.

Biblical Application

Discuss a biblical passage/story that you think is well-written and explain why.

There are several. The story of Joseph (Genesis) is an excellent short story with well-developed, credible characters, a fast-moving plot, and powerful themes.

Chapter 27 Test

I. Place these sections of this essay in the correct order: (80 points)

_____ There were two different themes between the two books. In *Frankenstein,* Mary Shelly shows the goodness of man and the evil of the world. In *Dr. Jekyll and Mr. Hyde,* Robert Louis Stevenson showed the inner evil of man. Both science fiction novels had drastically different themes.

_____ Mary Shelley's novel *Frankenstein* and R. L. Stevenson's novel *Dr. Jekyll and Mr. Hyde,* showed drastically different themes. In *Frankenstein,* Mary Shelly shows the goodness of mankind and the evil of the world. In *Dr. Jekyll and Mr. Hyde,* Robert Louis Stevenson shows the evil inside of man. Though both of the plots were the same, the themes were different. Not really. Shelley shows what happens when the "monster" does not accept his flaws. Stevenson shows the opposite. In that sense, Stevenson writes a more "Christian" novel, since Jekyll accepts responsibility for his actions and deals with it. Not so with the confused monster Frankenstein.

_____ *Dr. Jekyll and Mr. Hyde* showed a different theme. In that book, Robert Louis Stevenson shows the evil nature of man. Dr. Jekyll had two sides. One side was the kindly Dr. Jekyll. To this rule, Dr. Jekyll was . . . a large, well-made, smooth faced man of fifty . . . but with every mark of capacity and kindness. But the other side was Mr. Hyde. Mr. Hyde was pale and dwarfish, he gave an impression of deformity without any nameable malformation. Stevenson showed in his novel, the inner nature of man. Jekyll was a nice man, but inside he was evil. He had a dual nature. Though so profound a double-dealer, I was in no sense a hypocrite; both sides of me were in dead earnest. . . . In the end of the story, evil took over Jekyll. Mr. Hyde took over Dr. Jekyll, and evil was dominant.

_____ In *Frankenstein,* Mary Shelly creates a theme of the good of man and the evil of the world. One night, a scientist accidently creates a monster. I saw the dull yellow eye of the creature open; it breathed hard, and a convulsive motion agitated its limbs. After creating the monster, Victor Frankenstein ran away horrified at what he had done. He is "god playing." Shelley hates that. Unable to endure the aspect at which I had created, I rushed out of the room. . . . Frankenstein returned to his family, until one day he met the monster. The monster then told Frankenstein that he had been mistreated everywhere he went. . . . I was benevolent; my soul glowed with love and humanity, but am I not alone, miserably alone? The monster was kind to everyone he met. He helped a family and saved a woman from death. But he was mistreated. After he saved the woman, someone shot him. Everywhere he went he was mistreated.

II. Choose the best title for this essay (20 points):

A. Robert Louis Stevenson's Masterpiece
B. The Problem of Evil
C. Monsters Are Scary
D. The Horrors of 19th-Century London

Chapter 27 Test Answer Sample

I. Place these sections of this essay in the correct order: (80 points)

4 There were two different themes between the two books. In *Frankenstein,* Mary Shelly shows the goodness of man and the evil of the world. In *Dr. Jekyll and Mr. Hyde,* Robert Louis Stevenson showed the inner evil of man. Both science fiction novels had drastically different themes.

1 Mary Shelley's novel Frankenstein and R. L. Stevenson's novel *Dr. Jekyll and Mr. Hyde,* showed drastically different themes. In *Frankenstein,* Mary Shelly shows the goodness of mankind and the evil of the world. In *Dr. Jekyll and Mr. Hyde,* Robert Louis Stevenson shows the evil inside of man. Though both of the plots were the same, the themes were different. Not really. Shelley shows what happens when the "monster" does not accept his flaws. Stevenson shows the opposite. In that sense, Stevenson writes a more "Christian" novel, since Jekyll accepts responsibility for his actions and deals with it. Not so with the confused monster Frankenstein.

3 *Dr. Jekyll and Mr. Hyde* showed a different theme. In that book, Robert Louis Stevenson shows the evil nature of man. Dr. Jekyll had two sides. One side was the kindly Dr. Jekyll. To this rule, Dr. Jekyll was . . . a large, well-made, smooth faced man of fifty . . . but with every mark of capacity and kindness. But the other side was Mr. Hyde. *Mr. Hyde was pale and dwarfish, he gave an impression of deformity without any nameable malformation.* Stevenson showed in his novel, the inner nature of man. Jekyll was a nice man, but inside he was evil. He had a dual nature. Though so profound a double-dealer, I was in no sense a hypocrite; both sides of me were in dead earnest. . . . In the end of the story, evil took over Jekyll. Mr. Hyde took over Dr. Jekyll, and evil was dominant.

2 In *Frankenstein,* Mary Shelly creates a theme of the good of man and the evil of the world. One night, a scientist accidently creates a monster. I saw the dull yellow eye of the creature open; it breathed hard, and a convulsive motion agitated its limbs. After creating the monster, Victor Frankenstein ran away horrified at what he had done. He is "god playing." Shelley hates that. Unable to endure the aspect at which I had created, I rushed out of the room. . . . Frankenstein returned to his family, until one day he met the monster. The monster then told Frankenstein that he had been mistreated everywhere he went. . . . I was benevolent; my soul glowed with love and humanity, but am I not alone, miserably alone? The monster was kind to everyone he met. He helped a family and saved a woman from death. But he was mistreated. After he saved the woman, someone shot him. Everywhere he went he was mistreated.

II. Choose the best title for this essay (20 points):

C. Monsters Are Scary

Reading 1

To Kill a Mockingbird by Harper Lee

Chapter 28

First Thoughts

In 1991, the Library of Congress conducted a survey of book readers. Readers were asked to cite books that had made a difference in their lives. One of the books most often cited was Harper Lee's *To Kill a Mockingbird.* The only book ranked higher by readers was the Bible. In the last eight years that the author has evaluated SAT essays, the most often-cited literary source is *To Kill a Mockingbird.*

Chapter Learning Objectives

In chapter 28 we will . . .

1. Analyze the author and her times
2. Review narration and the credibility of the narrator
3. Evaluate the importance of the setting

Look Ahead for Friday

- Turn in all assignments.
- Continue to work on your novella.

Active Reading: To Kill a Mockingbird (Chapter I) by Harper Lee

Predict the end of the novel.

Answers will vary.

Daily Assignment

- Warm-up: Did you enjoy this novel?
- In your essay, use the words who and whom.
- Students will complete Concept Builder 28-A.
- Prayer journal: students are encouraged to write in their prayer journal every day.
- Finish the next book you have been assigned.
- Students should systematically review their vocabulary words daily.

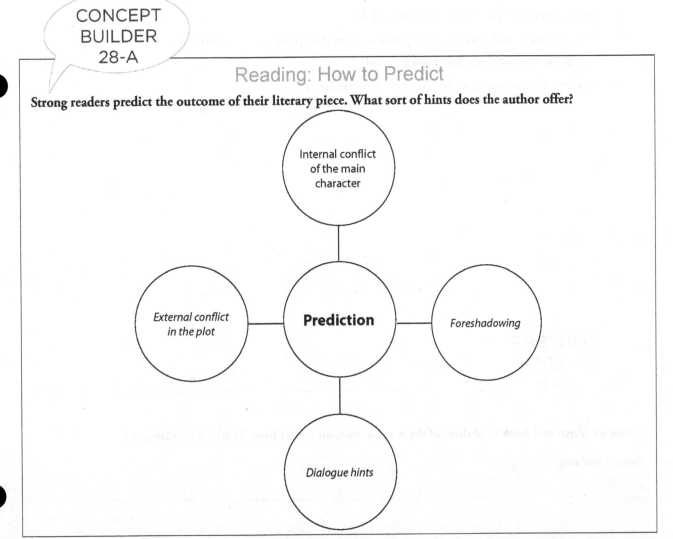

CONCEPT BUILDER 28-A

Reading: How to Predict

Strong readers predict the outcome of their literary piece. What sort of hints does the author offer?

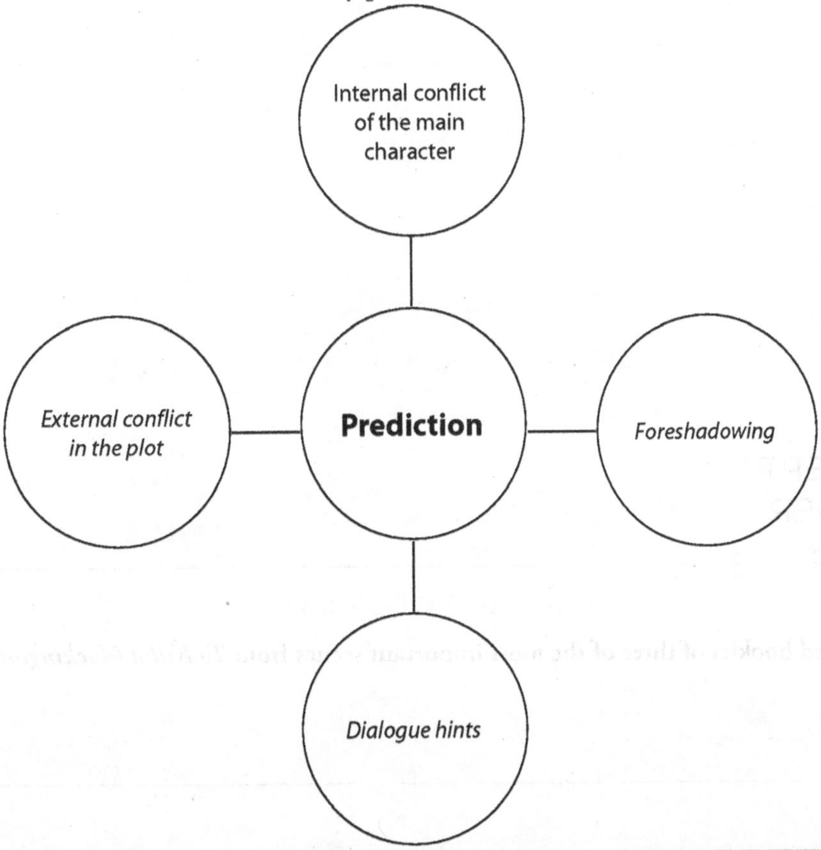

Lesson 2

The Author and Her Times

Daily Assignment

- Warm-up: Could someone from the north write this novel?
- Students will complete Concept Builder 28-B.
- Prayer journal: students are encouraged to write in their prayer journal every day.
- Finish the next book you have been assigned.
- Students should systematically review their vocabulary words daily.

CONCEPT BUILDER 28-B

Illustrated Book Review

Create an illustrated booklet of three of the most important scenes from *To Kill a Mockingbird*.

Answers will vary.

Setting: *To Kill a Mockingbird*

Daily Assignment

- Warm-up: How important was the setting to *To Kill a Mockingbird*?
- Students will complete Concept Builder 28-C.
- Prayer journal: students are encouraged to write in their prayer journal every day.
- Finish the next book you have been assigned.
- Students should systematically review their vocabulary words daily.

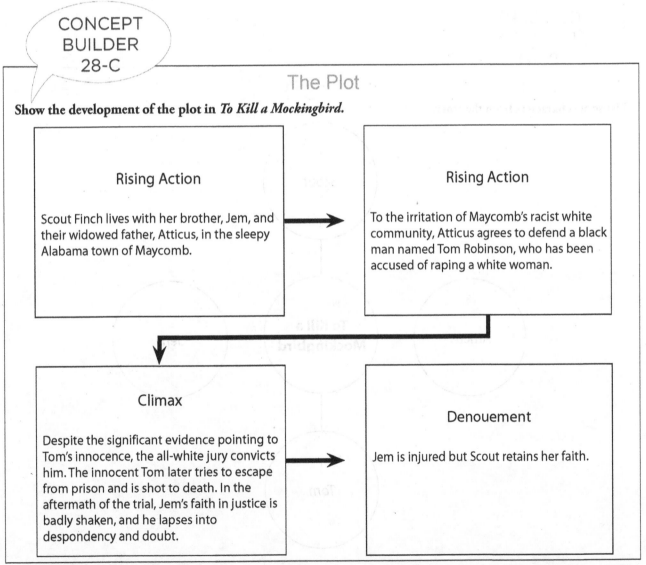

CONCEPT BUILDER 28-C

The Plot

Show the development of the plot in *To Kill a Mockingbird*.

Rising Action

Scout Finch lives with her brother, Jem, and their widowed father, Atticus, in the sleepy Alabama town of Maycomb.

→

Rising Action

To the irritation of Maycomb's racist white community, Atticus agrees to defend a black man named Tom Robinson, who has been accused of raping a white woman.

↓

Climax

Despite the significant evidence pointing to Tom's innocence, the all-white jury convicts him. The innocent Tom later tries to escape from prison and is shot to death. In the aftermath of the trial, Jem's faith in justice is badly shaken, and he lapses into despondency and doubt.

→

Denouement

Jem is injured but Scout retains her faith.

Lesson 4

First-Person Point of View

Daily Assignment

- Warm-up: What advantages does first-person narration offer Harper Lee as she tells her story?
- Students will complete Concept Builder 28-D.
- Prayer journal: students are encouraged to write in their prayer journal every day.
- Finish the next book you have been assigned.
- Students should systematically review their vocabulary words daily.

CONCEPT BUILDER 28-D

Characters

List some characters from the story.

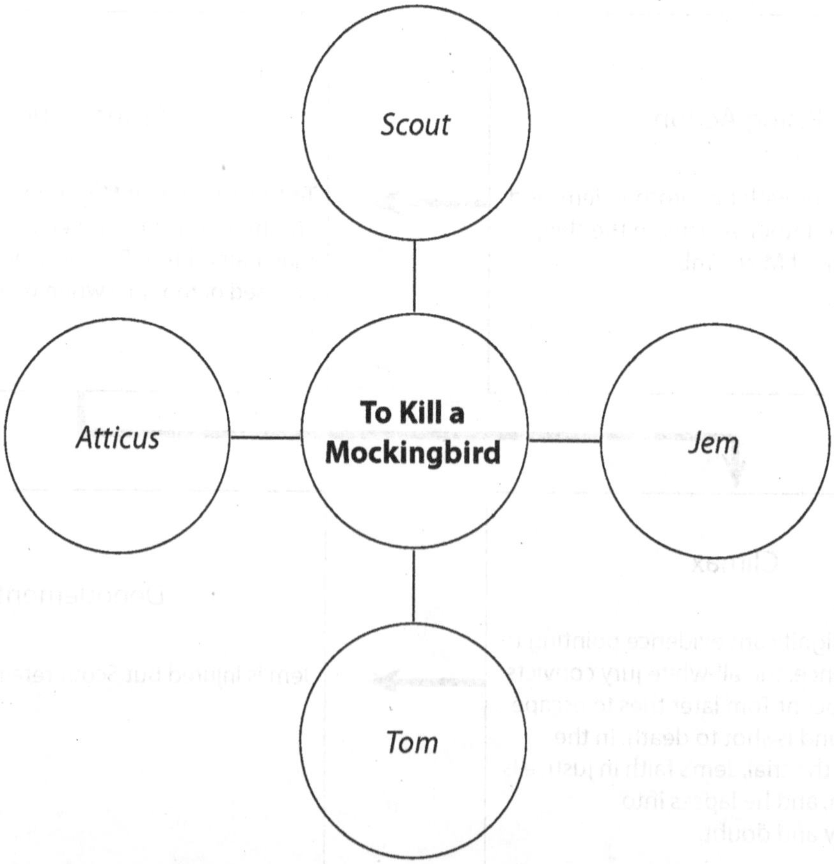

Student Essay

First-Person Narration in *The Unvanquished* by William Faulkner

Daily Assignment

- Warm-up: Write an encouraging letter to Scout.
- Students will complete Concept Builder 28-E.
- Prayer journal: students are encouraged to write in their prayer journal every day.
- Finish the next book you have been assigned.
- Students should systematically review their vocabulary words daily.

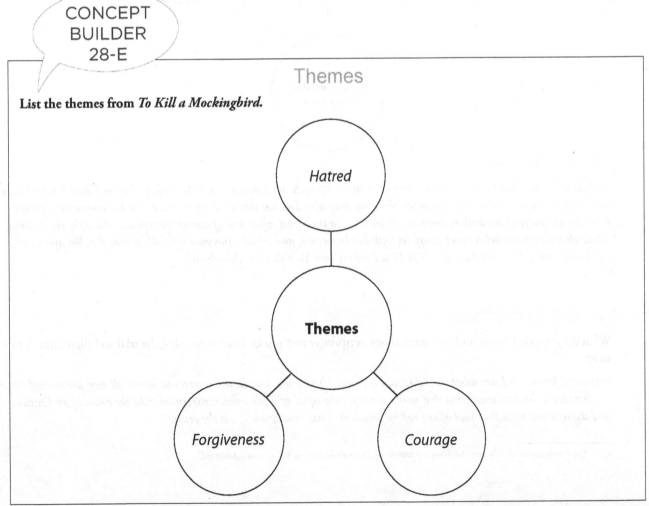

CONCEPT BUILDER 28-E

Themes

List the themes from *To Kill a Mockingbird.*

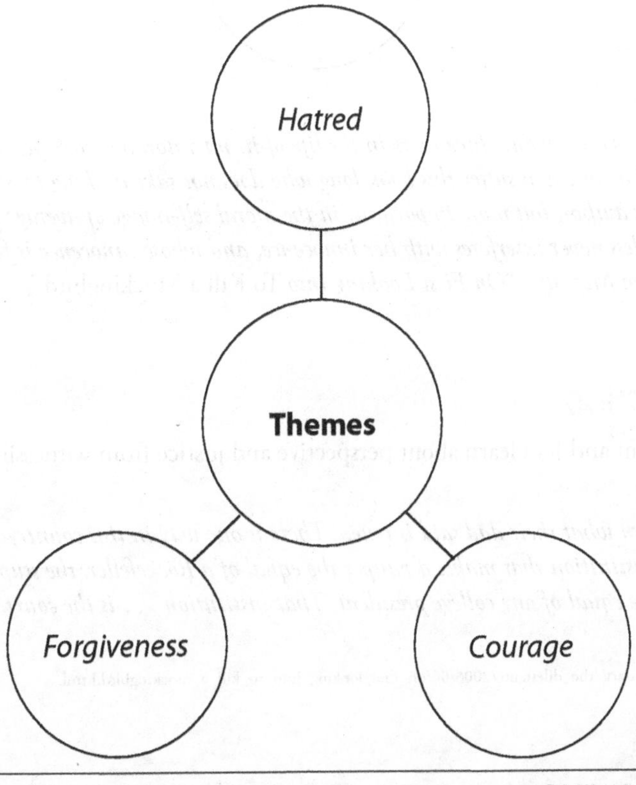

Chapter 28 Review Questions

Writing a Novella

Write a chapter in your novella. Credibility is an important question in narration. How credible is your narrator?

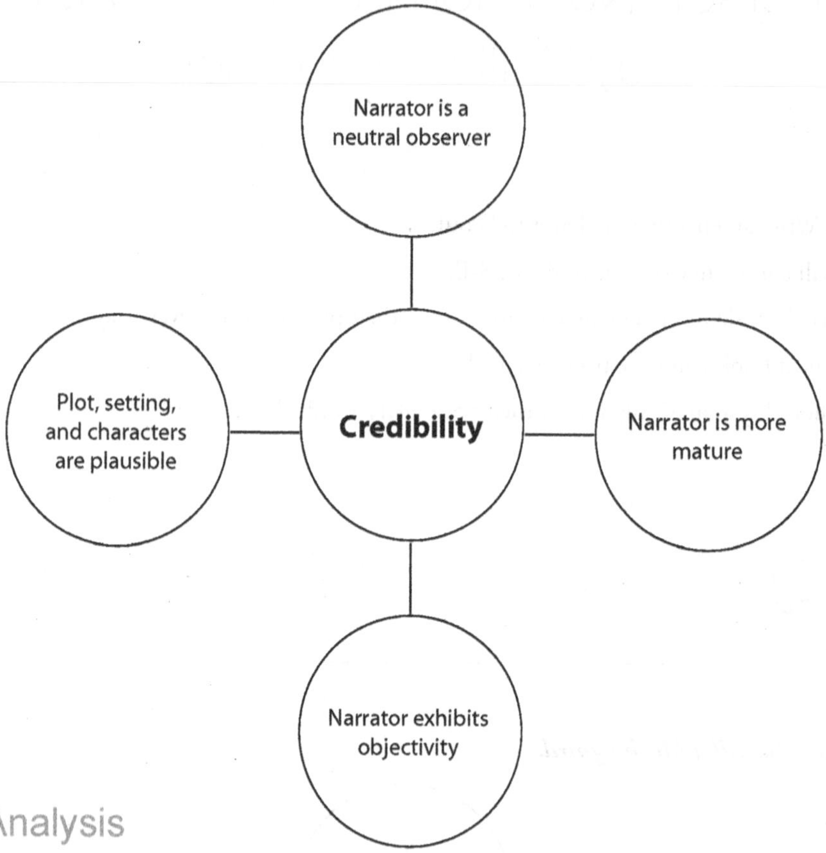

Literary Analysis

Is Scout a credible narrator?

To Kill a Mockingbird *covers roughly three years in the life of its narrator, a 6-to-9-year-old girl named Jean Louise Finch, nicknamed "Scout," and no one will suffer this book long who does not take a liking to Scout. She is a character famously made in the image of her author, but more important, in the moral self-image of average Americans: she is the clever child, whose cleverness nonetheless never interferes with her innocence, and whose innocence is finally a near-flawless arbiter of right and wrong. (Stephen Metcalfe, "On First Looking Into* To Kill a Mockingbird*")*[1]

Biblical Application

What do you think Scout and Jem learn about perspective and justice from witnessing the trial and their father's role in it?

Scout and Jem surely learn what their dad said is true. "There is one way in this country in which all men are created equal — there is one human institution that makes a pauper the equal of a Rockefeller, the stupid man the equal of an Einstein, and the ignorant man the equal of any college president. That institution . . . is the court."

---

1 http://www.slate.com/articles/arts/the_dilettante/2006/06/on_first_looking_into_to_kill_a_mockingbird.html.

Chapter 28 Test

I. Place these events in the order in which they occur. (75 points)

_____ Boo carries the wounded Jem back to Atticus's house, where the sheriff, in order to protect Boo, insists that Ewell tripped over a tree root and fell on his own knife. After sitting with Scout for a while, Boo disappears once more into the Radley house.

_____ Dill becomes fascinated with the Radley Place.

_____ Scout Finch lives with her brother, Jem, and their widowed father, Atticus, in the sleepy Alabama town of Maycomb.

_____ Scout and Jem find gifts apparently left for them in a knothole of a tree on the Radley property.

_____ Despite the significant evidence pointing to Tom's innocence, the all-white jury convicts him.

_____ Jem loses his pants and when he returns for them, he finds them mended and hung over the fence.

_____ The next winter, Jem and Scout find more presents in the tree, presumably left by the mysterious Boo. Nathan Radley eventually plugs the knothole with cement.

_____ Atticus agrees to defend a black man named Tom Robinson, who has been accused of assaulting a white woman.

_____ Atticus's sister, Alexandra, comes to live with the Finches the next summer. Dill, who is supposed to live with his "new father" in another town, runs away and comes to Maycomb.

_____ Later, Scout feels as though she can finally imagine what life is like for Boo. He has become a human being to her at last.

_____ Despite the verdict, Bob Ewell feels that Atticus and the judge have made a fool out of him, and he vows revenge.

_____ The innocent Tom later tries to escape from prison and is shot to death.

_____ On Dill's last night in Maycomb for the summer, the three sneak onto the Radley property, where Nathan Radley shoots at them.

_____ Ewell attacks Jem and Scout as they walk home from a Halloween party. Boo Radley intervenes, however, saving the children and stabbing Ewell fatally during the struggle.

_____ One summer, Jem and Scout befriend a boy named Dill, who has come to live in their neighborhood for the summer.

II. Discussion Question (25 points)

Jem and Scout are important dynamic, round characters. What does that mean?

Chapter 28 Test Answer Sample

I. Place these events in the order in which they occur. (75 points)

14 Boo carries the wounded Jem back to Atticus's house, where the sheriff, in order to protect Boo, insists that Ewell tripped over a tree root and fell on his own knife. After sitting with Scout for a while, Boo disappears once more into the Radley house.

3 Dill becomes fascinated with the Radley Place.

1 Scout Finch lives with her brother, Jem, and their widowed father, Atticus, in the sleepy Alabama town of Maycomb.

4 Scout and Jem find gifts apparently left for them in a knothole of a tree on the Radley property.

10 Despite the significant evidence pointing to Tom's innocence, the all-white jury convicts him.

6 Jem loses his pants and when he returns for them, he finds them mended and hung over the fence.

7 The next winter, Jem and Scout find more presents in the tree, presumably left by the mysterious Boo. Nathan Radley eventually plugs the knothole with cement.

8 Atticus agrees to defend a black man named Tom Robinson, who has been accused of assaulting a white woman.

9 Atticus's sister, Alexandra, comes to live with the Finches the next summer. Dill, who is supposed to live with his "new father" in another town, runs away and comes to Maycomb.

15 Later, Scout feels as though she can finally imagine what life is like for Boo. He has become a human being to her at last.

12 Despite the verdict, Bob Ewell feels that Atticus and the judge have made a fool out of him, and he vows revenge.

11 The innocent Tom later tries to escape from prison and is shot to death.

5 On Dill's last night in Maycomb for the summer, the three sneak onto the Radley property, where Nathan Radley shoots at them.

13 Ewell attacks Jem and Scout as they walk home from a Halloween party. Boo Radley intervenes, however, saving the children and stabbing Ewell fatally during the struggle.

2 One summer, Jem and Scout befriend a boy named Dill, who has come to live in their neighborhood for the summer.

II. Discussion Question (25 points)

Jem and Scout are important dynamic, round characters. What does that mean?

They are developed well by the narrator (round) and they change (dynamic).

Reading 2

To Kill a Mockingbird by Harper Lee

Chapter 29

First Thoughts

Atticus is known as one of the last moral characters in American literature. Yet, it is sad to me, that he is moral without the aid of the Church, God, or the clergy. All of these are absent in this story. This presages decades of woe for our country as we try to navigate our way through history without the aid of God or His Word. Let us pray that will change in the future.

Chapter Learning Objectives

In chapter 29 we will . . .

1. Understand how authors use conflict
2. Compare a book with its movie

Look Ahead for Friday

- Turn in all assignments.
- Continue to work on your novella.

Lesson 1

Critics' Corner

Daily Assignment

- Warm-up: What memories of your own childhood come to mind as you read about Scout's experiences?
- In your essay, use the words who and whom.
- Students will complete Concept Builder 29-A.
- Prayer journal: students are encouraged to write in their prayer journal every day.
- Finish the next book you have been assigned.
- Students should systematically review their vocabulary words daily.

CONCEPT BUILDER 29-A

The Setting

List the varied settings from the story.

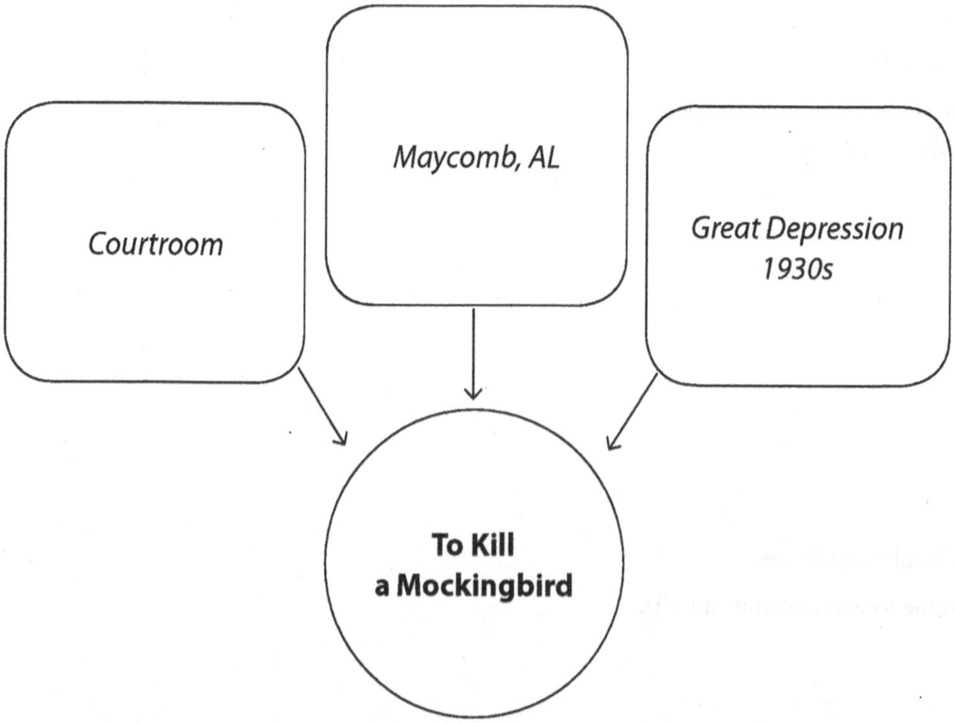

Lesson 2

Conflict

Daily Assignment

- Warm-up: Describe an internal conflict and an external conflict in your life.
- Students will complete Concept Builder 29-B.
- Prayer journal: students are encouraged to write in their prayer journal every day.
- Finish the next book you have been assigned.
- Students should systematically review their vocabulary words daily.

CONCEPT BUILDER 29-B

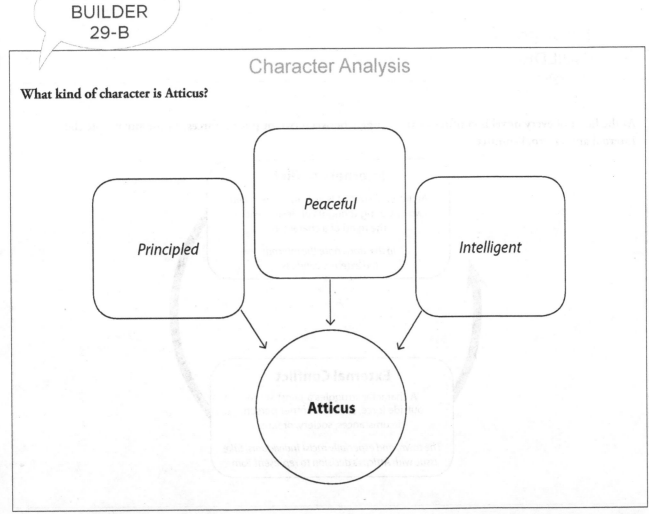

Character Analysis

What kind of character is Atticus?

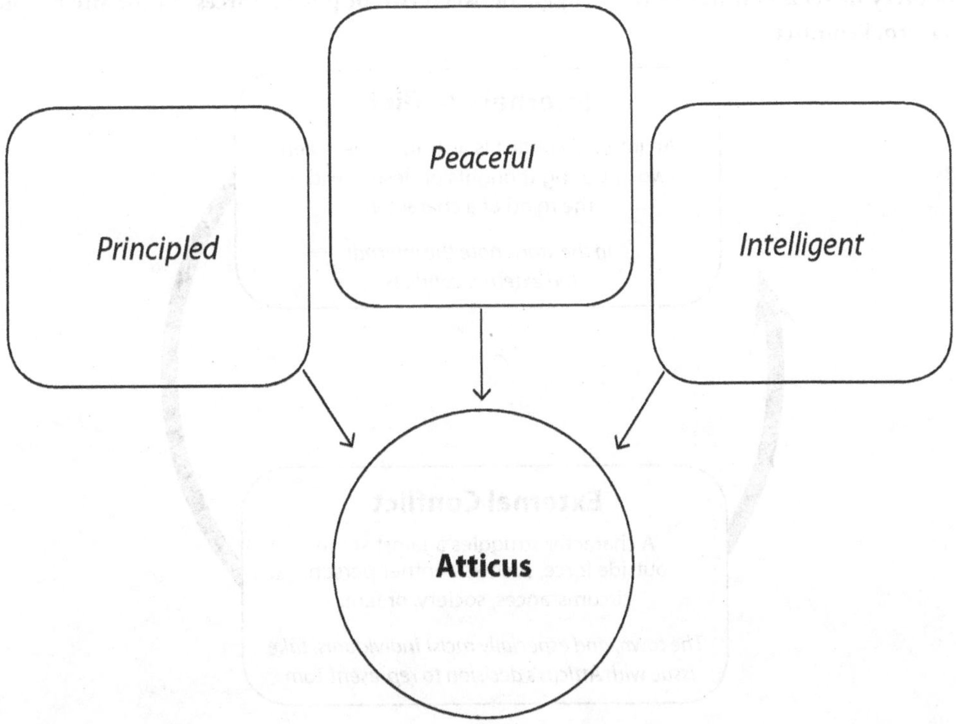

Lesson 3

Jim Crow South

Daily Assignment

- Warm-up: Give a few examples of Jim Crow laws.
- Students will complete Concept Builder 29-C.
- Prayer journal: students are encouraged to write in their prayer journal every day.
- Finish the next book you have been assigned.
- Students should systematically review their vocabulary words daily.

CONCEPT BUILDER 29-C

Conflict

At the heart of every novel is conflict — the struggle between two opposing forces. In the story, note the internal and external conflicts.

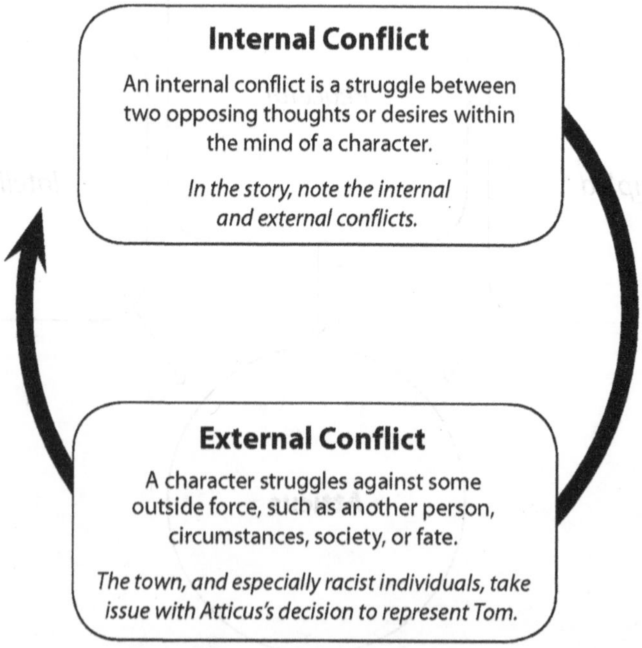
Internal Conflict
An internal conflict is a struggle between two opposing thoughts or desires within the mind of a character.
In the story, note the internal and external conflicts.
External Conflict
A character struggles against some outside force, such as another person, circumstances, society, or fate.
The town, and especially racist individuals, take issue with Atticus's decision to represent Tom.

Lesson 4

The Movie: A Review by Roger Ebert

Daily Assignment

- Warm-up: View the movie *To Kill a Mockingbird* and compare it to the book.
- Students will complete Concept Builder 29-D.
- Prayer journal: students are encouraged to write in their prayer journal every day.
- Finish the next book you have been assigned.
- Students should systematically review their vocabulary words daily.

CONCEPT BUILDER 29-D

Point of View

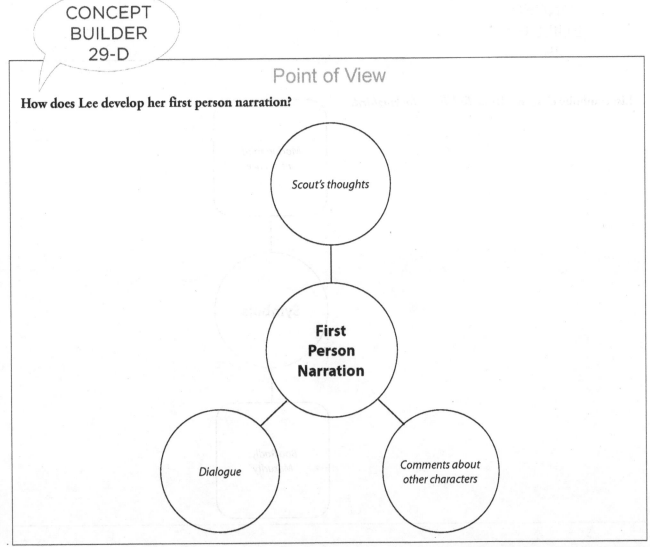

How does Lee develop her first person narration?

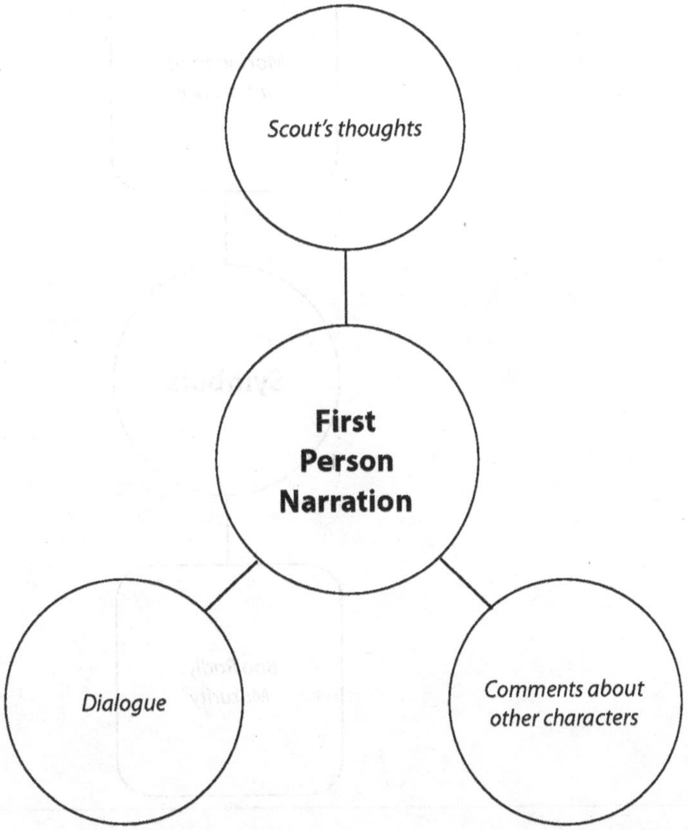

Student Essay

Characterization in the Book of Esther

Daily Assignment

- Warm-up: What is a book you enjoyed, as well as the movie it was made into?
- Students will complete Concept Builder 29-E.
- Prayer journal: students are encouraged to write in their prayer journal every day.
- Finish the next book you have been assigned.
- Students should systematically review their vocabulary words daily.

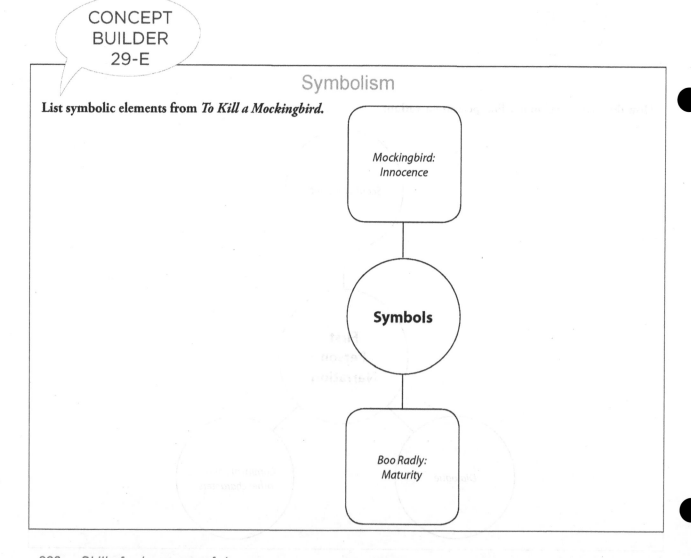

CONCEPT BUILDER 29-E

Symbolism

List symbolic elements from *To Kill a Mockingbird*.

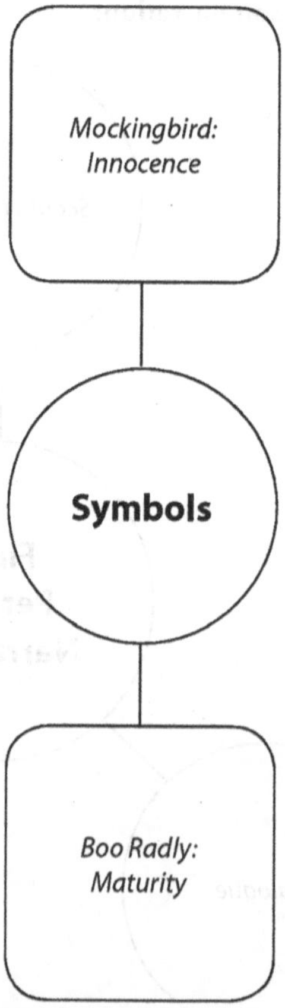

Chapter 29 Review Questions

Writing a Novella

Write a chapter in your novella. Do you use foreshadowing? It is a powerful literary tool.

In the following chart, here are a few uses of foreshadowing in *To Kill a Mockingbird.*

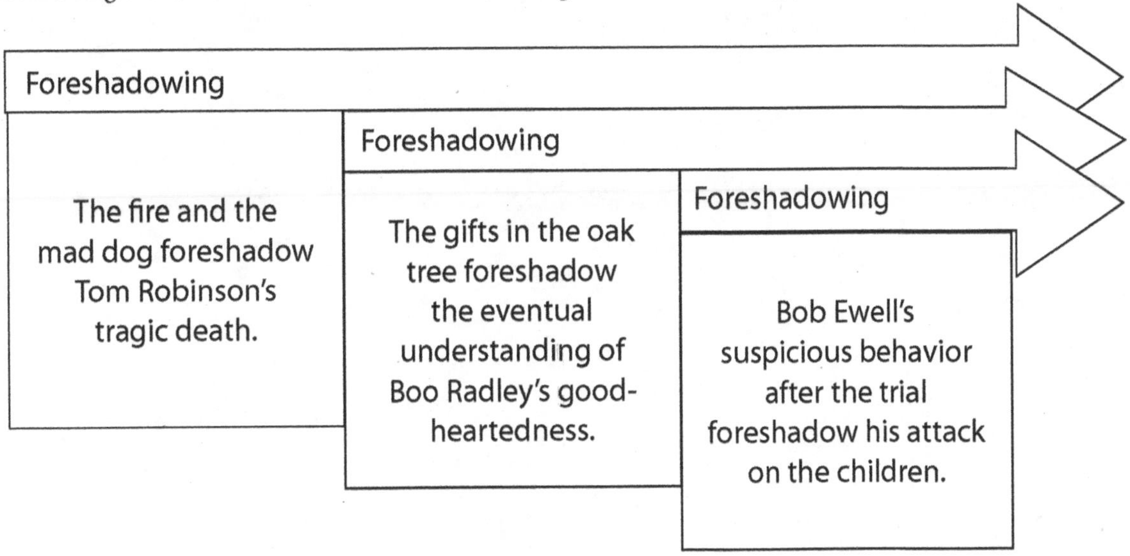
Foreshadowing
The fire and the mad dog foreshadow Tom Robinson's tragic death.
Foreshadowing
The gifts in the oak tree foreshadow the eventual understanding of Boo Radley's good-heartedness.
Foreshadowing
Bob Ewell's suspicious behavior after the trial foreshadow his attack on the children.

Literary Analysis

Write a letter to the editor of the local newspaper in Maycomb, Alabama, expressing your feelings about the trial of Tom Robinson.

Answers will vary.

Biblical Application

What does the Bible say about the races?

Ultimately, the Bible shows that we are all of one race, descended from Adam.

Chapter 29 Test

Pretend that you are Scout's cousin and you discover all the terrible things that have happened to her and to her small town. Write a letter encouraging her (100 points).

Chapter 29 Test Answer Sample

Pretend that you are Scout's cousin and you discover all the terrible things that have happened to her and to her small town. Write a letter encouraging her (100 points).

Answers will vary.

Working on Your Novella

Chapter 30

First Thoughts

This week you will be focusing more time on your novella.

Chapter Learning Objectives

In chapter 30 we will . . .

1. Review your novella.
2. Consider types of plots.
3. Develop the concept of climax.
4. Analyze allegories in the Bible.
5. Understand parody.

Look Ahead for Friday

- Turn in all assignments.
- Continue to work on your novella.

Lesson 1

Novella Review: The Beginning

Daily Assignment

- Warm-up: Revise your novella and make the beginning more interesting.
- Students will complete Concept Builder 30-A.
- Prayer journal: students are encouraged to write in their prayer journal every day.
- Finish the next book you have been assigned.
- Students should systematically review their vocabulary words daily.

CONCEPT BUILDER 30-A

Novella Review: The Beginning

How does each author begin his novel or short story?

A. Letter/frame story	*B*	"Off there to the right — somewhere — is a large island," said Whitney." It's rather a mystery —" "What island is it?" Rainsford asked. "The old charts call it 'Ship-Trap Island,' " Whitney replied." A suggestive name, isn't it? Sailors have a curious dread of the place. I don't know why. Some superstition—" "Can't see it," remarked Rainsford, trying to peer through the dank tropical night that was palpable as it pressed its thick warm blackness in upon the yacht. "You've good eyes," said Whitney, with a laugh," and I've seen you pick off a moose moving in the brown fall bush at four hundred yards, but even you can't see four miles or so through a moonless Caribbean night." (Richard Connell, "The Dangerous Game" http://www.classicshorts.com/stories/danger.html.)
B. Suspense	*A*	St. Petersburg, Dec. 11th, 17-- TO Mrs. Saville, England You will rejoice to hear that no disaster has accompanied the commencement of an enterprise which you have regarded with such evil forebodings. I arrived here yesterday, and my first task is to assure my dear sister of my welfare and increasing confidence in the success of my undertaking. I am already far north of London, and as I walk in the streets of Petersburg, I feel a cold northern breeze play upon my cheeks, which braces my nerves and fills me with delight. Do you understand this feeling? This breeze, which has travelled from the regions towards which I am advancing, gives me a foretaste of those icy climes. Inspirited by this wind of promise, my daydreams become more fervent and vivid. I try in vain to be persuaded that the pole is the seat of frost and desolation; it ever presents itself to my imagination as the region of beauty and delight. There, Margaret, the sun is forever visible, its broad disk just skirting the horizon and diffusing a perpetual splendor. (Mary Shelley, *Frankenstein,* http://www.authorama.com/frankenstein-1.html.)

Lesson 2

Types of Plots: Managing Time and Space

Daily Assignment

- Warm-up: Does your novella have an obvious progression from exposition to resolution?
- Students will complete Concept Builder 30-B.
- Prayer journal: students are encouraged to write in their prayer journal every day.
- Finish the next book you have been assigned.
- Students should systematically review their vocabulary words daily.

CONCEPT BUILDER 30-B

Types of Plots: Managing Time and Space

Match the plot elements in these excerpts from *Alice's Adventures in Wonderland*, by Lewis Carroll.

A. Falling Action	C	"So she sat on, with closed eyes, and half believed herself in Wonderland, though she knew she had but to open them again, and all would change to dull reality — the grass would be only rustling in the wind, and the pool rippling to the waving of the reeds — the rattling teacups would change to tinkling sheep-bells, and the Queen's shrill cries to the voice of the shepherd boy — and the sneeze of the baby, the shriek of the Gryphon, and all the other queer noises, would change (she knew) to the confused clamour of the busy farm-yard — while the lowing of the cattle in the distance would take the place of the Mock Turtle's heavy sobs. Lastly, she pictured to herself how this same little sister of hers would, in the after-time, be herself a grown woman; and how she would keep, through all her riper years, the simple and loving heart of her childhood: and how she would gather about her other little children, and make their eyes bright and eager with many a strange tale, perhaps even with the dream of Wonderland of long ago: and how she would feel with all their simple sorrows, and find a pleasure in all their simple joys, remembering her own child-life, and the happy summer days.
B. Climax	B	"Off with her head!" the Queen shouted at the top of her voice. Nobody moved. "Who cares for you?" said Alice, (she had grown to her full size by this time.) "You're nothing but a pack of cards!" At this the whole pack rose up into the air, and came flying down upon her: she gave a little scream, half of fright and half of anger, and tried to beat them off, and found herself lying on the bank, with her head in the lap of her sister, who was gently brushing away some dead leaves that had fluttered down from the trees upon her face.
C. Resolution	A	"Wake up, Alice dear!" said her sister; "Why, what a long sleep you've had!" "Oh, I've had such a curious dream!" said Alice, and she told her sister, as well as she could remember them, all these strange Adventures of hers that you have just been reading about; and when she had finished, her sister kissed her, and said, "It was a curious dream, dear, certainly: but now run in to your tea; it's getting late." So Alice got up and ran off, thinking while she ran, as well she might, what a wonderful dream it had been. But her sister sat still just as she left her, leaning her head on her hand, watching the setting sun, and thinking of little Alice and all her wonderful Adventures, till she too began dreaming after a fashion, and this was her dream: — First, she dreamed of little Alice herself, and once again the tiny hands were clasped upon her knee, and the bright eager eyes were looking up into hers — she could hear the very tones of her voice, and see that queer little toss of her head to keep back the wandering hair that would always get into her eyes — and still as she listened, or seemed to listen, the whole place around her became alive with the strange creatures of her little sister's dream. The long grass rustled at her feet as the White Rabbit hurried by — the frightened Mouse splashed his way through the neighbouring pool — she could hear the rattle of the teacups as the March Hare and his friends shared their never-ending meal, and the shrill voice of the Queen ordering off her unfortunate guests to execution — once more the pig-baby was sneezing on the Duchess's knee, while plates and dishes crashed around it — once more the shriek of the Gryphon, the squeaking of the Lizard's slate-pencil, and the choking of the suppressed guinea-pigs, filled the air, mixed up with the distant sobs of the miserable Mock Turtle.

Lesson 3

The Climax

Daily Assignment

- Warm-up: : Can you identify the climax(es) in your novella? Can you make it (them) even more pronounced and suspenseful?
- Students will complete Concept Builder 30-C.
- Prayer journal: students are encouraged to write in their prayer journal every day.
- Finish the next book you have been assigned.
- Students should systematically review their vocabulary words daily.

CONCEPT BUILDER 30-C

The Climax

In the short story, "The Most Dangerous Game," Richard Connell has his climax at the end of the story. The protagonist is being pursued by an evil man until the end of the short story. What is the climax? (Student text)

_____The reader is left hanging. We really don't know what happened.

__*X*__Rainsford and Zaroff fight but Rainsford prevails.

_____Both men fight to a draw.

Lesson 4

Allegories in the Bible

Daily Assignment

- Warm-up: Include at least one allegory in your novella.
- Students will complete Concept Builder 30-D.
- Prayer journal: students are encouraged to write in their prayer journal every day.
- Finish the next book you have been assigned.
- Students should systematically review their vocabulary words daily.

CONCEPT BUILDER 30-D

Allegories in the Bible

Match.

A. Galatians 4:24	C	The wilderness will blossom as the rose.
B. Judges 9:7–21	D	This passage compares the messianic kingdom to the wolf and the lamb dwelling together peacefully.
C. Isaiah 35	B	With dialogue and personification, Jotham warns the leaders of Shechem against seeking a king instead of relying on God's rule. "The thornbush said to the trees, 'If you really want to anoint me king over you, come and take refuge in my shade; but if not, then let fire come out of the thornbush and consume the cedars of Lebanon!'"
D. Isaiah 11:6–8	A	The Apostle Paul compares two covenants "These things are being taken figuratively [allegorically]: The women represent two covenants. One covenant is from Mount Sinai and bears children who are to be slaves: This is Hagar."

Lesson 5

Parody

Daily Assignment

- Warm-up: Is your novella humorous? Parody is a great way to make fun of something.
- Students will complete Concept Builder 30-E.
- Prayer journal: students are encouraged to write in their prayer journal every day.
- Finish the next book you have been assigned.
- Students should systematically review their vocabulary words daily.

CONCEPT BUILDER 30-E

Parody

Write a short letter to a sibling poking fun at some of the humorous attributes that he/she manifests in the family.

Answers will vary.

Chapter 30 Review Questions

Writing a Novella

Write a chapter in your novella. Pay particular attention to the literary elements that we studied this week.

Literary Analysis

Discuss the best beginning of a novel that you read.

Answers will vary.

Biblical Application

Analyze a biblical story of your choice. Point out rising action, climax, falling action, resolution.

Answers will vary.

Chapter 30 Test

Write a 500-word parody of a friend, historical period, or a historical figure. (100 points)

Chapter 30 Test

Write a 500-word parody of a friend, historical period, or a historical figure. (100 points)

Answers will vary.

Wisdom Literature in the Old Testament

Chapter 31

First Thoughts

Most of us prefer the historical elements of the Old Testament books and the entire New Testament. However, the poetry and wisdom books (Job through the Psalms) are some of the richest literature in the English language.

Chapter Learning Objectives

In chapter 31 we will . . .

1. Analyze the Book of Job
2. Analyze the Psalms and other Hebrew poetry

Look Ahead for Friday

- Turn in all assignments.
- Continue to work on your novella.

Lesson 1

The Book of Job

Daily Assignment

- Warm-up: What is your favorite verse(s) in Job? Why?
- Students will complete Concept Builder 31-A.
- Prayer journal: students are encouraged to write in their prayer journal every day.
- Finish the next book you have been assigned.
- Students should systematically review their vocabulary words daily.

CONCEPT BUILDER 31-A

Identify the Voices

The Book of Job consists of a prose prologue (introduction or preamble) and epilogue (speech) narrative framing poetic dialogues and monologues (speeches by one person to another person). Read carefully the Book of Job and identify the different speakers.

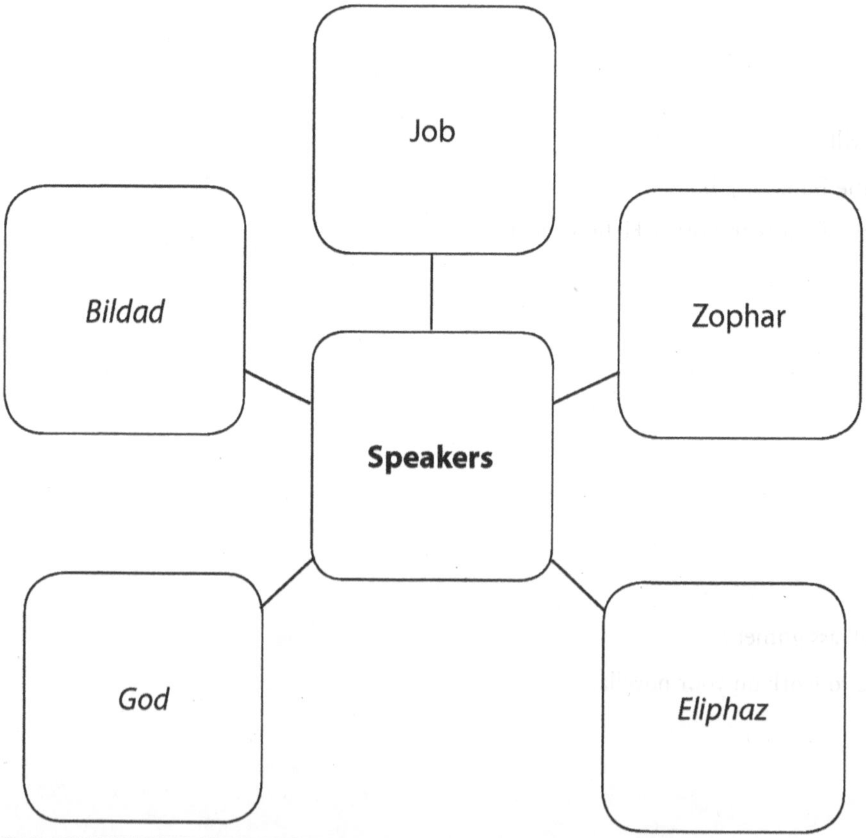

Lesson 2

Hebrew Poetry

Daily Assignment

- Warm-up: Write a six-line poem in the form of a traditional Hebrew poem.
- Students will complete Concept Builder 31-B.
- Prayer journal: students are encouraged to write in their prayer journal every day.
- Finish the next book you have been assigned.
- Students should systematically review their vocabulary words daily.

CONCEPT BUILDER 31-B

Hebrew Poetry

Match.

A. **Synonymous**: Both lines say the same thing but the idea is repeated for a matter of emphasis.	*B*	Blessed is the one who does not walk in step with the wicked (Psalm 1:1).
B. **Synthetic**: The second line builds upon or adds to the first line.	*C*	A righteous man is wise but a wicked man is foolish (Proverbs 14:16).
C. **Antithetic**: Line two is contrary to line one.	*A*	Rejoice in the Lord always. I will say it again: Rejoice! (Philippians 4:4).

Lesson 3

The Psalms

Daily Assignment

- Warm-up: What is your favorite psalm? Why?
- Students will complete Concept Builder 31-C.
- Prayer journal: students are encouraged to write in their prayer journal every day.
- Finish the next book you have been assigned.
- Students should systematically review their vocabulary words daily.

CONCEPT BUILDER 31-C

The Psalms

Match.

A. Book 1 — Psalm 1–41: These first psalms are considered prayers of David. All 40 psalms are attributed to him.	A	The LORD is my shepherd; I shall not want.
B. Book 2 — Psalm 42–72: The theme of these psalms is the suffering of the righteous and deliverance from iniquity and injustice.	E	Praise God in His sanctuary; praise Him in His mighty heavens.
C. Book 3 — Psalm 73–89: These psalms are historical psalms.	C	God is renowned in Judah; in Israel his name is great. His tent is in Salem, his dwelling place in Zion.
D. Book 4 — Psalm 90–106: These psalms focus on the reign of God.	D	Lord, you have been our dwelling place throughout all generations. Before the mountains were born or you brought forth the whole world, from everlasting to everlasting you are God.
E. Book 5 — Psalm 107–150: This final section focuses on the law of God.	B	Do you rulers indeed speak justly? Do you judge people with equity? No, in your heart you devise injustice, and your hands mete out violence on the earth.

Lesson 4

Psalm 23

Sermon

Daily Assignment

- Warm-up: Memorize Psalm 23.
- Students will complete Concept Builder 31-D.
- Prayer journal: students are encouraged to write in their prayer journal every day.
- Finish the next book you have been assigned.
- Students should systematically review their vocabulary words daily.

CONCEPT BUILDER 31-D

Psalm 23

What does God do for the believer in this psalm?

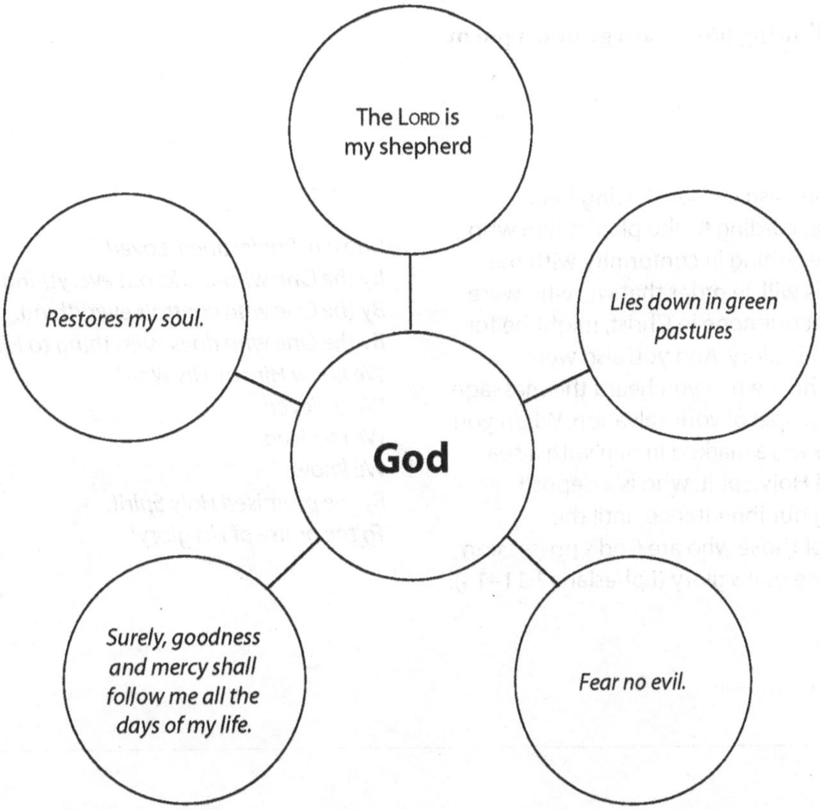

The LORD is my shepherd
Lies down in green pastures
Restores my soul.
God
Surely, goodness and mercy shall follow me all the days of my life.
Fear no evil.

Lesson 5

Other Poetry in the Bible

Daily Assignment

- Warm-up: Memorize one of the poems listed above.
- Students will complete Concept Builder 31-E.
- Prayer journal: students are encouraged to write in their prayer journal every day.
- Finish the next book you have been assigned.
- Students should systematically review their vocabulary words daily.

CONCEPT BUILDER 31-E

Poetry in the Bible

Change the following prose passage into a poem.

In him we were also chosen, having been predestined according to the plan of him who works out everything in conformity with the purpose of his will, in order that we, who were the first to put our hope in Christ, might be for the praise of his glory. And you also were included in Christ when you heard the message of truth, the gospel of your salvation. When you believed, you were marked in him with a seal, the promised Holy Spirit, who is a deposit guaranteeing our inheritance until the redemption of those who are God's possession — to the praise of his glory (Ephesians 1:11–14).

Chosen. Predestined. Loved.
By the One who works out everything.
By the One who controls everything.
By the One who does everything to His glory.
We know Him by His Word.
We believed.
We received.
We know.
By the promised Holy Spirit.
To the praise of His glory!

Chapter 31 Review Questions

Writing a Novella

Write a chapter in your novella.

Literary Analysis

Analyze a psalm or a proverb. What metaphors or other literary devices does the author use to make his/her point?

See sermon. Answers will vary.

Biblical Application

Write a letter to someone who does not know the Lord as Savior. Use Scripture to persuade him/her to commit his/her life to Christ.

Answers will vary.

Chapter 31 Test

I. Write a psalm. (40 points)

II. Write a proverb. (40 points)

III. Write a poem about a historical figure in the Bible. (20 points)

Chapter 31 Test Answer Sample

I. Write a psalm. (40 points)
Answers will vary.

II. Write a proverb. (40 points)
Answers will vary.

III. Write a poem about a historical figure in the Bible. (20 points)
Answers will vary.

The Bible

Chapter 32

First Thoughts

The Bible is the Word of God. It is written by the Holy Spirit through mankind. It is inspired and inerrant. Yet, at the same time it is literature.

Chapter Learning Objectives

In chapter 32 we will . . .

1. Understand biblical narration
2. Analyze the Bible as literature

Look Ahead for Friday

- Turn in all assignments.
- Continue to work on your novella.

Lesson 1

Biblical Obstacles

Daily Assignment

- Warm-up: What sort of obstacles must your protagonist overcome in your novella?
- Students will complete Concept Builder 32-A.
- Prayer journal: students are encouraged to write in their prayer journal every day.
- Finish the next book you have been assigned.
- Students should systematically review their vocabulary words daily.

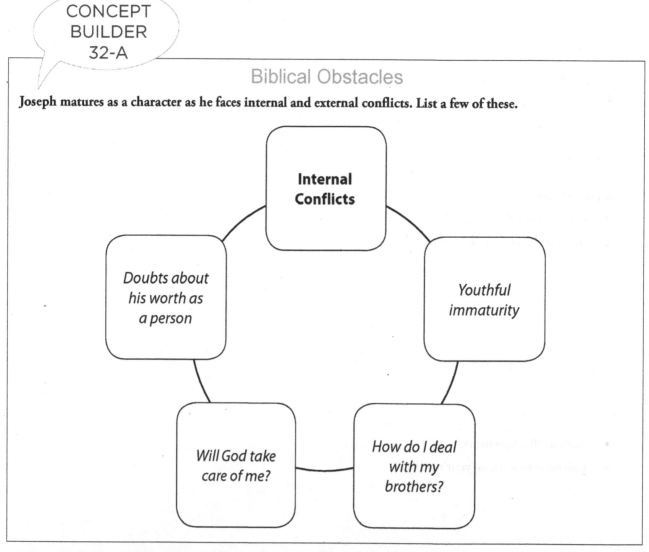

CONCEPT BUILDER 32-A

Biblical Obstacles

Joseph matures as a character as he faces internal and external conflicts. List a few of these.

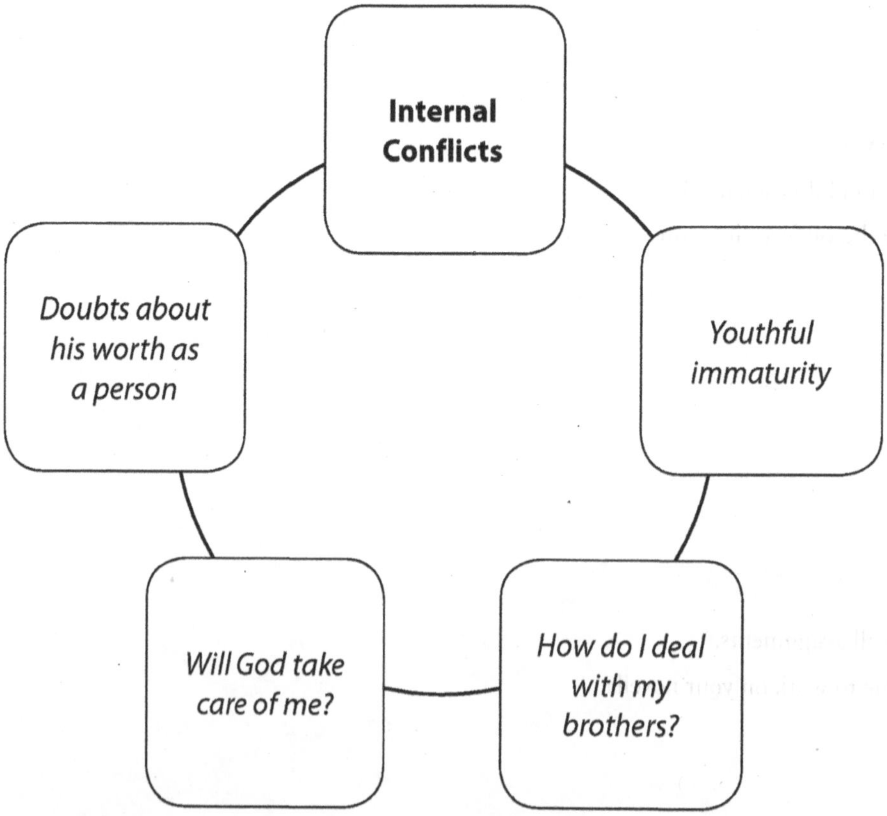

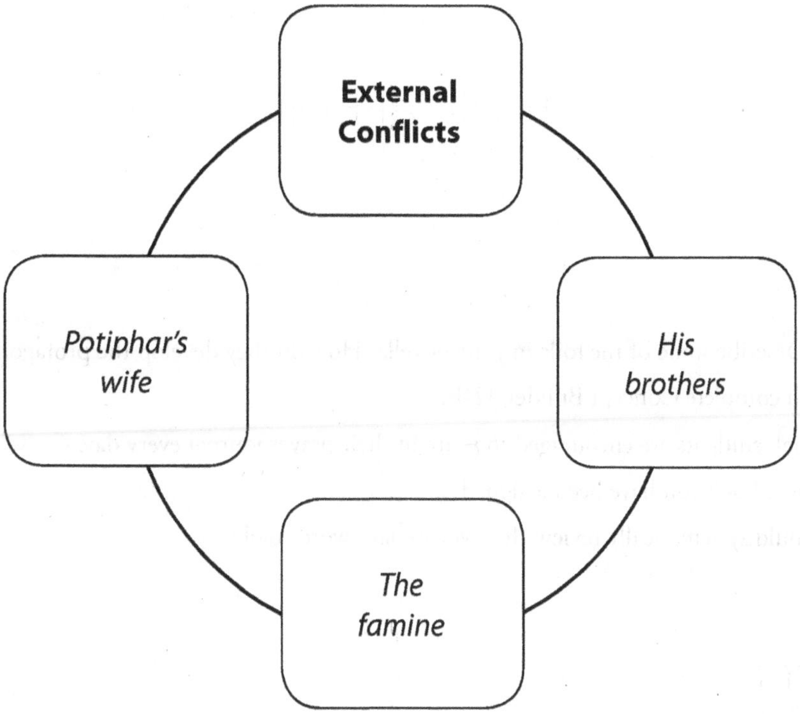
External Conflicts
Potiphar's wife
His brothers
The famine

Biblical Foils

Daily Assignment

- Warm-up: Describe some of the foils in your novella. How do they develop the protagonist?
- Students will complete Concept Builder 32-B.
- Prayer journal: students are encouraged to write in their prayer journal every day.
- Finish the next book you have been assigned.
- Students should systematically review their vocabulary words daily.

CONCEPT BUILDER 32-B

Biblical Foils

Aaron is a quiet but mostly loyal foil and brother to Moses. How does he help develop Moses as a character?

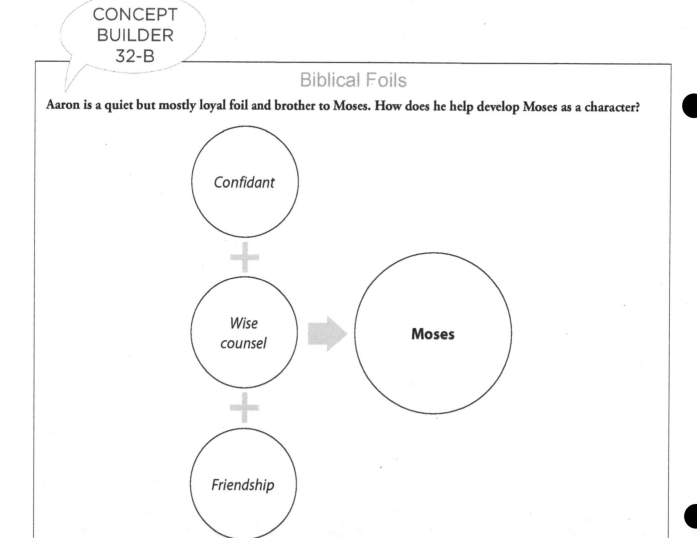

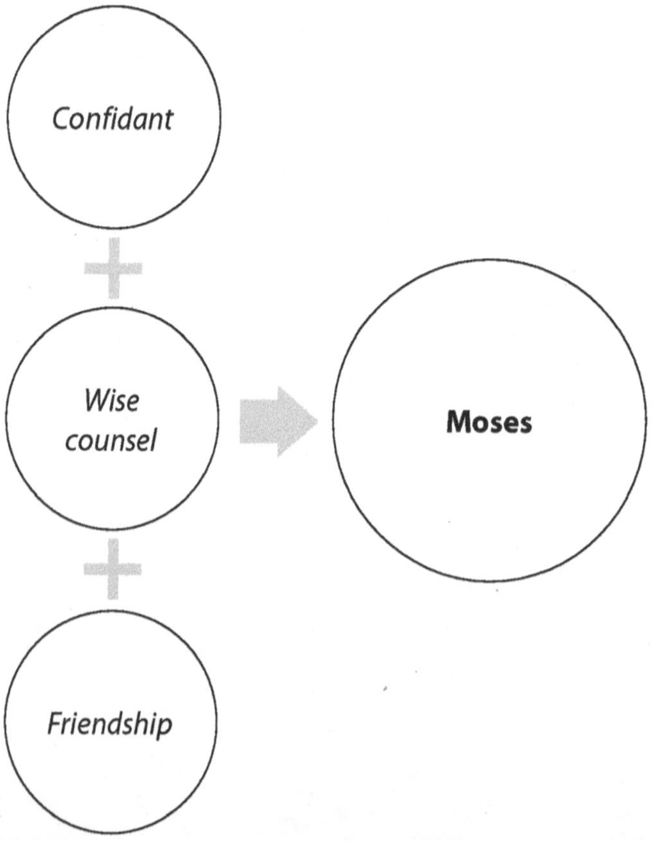

Lesson 3

Narration in the Bible

Daily Assignment

- Warm-up: Write a short parable.
- Students will complete Concept Builder 32-C.
- Prayer journal: students are encouraged to write in their prayer journal every day.
- Finish the next book you have been assigned.
- Students should systematically review their vocabulary words daily.

CONCEPT BUILDER 32-C

Narration in the Bible

What two narrative techniques are in the Book of Ezra?

The narrator of Ezra begins his book with third-person objective narration:

In the first year of Cyrus king of Persia, in order to fulfill the word of the LORD spoken by Jeremiah, the LORD moved the heart of Cyrus king of Persia to make a proclamation throughout his realm and also to put it in writing:

"This is what Cyrus king of Persia says:

" 'The LORD, the God of heaven, has given me all the kingdoms of the earth and he has appointed me to build a temple for him at Jerusalem in Judah. Any of his people among you may go up to Jerusalem in Judah and build the temple of the Lord, the God of Israel, the God who is in Jerusalem, and may their God be with them. And in any locality where survivors may now be living, the people are to provide them with silver and gold, with goods and livestock, and with freewill offerings for the temple of God in Jerusalem' " (Ezra 1:1–4).

Ezra arrived in Jerusalem in the fifth month of the seventh year of the king. He had begun his journey from Babylon on the first day of the first month, and he arrived in Jerusalem on the first day of the fifth month, for the gracious hand of his God was on him. For Ezra had devoted himself to the study and observance of the Law of the LORD, and to teaching its decrees and laws in Israel (Ezra 7:8–10).

In Ezra 8:15, the narration changes to first person, and Ezra himself tells the story. In chapter 10 the narration switches back to third-person objective. Here is some of Ezra 8:

I assembled them at the canal that flows toward Ahava, and we camped there three days. When I checked among the people and the priests, I found no Levites there. So I summoned Eliezer, Ariel, Shemaiah, Elnathan, Jarib, Elnathan, Nathan, Zechariah and Meshullam, who were leaders, and Joiarib and Elnathan, who were men of learning, and I ordered them to go to Iddo, the leader in Kasiphia. I told them what to say to Iddo and his fellow Levites, the temple servants in Kasiphia, so that they might bring attendants to us for the house of our God. Because the gracious hand of our God was on us, they brought us Sherebiah, a capable man, from the descendants of Mahli son of Levi, the son of Israel, and Sherebiah's sons and brothers, 18 in all; and Hashabiah, together with Jeshaiah from the descendants of Merari, and his brothers and nephews, 20 in all. They also brought 220 of the temple servants — a body that David and the officials had established to assist the Levites. All were registered by name.

There, by the Ahava Canal, I proclaimed a fast, so that we might humble ourselves before our God and ask him for a safe journey for us and our children, with all our possessions. I was ashamed to ask the king for soldiers and horsemen to protect us from enemies on the road, because we had told the king, "The gracious hand of our God is on everyone who looks to him, but his great anger is against all who forsake him." So we fasted and petitioned our God about this, and he answered our prayer (Ezra 8:15–23).

Lesson 4

Biblical Parables

Daily Assignment

- Warm-up: Write a short parable.
- Students will complete Concept Builder 32-D.
- Prayer journal: students are encouraged to write in their prayer journal every day.
- Finish the next book you have been assigned.
- Students should systematically review their vocabulary words daily.

CONCEPT BUILDER 32-D

Parables

What biblical lessons does the Prodigal Son parable teach?

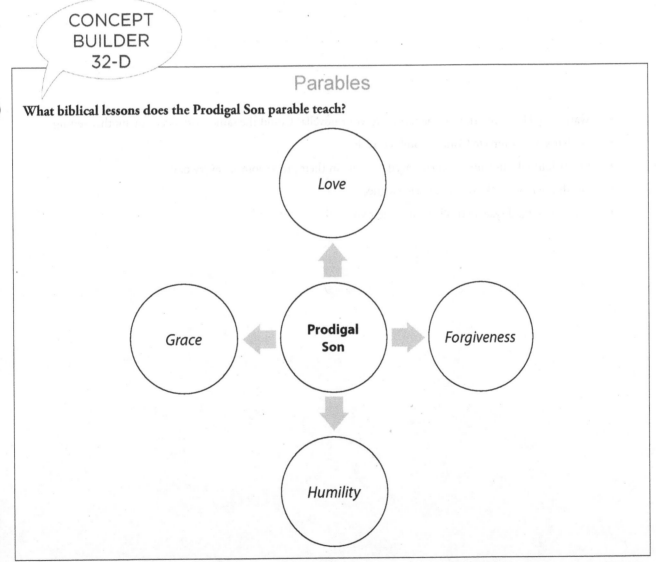

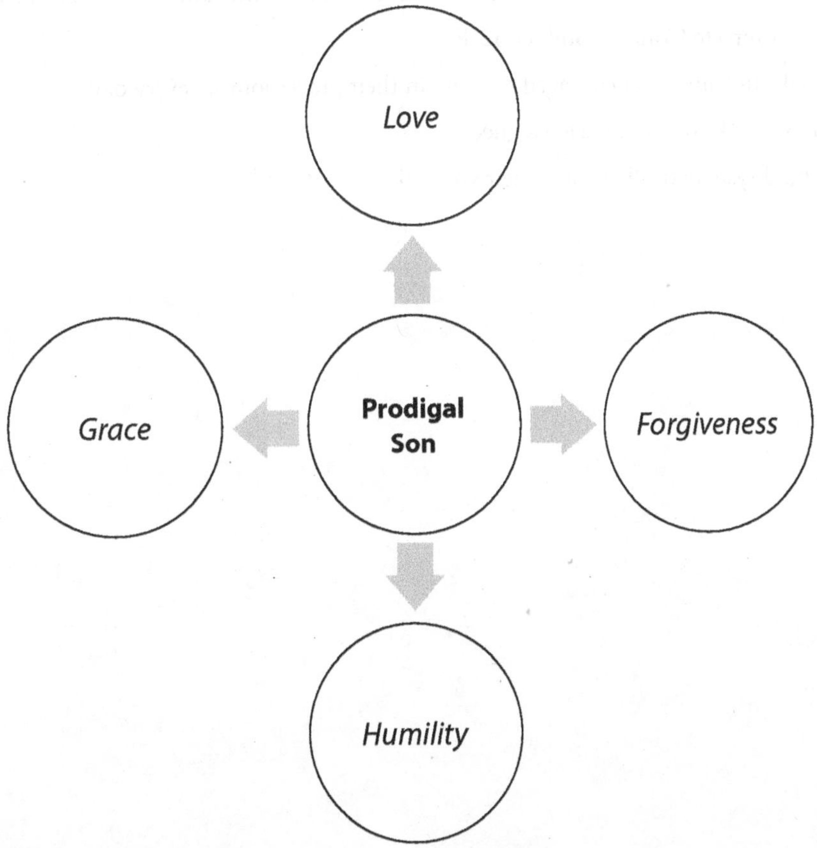

Lesson 5

Settings in the Bible

Daily Assignment

- Warm-up: How important is the setting to your novella? Could the same story occur in another setting?
- Students will complete Concept Builder 32-E.
- Prayer journal: students are encouraged to write in their prayer journal every day.
- Finish the next book you have been assigned.
- Students should systematically review their vocabulary words daily.

CONCEPT BUILDER 32-E

Settings in the Bible

How important is the setting in this biblical passage?

The prison setting is crucial to the tone and theme of this passage:

Paul in Prison: Philemon

Paul, a prisoner of Christ Jesus, and Timothy our brother,

To Philemon our dear friend and fellow worker — also to Apphia our sister and Archippus our fellow soldier — and to the church that meets in your home:

Grace and peace to you from God our Father and the Lord Jesus Christ.

I always thank my God as I remember you in my prayers, because I hear about your love for all his holy people and your faith in the Lord Jesus. I pray that your partnership with us in the faith may be effective in deepening your understanding of every good thing we share for the sake of Christ. Your love has given me great joy and encouragement, because you, brother, have refreshed the hearts of the Lord's people.

Therefore, although in Christ I could be bold and order you to do what you ought to do, yet I prefer to appeal to you on the basis of love. It is as none other than Paul — an old man and now also a prisoner of Christ Jesus—that I appeal to you for my son Onesimus, who became my son while I was in chains. Formerly he was useless to you, but now he has become useful both to you and to me

I am sending him — who is my very heart — back to you. I would have liked to keep him with me so that he could take your place in helping me while I am in chains for the gospel. But I did not want to do anything without your consent, so that any favor you do would not seem forced but would be voluntary. Perhaps the reason he was separated from you for a little while was that you might have him back forever — no longer as a slave, but better than a slave, as a dear brother. He is very dear to me but even dearer to you, both as a fellow man and as a brother in the Lord.

So if you consider me a partner, welcome him as you would welcome me. If he has done you any wrong or owes you anything, charge it to me. I, Paul, am writing this with my own hand. I will pay it back — not to mention that you owe me your very self. I do wish, brother, that I may have some benefit from you in the Lord; refresh my heart in Christ. Confident of your obedience, I write to you, knowing that you will do even more than I ask.

And one thing more: Prepare a guest room for me, because I hope to be restored to you in answer to your prayers.

Epaphras, my fellow prisoner in Christ Jesus, sends you greetings. And so do Mark, Aristarchus, Demas and Luke, my fellow workers.

The grace of the Lord Jesus Christ be with your spirit.

Chapter 32 Review Questions

Writing a Novella

Write a chapter in your novella.

Literary Analysis

Do a literary analysis essay of your favorite biblical story. In your essay, discuss the plot, characters, narration, tone, setting, and theme.

Answers will vary.

Biblical Application

Most apologists (defenders of the faith) of the 20th century were English teachers. Why does literary analysis help us write apologetics?

Answers will vary, but should include that good communication skills helps people make their message more clear.

Chapter 32 Test

Write a sermon on 1 Corinthian 13. (100 points)

Your sermon will be evaluated in these three areas:

Syntax and diction: grammar and style (25 points)

Organization: paragraphs, transitions, introduction, et al. (25 points)

Argument (50 points)

Chapter 32 Test Answer Sample

Write a sermon on 1 Corinthian 13. (100 points)

Your sermon will be evaluated in these three areas:

Syntax and diction: grammar and style (25 points)

Organization: paragraphs, transitions, introduction, et al. (25 points)

Argument (50 points)

Answers will vary.

Reading 1

The Hobbit by J.R.R. Tolkien

Chapter 33

First Thoughts

The Hobbit by J.R.R. Tolkien was published in 1937 as a children's book. It was met with great excitement and received several awards. At the request of his publishers, Tolkien set out to write a sequel to *The Hobbit.*

Chapter Learning Objectives

In chapter 33 we will . . .

1. Explore the author and his times
2. Review setting and point of view

Look Ahead for Friday

- Turn in all assignments.
- List and describe the characters in your novella.

Active Reading: *The Hobbit* (Chapter I) by J.R.R Tolkien

Why does Tolkien use second person?

Tolkien is trying to connect with readers.

Describe Gandalf.

"Tales and adventures sprouted up all over the place wherever he went, in the most extraordinary fashion. He had not been down that way under The Hill for ages and ages, not since his friend the Old Took died, in fact, and the hobbits had almost forgotten what he looked like. He had been away over The Hill and across The Water on business of his own since they were all small hobbit-boys and hobbit-girls."

Predict what will happen next.

Answers will vary.

Daily Assignment

- Warm-up: Would you join Bilbo Baggins on his quest?
- Students will complete Concept Builder 33-A.
- Prayer journal: students are encouraged to write in their prayer journal every day.
- Finish the next book you have been assigned.
- Students should systematically review their vocabulary words daily.

CONCEPT BUILDER 33-A

Illustrated Book Review

Create an illustrated booklet of three of the most important scenes from *The Hobbit*.

Answers will vary.

Lesson 2

The Author and His Times

Daily Assignment

- Warm-up: Discuss a time when it was very hard to forgive someone who offended you.
- Students will complete Concept Builder 33-B.
- Prayer journal: students are encouraged to write in their prayer journal every day.
- Finish the next book you have been assigned.
- Students should systematically review their vocabulary words daily.

CONCEPT BUILDER 33-B

The Author and His Times

World War I began (1914) while Tolkien was a student at Oxford University. After finishing his degree, Tolkien joined the Lancashire Fusiliers as a second lieutenant.

In 1916, Tolkien was sent to France, where he and his fellow soldiers fought in the Battle of the Somme, a vicious engagement in which over a million people were either killed or wounded. In fact, all but one of Tolkien's comrades was killed or wounded. World War I deeply affected his writing.

What do these descriptions illustrate elements of World War I?

Passages in Tolkien's Writings	World War I
Dead Marshes of Mordor	The bleak, dead land and trenches of World War I
The Hobbits	*Happy comrades*
The Shire	*Behind the trenches; land untouched by war*
Saruman, the corrupt wizard, devastates an ancient forest as he builds his army. The Elves, in contrast, live in harmony with nature, appreciating its beauty and power, and reflecting a sense of enchantment and wonder in their beautiful songs.	*Kaiser Wilhelm brings havoc on the land, destroying man and nature.*

Lesson 3

Point of View

Daily Assignment

- Warm-up: What advantages does third-person narration offer Tolkien as he tells his story?
- Students will complete Concept Builder 33-C.
- Prayer journal: students are encouraged to write in their prayer journal every day.
- Finish the next book you have been assigned.
- Students should systematically review their vocabulary words daily.

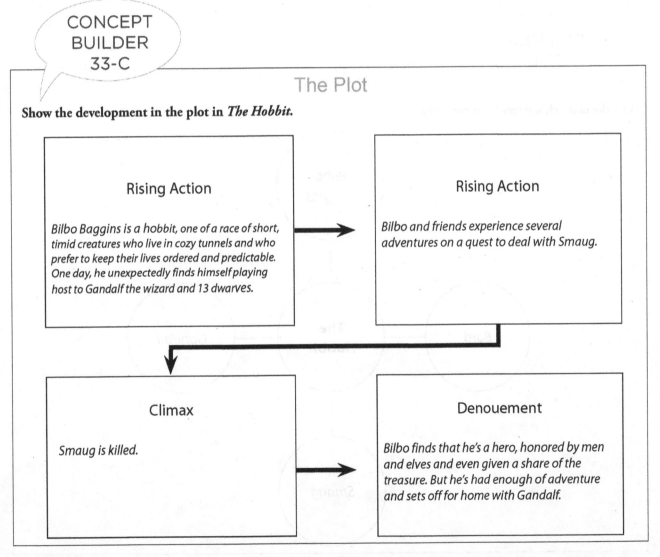

CONCEPT BUILDER 33-C

The Plot

Show the development in the plot in *The Hobbit*.

Rising Action

Bilbo Baggins is a hobbit, one of a race of short, timid creatures who live in cozy tunnels and who prefer to keep their lives ordered and predictable. One day, he unexpectedly finds himself playing host to Gandalf the wizard and 13 dwarves.

Rising Action

Bilbo and friends experience several adventures on a quest to deal with Smaug.

Climax

Smaug is killed.

Denouement

Bilbo finds that he's a hero, honored by men and elves and even given a share of the treasure. But he's had enough of adventure and sets off for home with Gandalf.

The Setting

Daily Assignment

- Warm-up: What sort of imaginary world would you like to live in if you could?
- Students will complete Concept Builder 33-D.
- Prayer journal: students are encouraged to write in their prayer journal every day.
- Finish the next book you have been assigned.
- Students should systematically review their vocabulary words daily.

CONCEPT BUILDER 33-D

Characters

List the main characters from the story.

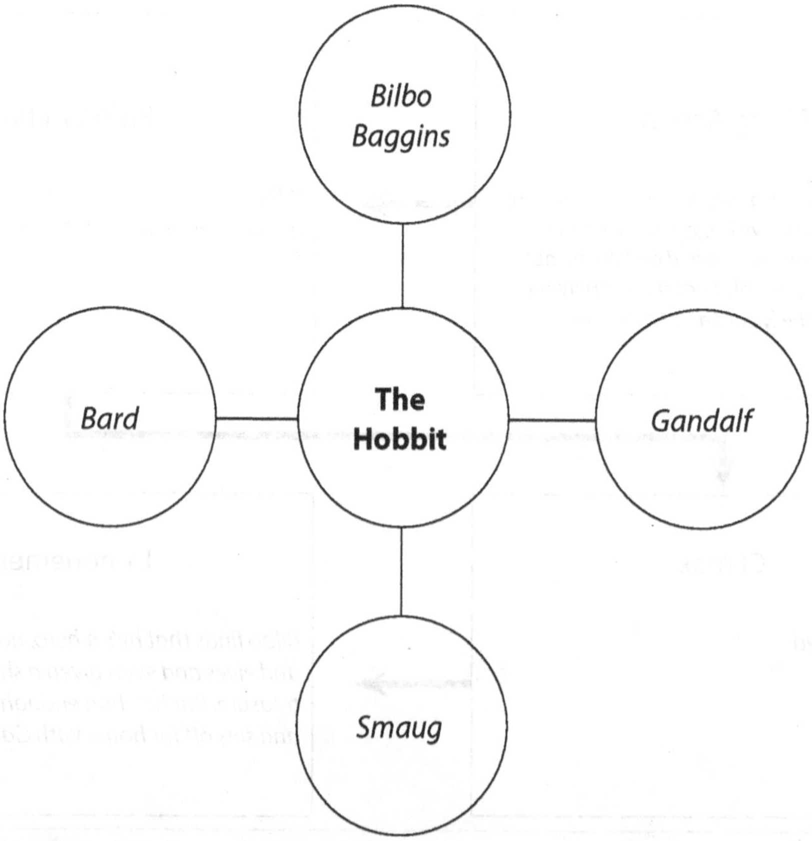

Student Essay
The Setting in Tolkien's Novels

Daily Assignment

- Warm-up: Who is your favorite character in the *The Lord of the Rings*?
- Students will complete Concept Builder 33-E.
- Prayer journal: students are encouraged to write in their prayer journal every day.
- Finish the next book you have been assigned.
- Students should systematically review their vocabulary words daily.

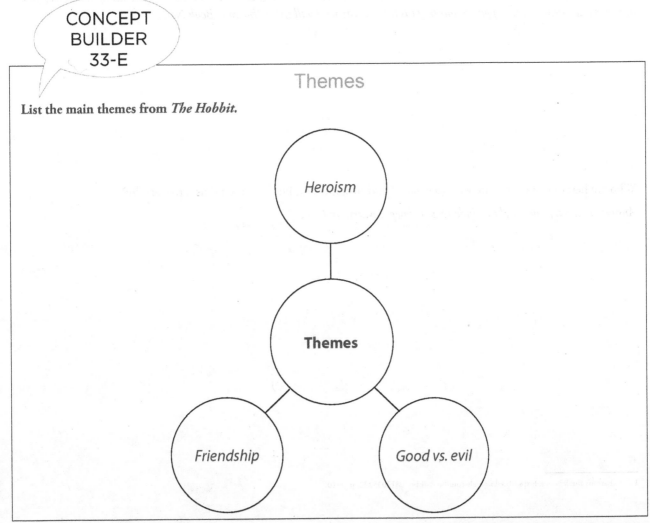

CONCEPT BUILDER 33-E

Themes

List the main themes from *The Hobbit*.

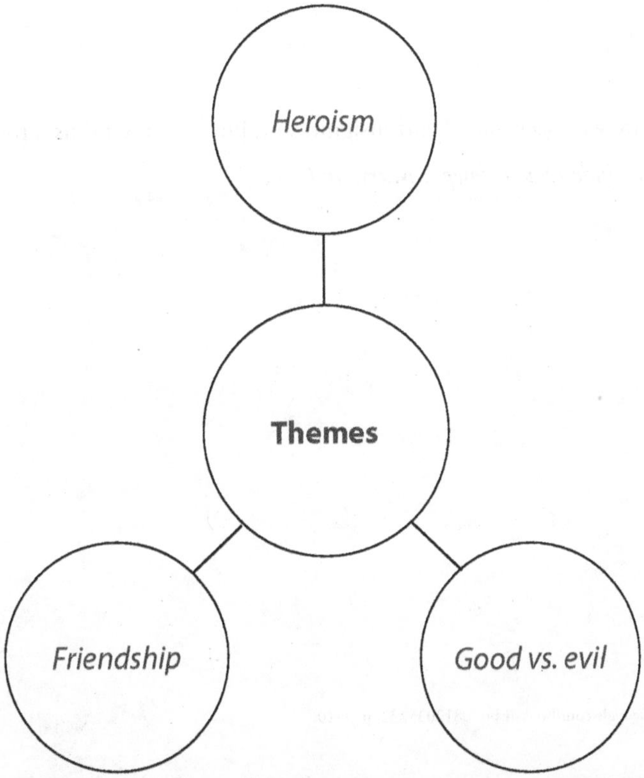

Chapter 33 Review Questions

Writing a Novella

Proofread your novella and make final changes.

Literary Analysis

In what way is Bilbo Baggins an anti-hero?

Bilbo finds that he's a hero, honored by men and elves and even given a share of the treasure. But he's had enough of adventure and sets off for home with Gandalf. Once there, he finds that his house and furnishings are being auctioned off, since everyone believed him dead. Finally, everything is straightened out and he's able to settle down again into his old, comfortable life. Although from then on, he's considered eccentric by his neighbors, he continues his friendship with elves and dwarves and the wizard, happily recounting his tales to any who will listen (Barron's Book Notes).[1]

Biblical Application

Who are heroes from Scripture who seem small and insignificant, but whom God uses powerfully?

Answers will vary, but might include David, Joseph, Mary, and others.

1 Barron's Book Notes, https://books.google.com/books?isbn=0812035232, p. 9–10.

Chapter 33 Test

I. Place these events in the order in which they occurred. (55 points)

_____ In Lake-town, Bard holds his ground. He kills the dragon with his last arrow and escapes before Smaug falls, smashing the town.

_____ Bilbo tries to end the dispute by stealing the Arkenstone, the piece of treasure most valued by the leader of the dwarves. He gives the jewel to Bard, hoping it can be used to force the dwarves to negotiate.

_____ Bilbo Baggins and the dwarfs, with Gandalf's help, plans to travel to the Lonely Mountain to recover the treasure that a dragon named Smaug stole from their people long ago.

_____ Just as war begins to break out, an army of goblins and wild wolves attack. The dwarves, elves, and men forget their differences and join together to keep from being killed.

_____ Bilbo himself isn't sure that he's happy about this arrangement.

_____ Bilbo's bravery wins him praise from all but the dwarves, who are furious with him. When more dwarves arrive from the north, they are determined to fight.

_____ Bilbo finds a magic ring that makes him invisible, and has several opportunities to use it to rescue the dwarves from danger and imprisonment.

_____ Bilbo and the dwarves finally reach Lonely Mountain.

_____ Furious that someone has dared steal a piece of his treasure, Smaug attacks the mountainside where the dwarves have their camp and Lake-town.

_____ Bilbo wants none of the treasure and returns home with Gandalf.

_____ Believing the dwarves are dead, an army of men, led by Bard, and an army of elves find to their surprise that the dwarves are still alive.

_____ Bard, because he killed the dragon, claims his rightful share of the treasure. When the dwarves refuse to surrender it, the army besieges the mountain.

_____ Bilbo has more confidence in himself now and not only steals a cup, but converses with the tricky Smaug.

II. Discussion Question (45 points)

Explain why Tolkien chose Bilbo Baggins as his protagonist.

Chapter 33 Test Answer Sample

I. Place these events in the order in which they occurred. (55 points)

7 In Lake-town, Bard holds his ground. He kills the dragon with his last arrow and escapes before Smaug falls, smashing the town.

10 Bilbo tries to end the dispute by stealing the Arkenstone, the piece of treasure most valued by the leader of the dwarves. He gives the jewel to Bard, hoping it can be used to force the dwarves to negotiate.

1 Bilbo Baggins and the dwarfs, with Gandalf's help, plans to travel to the Lonely Mountain to recover the treasure that a dragon named Smaug stole from their people long ago.

12 Just as war begins to break out, an army of goblins and wild wolves attack. The dwarves, elves, and men forget their differences and join together to keep from being killed.

2 Bilbo himself isn't sure that he's happy about this arrangement.

11 Bilbo's bravery wins him praise from all but the dwarves, who are furious with him. When more dwarves arrive from the north, they are determined to fight.

3 Bilbo finds a magic ring that makes him invisible, and has several opportunities to use it to rescue the dwarves from danger and imprisonment.

4 Bilbo and the dwarves finally reach Lonely Mountain.

6 Furious that someone has dared steal a piece of his treasure, Smaug attacks the mountainside where the dwarves have their camp and Lake-town.

13 Bilbo wants none of the treasure and returns home with Gandalf.

8 Believing the dwarves are dead, an army of men, led by Bard, and an army of elves find to their surprise that the dwarves are still alive.

9 Bard, because he killed the dragon, claims his rightful share of the treasure. When the dwarves refuse to surrender it, the army besieges the mountain.

5 Bilbo has more confidence in himself now and not only steals a cup, but converses with the tricky Smaug.

II. Discussion Question (45 points)

Explain why Tolkien chose Bilbo Baggins as his protagonist.

Bilbo is the small, shy protagonist representative of ordinary man. Adults and children can identify with this unassuming but brave man. Also, Bilbo rises to the occasion — he is brave when necessary — something all readers hope to attain.

Reading 2

The Hobbit by J.R.R. Tolkien

Chapter 34

First Thoughts

His Hobbit is both a bridge and a being — Hobbits connect readers with the world and with themselves. They give all readers, brave and timid ones, hope that they too can be brave, courageous, and adventurous. Moreover, the Hobbit is . . . more of a human than if he were one, as petit-bourgeois as if he caught the 8:15 commuter train. . . . The rather jolly virtues of the Hobbits are raised to solemn magnificence when it is realized that these virtues endow their possessors with the power to face and subdue the terrible and soul-destroying opposition of evil that besets them. It is the reluctant choice to face or not to face evil that raised Bilbo and more so his heir, Frodo, above even great Beowulf.[1]

1 William Ready, *The Tolkien Relation* (Chicago, IL: Regnery, 1968).

Chapter Learning Objectives

In chapter 34 we will . . .

1. Understand the use of song in *The Hobbit*
2. Review the concept of motif
3. Analyze the form and structure of *The Hobbit*
4. Evaluate the way Tolkien uses female characters in his novels

Look Ahead for Friday

- Turn in all assignments.
- List and describe the characters in your novella.

Critics' Corner

Daily Assignment

- Warm-up: What are some Christian motifs in *The Hobbit*?
- Students will complete Concept Builder 34-A.
- Prayer journal: students are encouraged to write in their prayer journal every day.
- Finish the next book you have been assigned.
- Students should systematically review their vocabulary words daily.

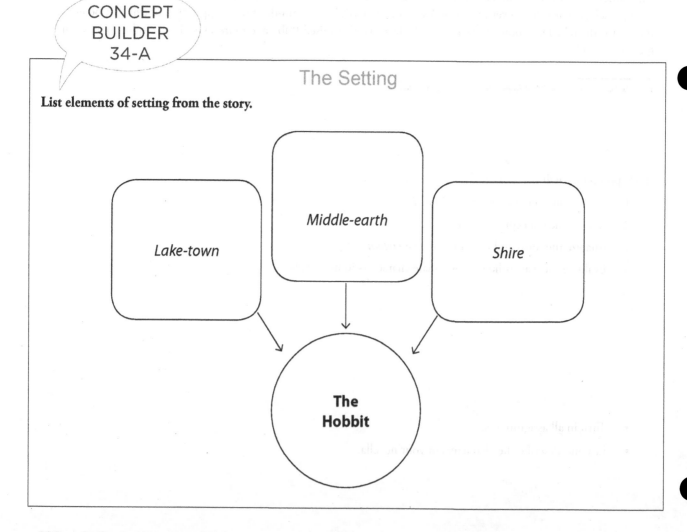

CONCEPT BUILDER 34-A

The Setting

List elements of setting from the story.

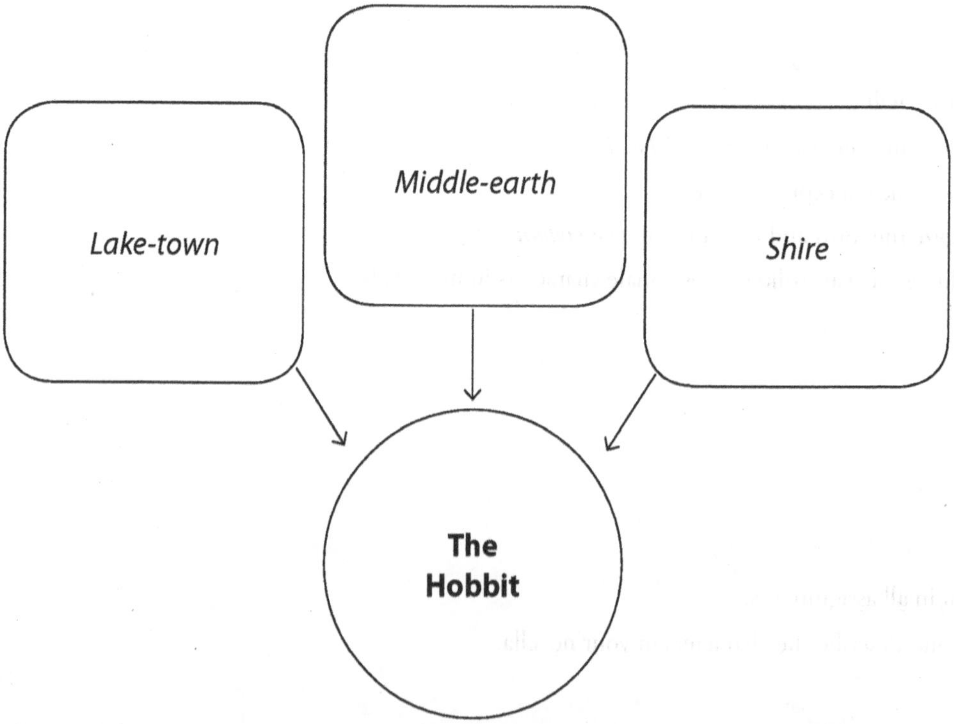

Lesson 2

The Use of Song

Daily Assignment

- Warm-up: Write a song that describes who you are or a journey you have taken.
- Students will complete Concept Builder 34-B.
- Prayer journal: students are encouraged to write in their prayer journal every day.
- Finish the next book you have been assigned.
- Students should systematically review their vocabulary words daily.

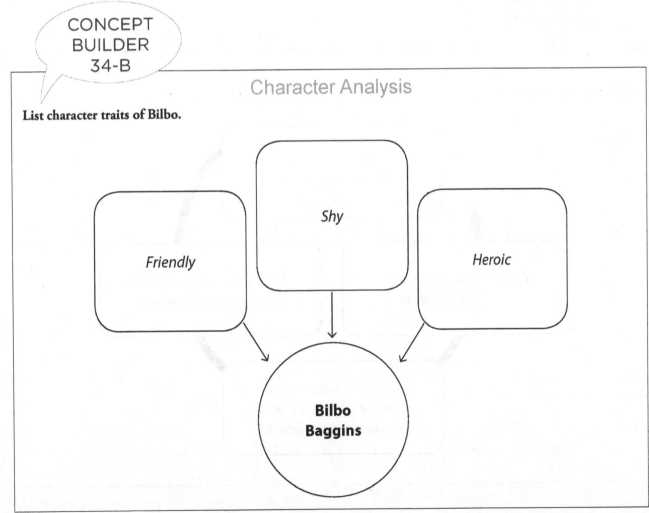

CONCEPT BUILDER 34-B

Character Analysis

List character traits of Bilbo.

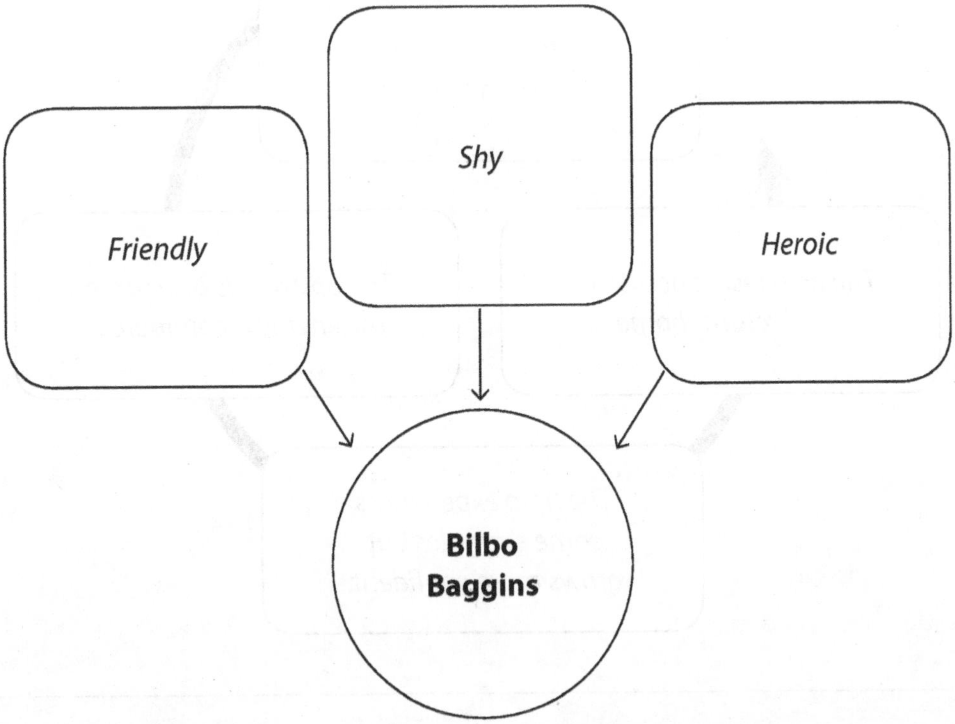

Form and Structure

Daily Assignment

- Warm-up: What is the form and structure of *The Hobbit*?
- Students will complete Concept Builder 34-C.
- Prayer journal: students are encouraged to write in their prayer journal every day.
- Finish the next book you have been assigned.
- Students should systematically review their vocabulary words daily.

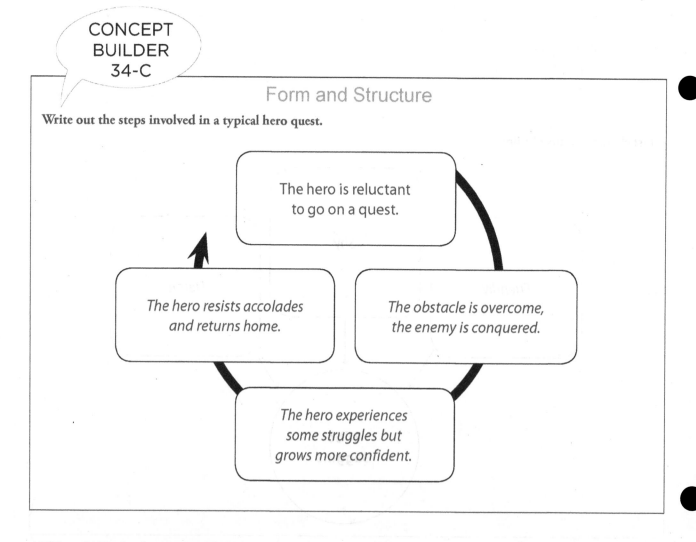

CONCEPT BUILDER 34-C

Form and Structure

Write out the steps involved in a typical hero quest.

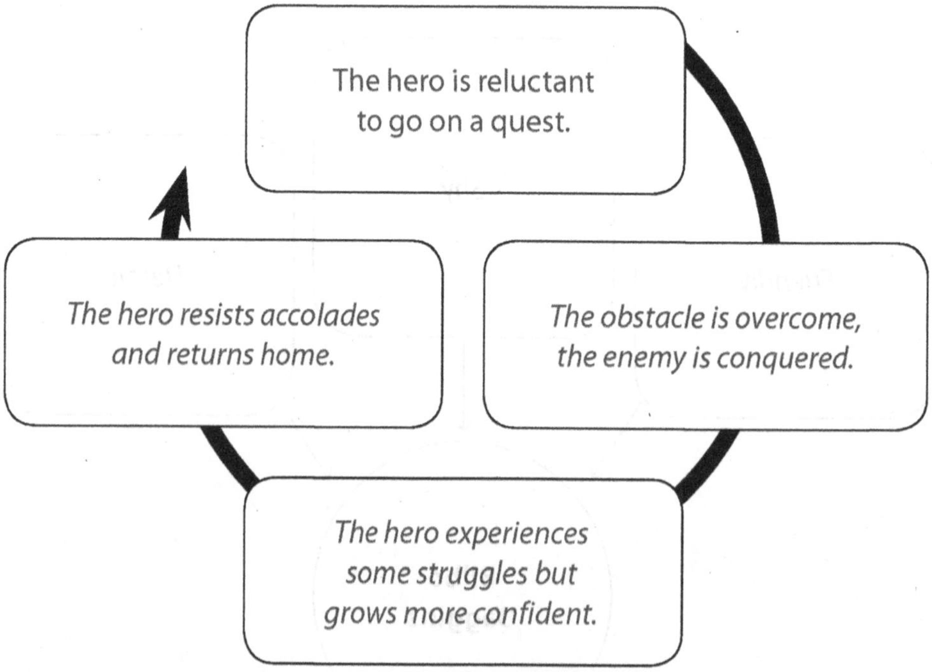

The hero is reluctant to go on a quest.
The obstacle is overcome, the enemy is conquered.
The hero experiences some struggles but grows more confident.
The hero resists accolades and returns home.

Lesson 4

Motif

Daily Assignment

- Warm-up: Describe a journey or quest that changed your life.
- Students will complete Concept Builder 34-D.
- Prayer journal: students are encouraged to write in their prayer journal every day.
- Finish the next book you have been assigned.
- Students should systematically review their vocabulary words daily.

CONCEPT BUILDER 34-D

Point of View

Discuss the development of the point of view.

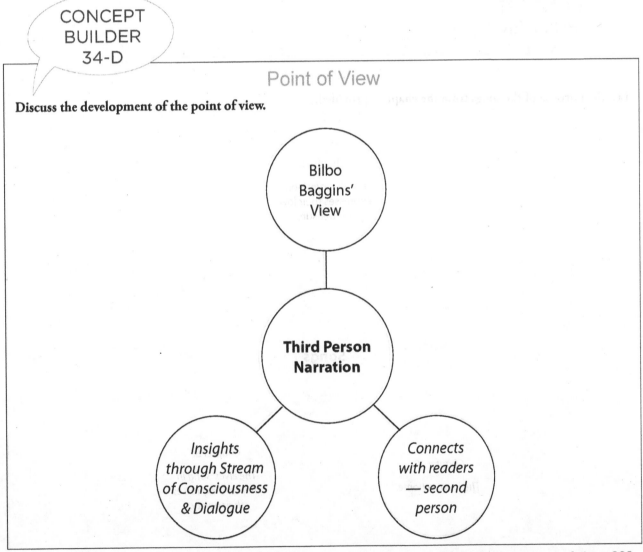

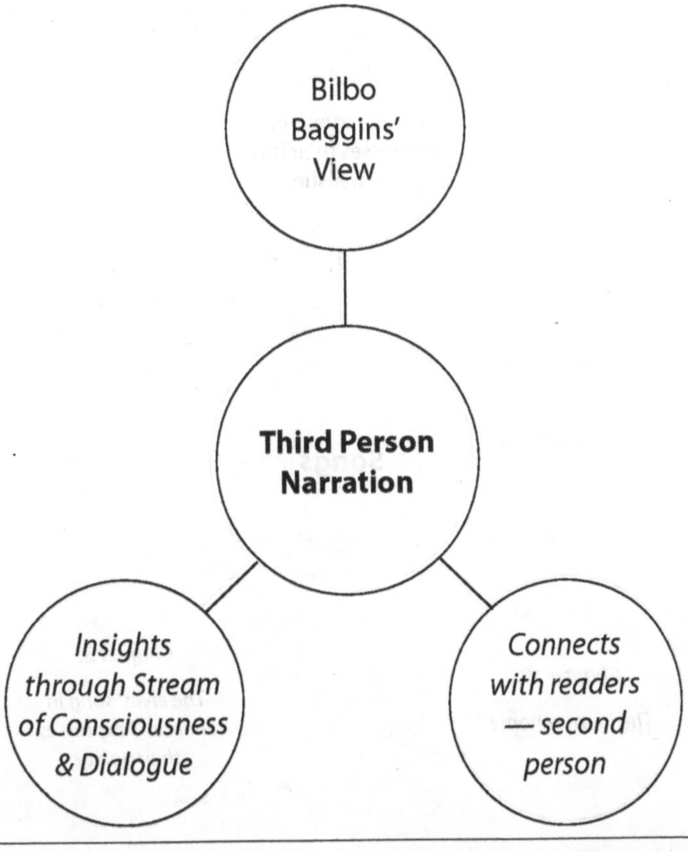

Lesson 5

Student Essay
The Setting in Tolkien's Novels

Daily Assignment

- Warm-up: Did you enjoy this novel? Why or why not?
- Students will complete Concept Builder 34-E.
- Prayer journal: students are encouraged to write in their prayer journal every day.
- Finish the next book you have been assigned.
- Students should systematically review their vocabulary words daily.

CONCEPT BUILDER 34-E

Use of Songs

List the purpose of the songs from the chapters provided.

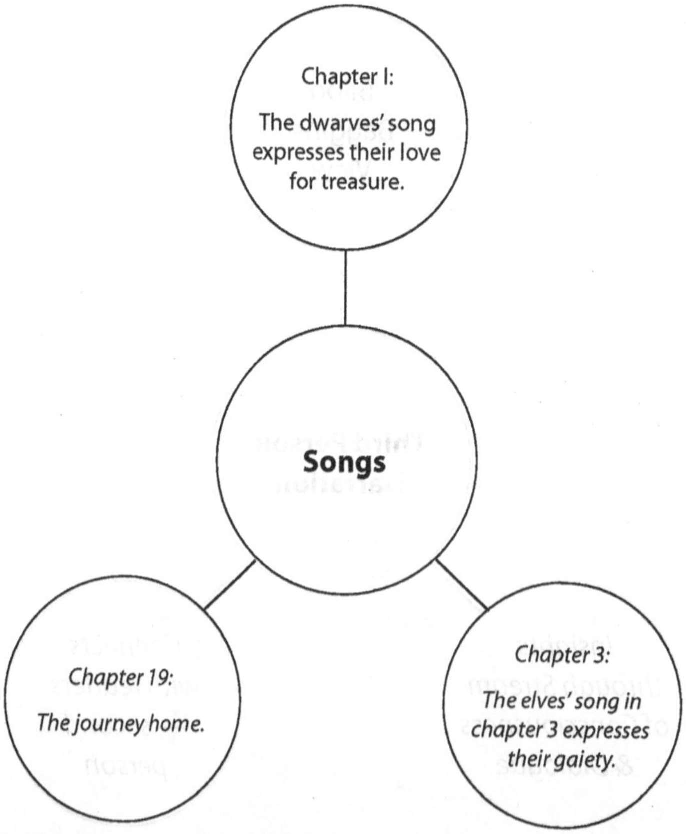
Chapter I:
The dwarves' song expresses their love for treasure.
Songs
Chapter 19:
The journey home.
Chapter 3:
The elves' song in chapter 3 expresses their gaiety.

Chapter 34 Review Questions

Writing a Novella

Proofread your novella and make final changes. Here are a few ways you may want to end your novella:

- You need to tie together loose ends, but do not do so artificially. Your novella does not have to end with a "happily ever after" ending.
- End with a dramatic, surprising event.
- End with a meaningful self-realization that the narrator has. For example, one novel I wrote with the narrator being satisfied with his life:

On this day I had Anna and whatever time God had given us to be together on this earth. And it was more than enough (Stobaugh, *Growing Up White*, p. 308).

- Don't forget to end the book.

Literary Analysis

How does Tolkien draw readers into his imaginary world?

Tolkien draws readers into his fictional world by creating the impression that Middle-earth is a real place. He describes in detail the landscape, filling it with the familiar plants and animals of earth. The books, on one level, are a tour through Middle-earth. Readers learn the names and background of different landmarks. Readers also meet the inhabitants of Middle-earth and learn something about their customs and histories. Readers will probably enjoy these details, even though most are not essential to the plot.

Biblical Application

Should Christians avoid fantasy?

One critic explains, "It should be obvious that this warning doesn't apply to the works of C.S. Lewis, J.R.R. Tolkien, George MacDonald, and other writers of fantasy-fiction. These authors are primarily artists, not self-proclaimed "prophets" or teachers and promoters of new religious doctrines. Nobody "believes in" The Lord of the Rings *or* The Chronicles of Narnia *in the same way they "believe in" the Bible, nor did the creators of these stories intend that anybody should. Yes, these tales are intended to reflect and embody many important Christian ideas. But they do it thematically, symbolically, and imaginatively, somewhat in the style of the parables of Jesus. They are not meant to be taken as "true" in and of themselves, in the same way that the narratives of Matthew, Mark, Luke, and John are "true."*[1]

1 Focus on the Family, "Questions about Christian Fantasy/Fiction, http://family.custhelp.com/app/answers/detail/a_id/26487/-/questions-about-christian-fantasy%2Ffiction.

Chapter 34 Test

Write a play about *The Hobbit.* (100 points)

Unlike prose fiction (novels, short stories) and poetry, drama is to be performed, and the creation of a play performance is a joint work, involving input from producers, directors, actors, choreographers, and in some cases, such as Tennessee Williams's *The Glass Menagerie,* the audience. Even though a play has a written script, every performance of a play is different, involving a unique interpretation of the play text. Casting, set, and costume design, the "blocking" or physical interaction of the actors, and the timing, phrasing, and tone of every speech affect the outcome. Prose fiction and poetry do not allow for such interpretative latitude.

Generally speaking drama has no point of view, no narrator. This is significantly different from prose fiction. Description in drama is determined by stage directions, the set, characters, and props.

In prose fiction, exposition may occur in any number of different milieus, such as dialogue, narrative descriptions, plot action, and so forth. In drama, exposition generally emerges only through dialogue. In other words, the story, unless it is mime, is told by the characters to other characters.

A character is an imaginary person who takes part in the action of a play. Drama tends to simplify the personalities of characters, often relying on stereotypes quickly to reveal and draw contrasts among characters. A playwright does not have 400 pages to tell his story. He needs to identify and to develop all his literary elements with a few lines, or he will lose his audience.

Chapter 34 Test Answer Sample

Write a play about *The Hobbit.* (100 points)

Answers will vary

Skills for Language Arts

Chapter Tests

Chapter 1 Test

Discussion Question (100 points)

Compare these two Bible passages to the Elijah passage (1 Kings 18).

Exodus 7:8–13

The LORD said to Moses and Aaron, "When Pharaoh says to you, 'Perform a miracle,' then say to Aaron, 'Take your staff and throw it down before Pharaoh,' and it will become a snake." So Moses and Aaron went to Pharaoh and did just as the LORD commanded. Aaron threw his staff down in front of Pharaoh and his officials, and it became a snake. Pharaoh then summoned wise men and sorcerers, and the Egyptian magicians also did the same things by their secret arts: Each one threw down his staff and it became a snake. But Aaron's staff swallowed up their staffs. Yet Pharaoh's heart became hard and he would not listen to them, just as the LORD had said.

1 Samuel 17:45–50

David said to the Philistine, "You come against me with sword and spear and javelin, but I come against you in the name of the LORD Almighty, the God of the armies of Israel, whom you have defied. This day the LORD will deliver you into my hands, and I'll strike you down and cut off your head. This very day I will give the carcasses of the Philistine army to the birds and the wild animals, and the whole world will know that there is a God in Israel. All those gathered here will know that it is not by sword or spear that the LORD saves; for the battle is the LORD's, and he will give all of you into our hands." As the Philistine moved closer to attack him, David ran quickly toward the battle line to meet him. Reaching into his bag and taking out a stone, he slung it and struck the Philistine on the forehead. The stone sank into his forehead, and he fell facedown on the ground. So David triumphed over the Philistine with a sling and a stone; without a sword in his hand he struck down the Philistine and killed him.

	Plot (Story)	Theme(s)	Setting
1 Kings 18	A moody prophet reveals the apostasy of Israel.		
Exodus 17	Moses confronts Pharaoh and God frees the people.		
1 Samuel 17	A young, unspectacular boy kills Israel's opponent and saves the nation.		

Chapter 2 Test

Matching (40 points)

A. Protagonist	_____ Elijah
B. Foil	_____ King Ahab
C. Antagonist	_____ Obadiah
D. Non-Personal Antagonist	_____ God
	_____ Baals
	_____ Fire

Letter (60 points total)

In spite of recent triumphs, Elijah is discouraged. Write him a letter encouraging him. Your letter will be evaluated in these three areas:

- Syntax and diction: grammar and style (10 points)
- Organization: paragraphs, transitions, introduction, et al. (20 points)
- Argument (30 points)

Chapter 3 Test

Essay (100 points total)

I. Circle words that describe Elijah. Box words that describe Jezebel. What does this tell you about these sworn enemies?

Character

Melancholic	**Choleric**
moody	touchy
anxious	restless
rigid	aggressive
sober	excitable
pessimistic	changeable
reserved	impulsive
unsociable	optimistic
quiet	active

Phlegmatic	**Sanguine**
passive	sociable
careful	outgoing
thoughtful	talkative
peaceful	responsive
controlled	easy-going
reliable	lively
even-tempered	carefree
calm	leadership

II. Take the same box and star words that describe your novella protagonist.

III. Take the same box and check words that describe your personality.

IV Now write a one-page essay comparing Elijah, Jezebel, your novella protagonist, and yourself. What did you learn about each character?

Your essay will be evaluated in these three areas:

- Syntax and diction: grammar and style (25 points)
- Organization: paragraphs, transitions, introduction, et al. (25 points)
- Argument (50 points)

Chapter 4 Test

Grammar (25 points)

I. Circle the linking verbs in the following sentences.

A. I am a teacher.

B. I appear to be sick.

C. You were not ready!

D. They seem to be nearly finished.

E. The soldiers are brave.

II. Identify the point of view in these passages (25 points)

A. First Person	____ Over the years, though, Margaret grew comfortable with her God. And that was all right too. They talked to each other and no doubt they loved each other, but practically speaking, she now wondered what sort of relationship that they had. Compatibility, though, did not inevitably lead to passion. And that was what she felt toward her God now: passion.
B. Third Person Objective	____ Over the years, though, Margaret appeared to grow comfortable with her God. And that was all right too. Many saw her praying out loud.
C. Omniscient Narration	____ I grew comfortable with God. And that was all right with me. I talked with Him. I trusted Him.

III. Explain what point of view you are choosing for your novella and explain why. (50 points total)

Your essay will be evaluated in these three areas:

Syntax and diction: grammar and style (10 points)

Organization: paragraphs, transitions, introduction, et al. (15 points)

Argument (25 points)

Chapter 5 Test

I. Choose the best word for the vocabulary word in context (30 points, 6 points/word).

The pejorative comment hurt my feelings.

A. Friendly

B. Gentle

C. Negative

D. Thoughtless

His perspicuity helped us solve the knotty problem.

A. Insightful . . . difficult.

B. Stupidity . . . easy.

C. Enthusiasm . . . potential.

D. Laziness . . . impossible.

The aplomb of the dancer allowed her to recover from her injury quicker.

A. Skill

B. Mood

C. Smile

D. Composure

The criminal did break the law, but he showed no malfeasance toward his victim.

A. Hard feelings

B. Evil

C. Love

D. Calmness

II. Verb Tenses

Every verb has six tenses: present tense, past tense, future tense, present perfect tense, past perfect tense, and future perfect tense. Complete the following chart (36 points, 2 points each):

Present Tense

Singular	Plural
I sing	We _____
You _____	You _____
He, She, It _____	They _____

Past Tense

Singular	Plural
I ____	We ____
You ____	You ____
He, She, It ____	They ____

Future Tense

Singular	Plural
I will ____	We will ________
You will ________	You will ________
He, She, It will ________	They will ________

Present Perfect Tense

Singular	Plural
I have ________	We have ________
You have ________	You have ________
He, She, It has ____	They have ________

Past Perfect Tense

Singular	Plural
I had ________	We had ________
You had ________	You had ________
He, She, It had ________	They had ________

Future Perfect Tense

Singular	Plural
I will have ________	We will have ________
You will have ________	You will have ________
He, She, It will have ________	He, She, It will have ________

III. How important is the setting to *The Yearling*? Could the story occur, say, in your hometown? Why or why not? (34 points total)

Your essay will be evaluated in these three areas:

Syntax and diction: grammar and style (10 points)

Organization: paragraphs, transitions, introduction, et al. (10 points)

Argument (14 points)

Chapter 6 Test

I. Organize the events in the order in which they occur. (65 points)

Organize the events in the novel in the order in which they occur.

_____ Thénardier's daughter Eponine, who is in love with Marius, helps Marius discover Cosette's whereabouts.

_____ Javert shows up to arrest Valjean while Valjean is at Fantine's bedside, and Fantine dies from the shock.

_____ Javert agrees. Javert feels tormented, torn between his duty to his profession and the debt he owes Valjean for saving his life. Ultimately, Javert lets Valjean go and throws himself into the river, where he drowns.

_____ After a few years, Valjean again escapes from prison and heads to Montfermeil, where he is able to buy Cosette from the Thénardiers.

_____ The convict Jean Valjean is released from a French prison after serving nineteen years for stealing a loaf of bread and for subsequent attempts to escape from prison. Myriel covers for Valjean, claiming that stolen silverware was a gift.

_____ Marius Pontmercy moves out of Gillenormand's house and lives as a poor young law student. While in law school, Marius associates with a group of radical students.

_____ The Thénardiers agree to look after Cosette as long as Fantine sends them a monthly allowance.

_____ Valjean manages to intercept a note and sets out to save the life of the man his daughter loves.

_____ Valjean arrives at the barricade and volunteers to execute Javert. When alone with Javert, however, Valjean instead secretly lets him go free.

_____ Marius and Cosette rush to dying Valjean's side. Valjean dies in peace.

_____ When Valjean emerges hours later, Javert immediately arrests him. Valjean pleads with Javert to let him take the dying Marius to Marius's grandfather.

_____ Marius sees Cosette at a public park. It is love at first sight, but the protective Valjean does his utmost to prevent Cosette and Marius from ever meeting.

_____ Marius decides to join his radical student friends, who have started a political uprising. Armed with two pistols, Marius heads for the barricades.

II. Discussion Question (35 points)

Why does Javert take his own life?

Chapter 7 Test

I. Matching (30 points)

A. Ethos	_______	emotional appeal, persuades readers by appealing to their emotions
B. Pathos	_______	the appeal to logic, convinces an audience through the use of logic or reason
C. Logos	_______	the ethical appeal, means to convince an audience of the author's credibility or character

II. Choose the correct pronoun. (60 points)

1. Each of the criminals had (his, their) motivation.
2. John and Mary planned (his and her, their) vacation.
3. Did Smith or Jones announce (his, their) intent to run for governor?
4. Neither my baseball nor my bat was returned to (its, their) original location.
5. Everyone turned in (his or her, their) assignments.
6. All of the lawyers turned in (his or her, their) briefs to the judge.
7. If any one of the students has misplaced (his or her, their) library card, (he or she, they) can pay a fine and get a replacement.
8. In the 19th century many states did not treat (its, their) public employees fairly.
9. Both of the children have made (her, their) desires known.
10. Every one of the female debaters knows (her, their) arguments by heart.
11. Either Sharon or her sisters will reveal (her, their) plans.
12. The losing captains thanked (his, their) special unit.
13. Mark's parents asked Mark if everything was in (its, their) place.
14. Neither of the workers wore clothing suitable for (his or her, their) job.

III. Discuss an example of symbolism in *Les Miserables.* (10 points)

There are several instances of symbolism. Probably the most famous is the candlesticks, which represent the redemption and grace of God that Javert himself experiences, and then gives to others.

Chapter 8 Test

I. Organize the events in the novel in the order in which they occur. (40 points)

________ Two nights before the departure, Pip receives a mysterious message to go to his own home village, where he is attacked by Orlick. Herbert rescues him, but he's still battered and sore when they set off down the river. Suffering has given Estella human feelings at last, and she is kind to Pip. As they walk away hand in hand, it looks as though they will finally get together.

________ In a village cemetery, a small boy, Pip, is accosted by a runaway convict who demands food and a file to saw off his leg iron.

________ Back in London, Pip learns that Magwitch once had a baby girl, but she was abandoned by her mother. Piecing together evidence, Pip realizes with shock that Estella was that baby girl. The time comes to take Magwitch away.

________ Returning to England many years later, Pip visits Miss Havisham's house, which has been pulled down. Estella is there, too. Her husband Drummle, who treated her badly, has died.

________ Pip visits Miss Havisham, to tell her he's lost his fortune; Estella is there, and he learns that she's going to marry Drummle. Dejected, Pip returns to London to learn that Compeyson is there, too, and is hunting down Magwitch. Herbert, Pip, and Jaggers' clerk Wemmick hatch a plan to take Magwitch in a rowboat down river, where he can board a ship bound for Germany. Pip agrees to go abroad with Magwitch, since he feels he has no future left in England. Miss Havisham asks to see Pip one more time.

________ Pip falls in love with Estella and becomes self-conscious about his low social class and unpolished manners. From then on, his abiding dream is to be a gentleman. He is bitterly disappointed when he becomes a teenager and Miss Havisham sees nothing better for him than to become apprenticed to his brother-in-law Joe at his blacksmith's forge.

________ Miss Havisham was deeply affected by Pip's outburst to Estella, and she is full of remorse for her selfish scheme; she begs Pip to forgive her. He does so, but just as he is leaving, she bends over the fire and then suddenly goes up in a pillar of flame. Pip rescues her, but she never recovers.

________ Magwitch tells Pip and Herbert his history. The convict Magwitch was fighting with on the marshes was his partner, Compeyson, who gave evidence against Magwitch to save his own skin. Pip and Herbert realize that Compeyson is the same man who deserted Miss Havisham on her wedding day.

II. Discussion Question (60 points)

Pip is one of the most complicated characters in western literature. The different elements of Pip's personality seem to be constantly in conflict. Explain.

Chapter 9 Test

I. Rewrite the following paragraphs removing unnecessary thoughts and sentences (75 points, 15 points each).

A. Adoption is an important theme in the Bible. I have an adopted sister and brother. The subject of orphans and adoption finds its way into numerous portions throughout both Old and New Testaments. The biblical understanding of adoption is interesting to explore.

B. There are many ways the theme of adoptions roots itself in the Bible. One of these ways is through Moses and Esther. This hero and heroine were both adopted, Moses by the Pharaoh's daughter. In the cartoon I saw, Pharaoh's daughter loved Moses. When the child grew older, she brought him to Pharaoh's daughter, and he became her son. She named him Moses, "Because," she said, "I drew him out of the water" (Exodus 2:10; HCSB), and Esther by Mordecai. Mordecai was the legal guardian of his cousin Hadassah (that is, Esther), because she didn't have a father or mother. . . . When her father and mother died, Mordecai had adopted her as his own daughter (Esther 2:7; HCSB). Much good came out of this, as they were both involved in saving God's people, Israel. Israel, as you know, is the nation with whom God made a covenant.

C. God frequently commands His people, and Christ commands His followers, to care for orphans. In fact, there are approximately 30 references in the New International Version to taking care of "orphans" or "the fatherless." And you should see how many times God tells husbands to love their wives! One of these references is found in Psalm 82:3: "Defend the weak and the fatherless; uphold the cause of the poor and the oppressed." Adoption is a significant way of caring for the fatherless, and is very much in line with God's commands.

D. A young woman in her 20s takes verses like Psalm 82:3 very seriously. She runs an outreach in Uganda for impoverished and orphaned children. It's called Amazima, which means "the truth" in Luganda, one of many languages spoken in Uganda. The program helps kids pay their school tuition, and equips them with school supplies. This woman has also adopted 13 daughters before the age of 21. She also loves to drive a Chevrolet.

E. The New Testament offers us another understanding of adoption. In Galatians 4:4–7, Paul states, "When the time came to completion, God sent His Son, born of a woman, born under the law, to redeem those under the law, so that we might receive adoption as sons. And because you are sons, God has sent the Spirit of His Son into our hearts, crying, 'Abba, Father!' So you are no longer a slave but a son, and if a son, then an heir through God" (HCSB). First John 3:1 says, "See what great love the Father has lavished on us, that we should be called children of God! And that is what we are!" These verses, and others, give us ample reason to believe that God made it possible for us to be adopted into His family through Christ's sacrifice on the Cross. But that does not mean you can have anything you want. No, you have to ask Him for it. He is our perfect father no matter what our family situation is, no matter who we are or where we've come from, or if we're saints or sinners — we are the children of God! This is a life-changing sense of adoption for those with a loving earthly father and those without, to have a Heavenly Father to guide them, love them, "embrace" them when they succeed, and pick them up when they fall. (Margo)

II. When does coincidence work in a novel and when does it not work? (25 points)

Your essay will be evaluated in these three areas:

Syntax and diction: grammar and style (5 points)

Organization: paragraphs, transitions, introduction, et al. (5 points)

Argument (15 points)

Chapter 10 Test

I. Develop at least three biblical themes in *Winnie the Pooh* (25 points).

II. Discuss the use of transitions in every paragraph in this essay (75 points, 12 points each)

In *Cold Sassy Tree,* Olive Ann Burns chooses a young boy to be her narrator. Though the reader may at first have doubts about the neutrality and reliability of this narrator, he is a reliable and trustworthy character. Throughout the book's course, he impartially reveals incidents that hurt him, and makes an effort to leave no detail untold.

Cold Sassy Tree carries with it the feel of a personal letter or diary — the narrator, a young boy, makes no effort to hide anything. Indeed, he even relates what is possibly the most embarrassing incident of his youth:

I was kissing Lightfoot! . . . Just then God spoke out loud in the voice of Miss Alice Ann. "Will Tweedy, you ought to be ashamed!" said God. I looked up and there He stood in a pink and white poky-dot dress, pointing His plump forefinger at us.

Furthermore, Will Tweedy, the narrator, makes no effort to present himself as the perfect child. Indeed, he narrates all events to the reader with perfect neutrality — both those that flatter him, and those that hurt him. Because of Will's willingness to tell even his most embarrassing tales, the reader feels comfortable trusting him with other details.

Through Will, the reader is privy to even the smallest detail of life in *Cold Sassy Tree:*

Grandpa and Miss Love stood there watching me read what it said under the picture: "PIERCE, 8 h.p., Geo. N. Pierce Co., Buffaly, N.Y. Price $900, without top; seats 4 persons, doors in back only; single, water-cooled cylinder; jump spark ignition, planetary transmission, 3 speeds; wt. 1,250 pound."

Also, this abundance of detail not only draws the reader into the story, but builds a relationship of trust between the reader and Will, the narrator. After all, if Will tells the reader what kind of ignition and what type of transmission Grandpa's automobile has, surely he can be trusted not to leave out other details important to the plot.

In *Cold Sassy Tree,* Olive Ann Burns chooses an ideal narrator. He is unscrupulous in his narration; impartially revealing all of the events in *Cold Sassy Tree* to the reader. Furthermore, he records in meticulous detail every minor incident—both drawing the reader into the story and adding to his reliability. (Daniel)

Chapter 11 Test

Write a fantasy story for your younger brother/sister or a friend. In your story illustrate through the plot, dialogue, etc., an important theme, such as love, forgiveness, or perseverance. (100 points)

Chapter 12 Test

I. Discussion Questions (60 points)

Why was *The Song of Hiawatha* so popular among Americans?

II. Write a six-line poem with rhythm and meter (40 points).

Chapter 13 Test

I. In a 300-word essay, describe Hiawatha as a peacemaker and a warrior. (50 points)

Your essay will be evaluated in these three areas:

Syntax and diction: grammar and style (10 points)

Organization: paragraphs, transitions, introduction, et al. (10 points)

Argument (30 points)

Chapter 14 Test

I. Organize the events in the order in which they occur. (60 points)

________ Meanwhile, he saves Weena.

________ In the year A.D. 802,701, he finds himself in a paradisiacal world of small humanoid creatures called Eloi.

________ He then returns, exhausted, to the present time. The next day, he leaves again, but never returns.

________ Many Morlocks die in the fire, and Weena is killed too.

________ That night, retreating from the Morlocks through a giant wood, he accidentally starts a fire.

________ The next week, the guests return, and the Time Traveler begins his story.

________ The Time Traveler goes down into the world of Morlocks to try to retrieve his time machine.

________ The Time Traveler produces a miniature time machine and makes it disappear.

________ In the night, he sees white human-like creatures called the Morlocks take the Eloi.

________ He goes to what he calls the Palace of Green Porcelain, which turns out to be a museum.

________ The Time Traveler returns home.

II. Discussion Question (40 points)

Discuss what a frame story is and how it is used with effectiveness in this novella (short novel).

Chapter 15 Test

I. Matching (60 points)

A. "The fire burned brightly, and the soft radiance of the incandescent lights in the lilies of silver caught the bubbles that flashed and passed in our glasses" (p. 1). ________ Personification

B. ". . . his lips moving as one who repeats mystic words" (p. 3). ________ Metaphor

C. "At once, like a lash across the face, came the possibility of losing my own age, of being left helpless in this strange new world" (p. 39). ________ Simile

D. "I felt as if I was in a monstrous spider's web" (p. 86) ________ Imagery

E. "That is the germ of my great discovery" (p. 5). ". . . almost see through it the Morlocks on their anthill going hither and thither . . ." (p. 69).

F. "There was a breath of wind . . ." (p. 8).
". . . with the big open portals that yawned before me shadowy and mysterious" (p. 28).
"The red tongues that went licking up my heap of wood . . ." (p. 83).

II. Write an essay predicting what the world will be like in 150 years (40 points).

Your essay will be evaluated in these three areas:

Syntax and diction: grammar and style (10 points)

Organization: paragraphs, transitions, introduction, et al. (10 points)

Argument (20 points)

Chapter 16 Test

I. Conflicts in characters: Matching (50 points)

______ Person versus fate	A. Samson
______ Person versus oneself	B. David and Goliath
______ Person versus person	C. Job
______ Person versus culture	D. Lot
______ Person versus nature	E. Joshua

II. Identify the following characters as round (A) or flat (B). (50 points)

______ Lot

______ Miriam

______ Abraham

______ Moses

______ Elizabeth

______ Joseph

______ Pharaoh

______ Daniel

______ Jacob

______ Obadiah

Chapter 17 Test

I. Spell the following words correctly: (60 points)

Ocasionally

Accomodation

Recieve

Murmer

Judgement

Monkay

Surgury

Confiscat

panorima

partality

Dandalion

pasttime

II. Match (40 points)

A. Interrogate ______ Find connections between information

B. Discover ______ Collect data; interview

C. Research ______ Brainstorm: What if?

D. Cluster ______ Who? What? When? How?

Chapter 18 Test

Essay (100 points)

Benet's classic is historical fiction — he admits that he is not writing an accurate, historical novel. Still, most readers consider it to be fact. Where does Benet get it right and get it wrong in his epic story of the American Civil War?

Your essay will be evaluated in these three areas:

Syntax and diction: grammar and style (25 points)

Organization: paragraphs, transitions, introduction, et al. (25 points)

Argument (50 points)

Chapter 19 Test

Write a letter to John Brown a few weeks before he leads his revolt. Support him or persuade him to change his mind. You decide! Follow the following format: (100 points)

1. Greeting

   The greeting or salutation is where you identify the recipient of the letter.

2. Body

   The body is where you write the content of the letter.

3. Closing

   The closing lets the reader know that you are finished with your letter.

Chapter 20 Test

I. Discussion Question (75 points)

Discuss the importance of the setting to "The Legend of Sleepy Hollow."

Your essay will be evaluated in these three areas:

Syntax and diction: grammar and style (15 points)

Organization: paragraphs, transitions, introduction, et al. (15 points)

Argument (45 points)

II. Fill in the following components of the setting in Irving's short novel: (25 points)

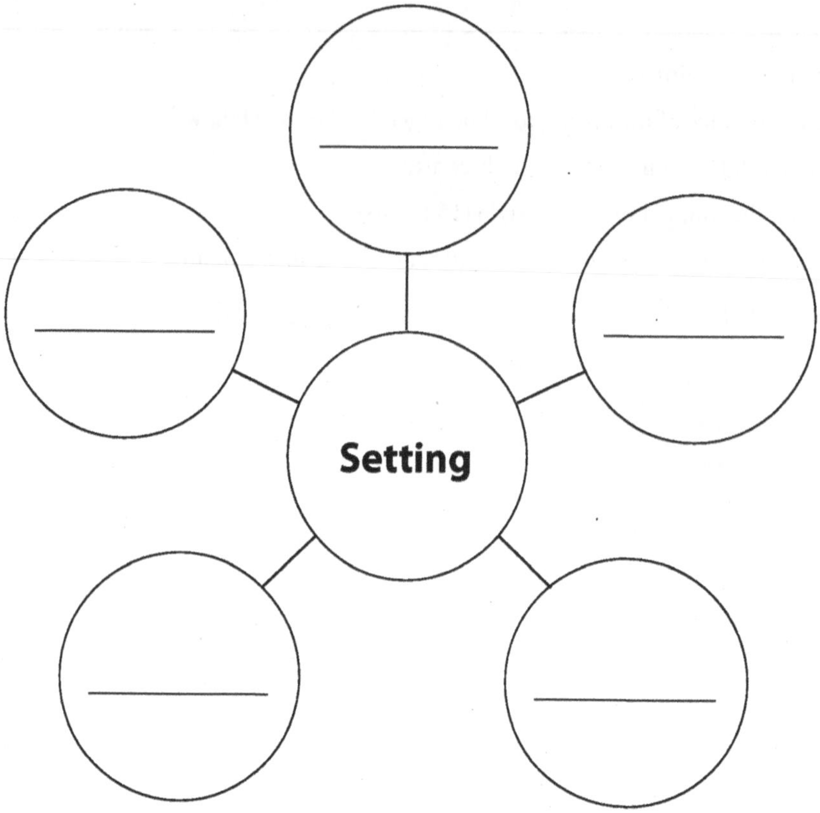

Chapter 21 Test

I. True or False. (50 points)

_____ Romanticism is just another form of Christianity.

_____ Romanticism, and its American version, transcendentalism, posits that God is nature and that "It" is good. The more natural things are, the better.

_____ Nature is inherently good. Nature alone is the ultimate reality. In other words, nature is the romantic god.

_____ Man is essentially a simple, stupid animal, too stupid to be controlled by absolute, codified truth (as one would find in the Bible).

_____ Human intuition replaces the Holy Spirit. Depending upon the demands on individual lives, truth and good are relative and changing.

II. Discussion Question (50 points)

Irving describes Ichabod Crane: "He was, in fact, an odd mixture of small shrewdness and simple credulity. His appetite for the marvelous, and his powers of digesting it, were equally extraordinary; and both had been increased by his residence in this spellbound region." Explain.

Your essay will be evaluated in these three areas.

Syntax and diction: grammar and style (15 points)

Organization: paragraphs, transitions, introduction, et al. (15 points)

Argument (20 points)

Chapter 22 Test

Discussion Question (100 points)

Life with Father, at its most basic level, is a memoir full of disparate stories only connected by the same characters and the same narrator. Along the way readers learn a lot about both. What can readers discern about the characters and narrator in this passage?

Your essay will be evaluated in these three areas:

Syntax and diction: grammar and style (25 points)

Organization: paragraphs, transitions, introduction, et al. (25 points)

Argument (50 points)

"Dad, where are we?"

I was nine years old and with my dad in Southeast Arkansas' Devil's Den Swamp hunting whitetail deer, and as usual, we arrived way too early.

"Nice night, dad," I sarcastically quipped. Perhaps it was an insight to my dad's personality that his nine-year-old son was already a cynic.

Nothing about this morning resembled its raison d'être. I stared into the heavens and contemplated the absurdity of our situation.

The Devil's Den Swamp was a thousand acre quagmire. It was the last wheeze of antediluvian mayhem in the wild Mississippi River Delta before pilgrims entered the subdued lowland piedmont.

Other little boys, waiting for trophy bucks, were relaxing in comfortable shelters on the edge of Milo maze fields. But no, not me. I was sloshing around in the Devil Den's Swamp.

With no hint of dawn, Dad and I languished in a slough of despair.

"We are right where we should be, Jacob." Dad smiled. "If we follow the North Star we shall surely be near the deer stand before dawn."

"Okay, Dad," I muttered deferentially.

We were doing no such thing. We were following Venus. Venus, squatting on the right of the first quarter moon, had been in the same place for millennium. Nowhere near the North Star.

We were following Venus, not the North Star, but I discerned that it was not propitious to challenge Dad's misapprehension of the universe.

My dad was 28-year-old dad Martin Stevens. Dad, five feet eight inches tall, wore heavy canvas camouflage pants and a grey flannel shirt. He wore his favorite green knee high rubber boots with tiny brand name red balls peering over the top of murky swamp water. In truth, he looked more like my older brother than my dad.

"Dad, where are we?"

"I don't know, but we are following the North Star so we are fine."

There was quicksand in the Devil's Den. I wondered if Dad remembered that. I knew a lot about quicksand—it regularly gobbled up unwary travelers in Saturday morning Tarzan movies.

Three years ago, while duck hunting, Jedidiah Morris walked into the Devil's Den and never returned. Old-timers claimed he fell into quicksand and disappeared forever. I was certain, this morning, that I would step on old, slimy, Jedidiah's head.

We were headed to the "deer stand" which was a euphemism for a rickety wooden structure strapped to an ancient Pin Oak Tree. Earlier that spring, fighting bloodthirsty mosquitoes and angry water moccasins, we built our deer stand on an obscure Indian mound in the middle of the Devil's Den.

Remote and unapproachable by man and deer alike, on this early November, the deer stand awaited our arrival and the debut of the first deer-hunting trip of the season.

I, Jacob Stevens, too wore camouflage attire, although I had pinned captain bars to my authentic Marine fatigue camouflage shirt. I was a captain in the Corps but I expected to be promoted any day, like my cousin Major Eddy Jones, a U. S. Marine Phantom II jet pilot who flew beer between Manila and Saigon. Even at age nine I knew it was a terrible waste to use a genuine American hero like Uncle Eddy and his superior flying machine the Phantom II to transport Budweiser when both hero and machine could be more profitably used to bomb the Charley.[1]

1 James P. Stobaugh, *Growing Up White* (New York: Harvard Square Editions, 2014), p. 9–10.

Chapter 23 Test

I. Narration Strategies: Matching (30 points)

A. Third Person Reminiscences: The narrator remembers important events in his life as they relate to his father and his family. Of course, readers must judge if these are reliable. That can be ascertained by the amount of details offered and of objectivity employed.

B. Stream of Consciousness: This is a literary technique that authors use to let the reader see into the mind of the narrator. This is a favorite strategy for first person narrators. Sometimes the narrator will even speak to himself and thereby reveal important details.

C. Dialogue: As the characters speak to one another we learn a lot about the story and the characters in it.

______ The dancers were whirling in David's head as they whirled on the dance floor

______ The weary pilgrim remembered the first time God delivered him, and he gave thanks.

______ "I will never forgive him!" Mary cried. "Never!"

II. Matching. Identify the types of humor in this passage. Answers may be used more than once. (70 points)

A. When Jake and Anna first arrived, Davy phoned and asked to speak to Jake.
Anna answered. "Hi Davy. Pastor Jake is not home. May I help you?"
Davy was reticent, maybe even a little insulted, to speak to what he thought was the B team.

B. "I am going to kill myself. Right now!"
"No wait, Davy. Let's talk!" Anna pleaded.
"Ok," Davy, in obvious stress, responded.
Anna, meanwhile, was motioning to Grace to come to her.

C. She wrote on a piece of paper, "See if Dad is outside. Bring him. Hurry!"
"Davy, can you tell me why you are so upset?"
"No one likes me, Anna. No one likes me."
"I like you, Davy, and so does Pastor Jake."
"You don't count. You have to like me because you are my pastor."

D. Anna was growing more concerned.
"What can I do to save his life?" She thought.
"Davy, how are you feeling, right now?" Anna asked.
"Depressed. Oh Anna! I am going to hurt myself right now!"
And then Davy screamed into the telephone.
"No! Don't," Anna cried. "Stop!"
By this time Anna was crying. Nathan and Emily were crying too. Everyone was crying!
"Davy, please! Let's pray!"
Only silence was on the other end of the phone line.

______ Irony

______ Exaggeration

______ Dialogue

E. Anna was sure Davy was dead. The police would come and find him lying in a pool of blood and it would be her fault. She did it. She pushed him over the edge.
"Davy?" Anna tried one last time before she called the police.
Nathan and Emily were alternately crying loudly and praying in their small voices.
Only silence.
Then Anna heard a sound. It sounded like keys jingling.
"Davy?"
"Oh yes, sorry, Anna. What did you say?"
Anna sighed. "Now Davy, wait where you are. I want to pray with you and then I will phone the police."

F. "I would like to, Anna. Thanks. But I have no time. I have to go to the bank. Will miss the bus if I talk any longer. Thanks for the offer though. Bye."
Davy hung up.

G. Anna held the phone in disbelief.
Suddenly Grace and Jake burst into the room.
Anna looked up and hit Jake hard on the arm.
"What? What?" Jake asked in consternation.
"Your stupid, crazy congregation!" was all that Anna could say.

______ Irony

______ Exaggeration

______ Dialogue

Chapter 24 Test

I. Place these events in the order in which they occur: (75 points)

_____ The fish pulls Santiago's skiff out to sea like a child pulling a toy wagon.

_____ Santiago rows his boat far beyond normal fishing waters, hoping to end his string of bad luck with a really huge catch.

_____ Santiago begins to see the reflected glare of Havana lights. But the sharks now come in a pack. He fights them with a club and even with the skiff's tiller, but they strip the remaining flesh from the marlin.

_____ His deepest line shows signs of a fish nibbling at the bait, and he catches a huge fish.

_____ Santiago, the "old man," has gone 84 days without catching a fish.

_____ Santiago increases tension on the line to the breaking point, attempting to make the fish jump. The line has been stretched over his back for hours now.

_____ Manolin had been Santiago's apprentice, but the boy's parents have made him work on another fishing boat because Santiago has "bad luck." But he's still loyal to Santiago and helps the old man prepare for an attempt to catch "the big one."

_____ The fish surfaces for the first time. Santiago sees he has hooked a marlin "longer than the skiff."

_____ The great marlin is jumping. This is good because its air sacs will fill and the fish won't sink to the bottom and die, unable to be pulled back up.

_____ The marlin begins to circle the boat rather than tow it. This is a major breakthrough in the struggle to bring in the fish.

_____ Tourists look with detached amusement at the skeletal remains of Santiago's three-day battle.

_____ Santiago kills it with his harpoon. Since the fish is much longer than the skiff, it must be lashed to the side rather than towed behind. Santiago puts up the mast and sets sail to the southwest, back toward Havana.

_____ Manolin tends to the spent, pain-ridden old man and vows to fish with him again.

_____ While killing a shark that is consuming his catch, he loses his harpoon. Now there is a massive trail of blood and scent in the water, which will inevitably attract other sharks.

_____ So now he pilots his small craft home, bringing only a huge skeleton.

II. Discussion Question (25 points)

Discuss the theme of suffering in this book.

Chapter 25 Test

Create a short story of a similar situation that captures the theme of this short novel. (100 points)

Chapter 26 Test

Discussion Questions (50 points each)

How does Poe build suspense in "The Cast of the Amontillado"?

Who is the audience at the end of the story?

Chapter 27 Test

I. Place these sections of this essay in the correct order: (80 points)

_____ There were two different themes between the two books. In *Frankenstein*, Mary Shelly shows the goodness of man and the evil of the world. In Dr. Jekyll and Mr. Hyde, Robert Louis Stevenson showed the inner evil of man. Both science fiction novels had drastically different themes.

_____ Mary Shelley's novel *Frankenstein* and R. L. Stevenson's novel *Dr. Jekyll and Mr. Hyde*, showed drastically different themes. In *Frankenstein*, Mary Shelly shows the goodness of mankind and the evil of the world. In *Dr. Jekyll and Mr. Hyde*, Robert Louis Stevenson shows the evil inside of man. Though both of the plots were the same, the themes were different. Not really. Shelley shows what happens when the "monster" does not accept his flaws. Stevenson shows the opposite. In that sense, Stevenson writes a more "Christian" novel, since Jekyll accepts responsibility for his actions and deals with it. Not so with the confused monster Frankenstein.

_____ *Dr. Jekyll and Mr. Hyde* showed a different theme. In that book, Robert Louis Stevenson shows the evil nature of man. Dr. Jekyll had two sides. One side was the kindly Dr. Jekyll. To this rule, Dr. Jekyll was . . . a large, well-made, smooth faced man of fifty . . . but with every mark of capacity and kindness. But the other side was Mr. Hyde. Mr. Hyde was pale and dwarfish, he gave an impression of deformity without any nameable malformation. Stevenson showed in his novel, the inner nature of man. Jekyll was a nice man, but inside he was evil. He had a dual nature. Though so profound a double-dealer, I was in no sense a hypocrite; both sides of me were in dead earnest. . . . In the end of the story, evil took over Jekyll. Mr. Hyde took over Dr. Jekyll, and evil was dominant.

_____ In *Frankenstein*, Mary Shelly creates a theme of the good of man and the evil of the world. One night, a scientist accidently creates a monster. I saw the dull yellow eye of the creature open; it breathed hard, and a convulsive motion agitated its limbs. After creating the monster, Victor Frankenstein ran away horrified at what he had done. He is "god playing." Shelley hates that. Unable to endure the aspect at which I had created, I rushed out of the room. . . . Frankenstein returned to his family, until one day he met the monster. The monster then told Frankenstein that he had been mistreated everywhere he went. . . . I was benevolent; my soul glowed with love and humanity, but am I not alone, miserably alone? The monster was kind to everyone he met. He helped a family and saved a woman from death. But he was mistreated. After he saved the woman, someone shot him. Everywhere he went he was mistreated.

II. Choose the best title for this essay (20 points):

A. Robert Louis Stevenson's Masterpiece

B. The Problem of Evil

C. Monsters Are Scary

D. The Horrors of 19th-Century London

Chapter 28 Test

I. Place these events in the order in which they occur. (75 points)

_____ Boo carries the wounded Jem back to Atticus's house, where the sheriff, in order to protect Boo, insists that Ewell tripped over a tree root and fell on his own knife. After sitting with Scout for a while, Boo disappears once more into the Radley house.

_____ Dill becomes fascinated with the Radley Place.

_____ Scout Finch lives with her brother, Jem, and their widowed father, Atticus, in the sleepy Alabama town of Maycomb.

_____ Scout and Jem find gifts apparently left for them in a knothole of a tree on the Radley property.

_____ Despite the significant evidence pointing to Tom's innocence, the all-white jury convicts him.

_____ Jem loses his pants and when he returns for them, he finds them mended and hung over the fence.

_____ The next winter, Jem and Scout find more presents in the tree, presumably left by the mysterious Boo. Nathan Radley eventually plugs the knothole with cement.

_____ Atticus agrees to defend a black man named Tom Robinson, who has been accused of assaulting a white woman.

_____ Atticus's sister, Alexandra, comes to live with the Finches the next summer. Dill, who is supposed to live with his "new father" in another town, runs away and comes to Maycomb.

_____ Later, Scout feels as though she can finally imagine what life is like for Boo. He has become a human being to her at last.

_____ Despite the verdict, Bob Ewell feels that Atticus and the judge have made a fool out of him, and he vows revenge.

_____ The innocent Tom later tries to escape from prison and is shot to death.

_____ On Dill's last night in Maycomb for the summer, the three sneak onto the Radley property, where Nathan Radley shoots at them.

_____ Ewell attacks Jem and Scout as they walk home from a Halloween party. Boo Radley intervenes, however, saving the children and stabbing Ewell fatally during the struggle.

_____ One summer, Jem and Scout befriend a boy named Dill, who has come to live in their neighborhood for the summer.

II. Discussion Question (25 points)

Jem and Scout are important dynamic, round characters. What does that mean?

Chapter 29 Test

Pretend that you are Scout's cousin and you discover all the terrible things that have happened to her and to her small town. Write a letter encouraging her (100 points).

Chapter 30 Test

Write a 500-word parody of a friend, historical period, or a historical figure. (100 points)

Chapter 31 Test

I. Write a psalm. (40 points)

II. Write a proverb. (40 points)

III. Write a poem about a historical figure in the Bible. (20 points)

Chapter 32 Test

Write a sermon on 1 Corinthian 13. (100 points)

Your sermon will be evaluated in these three areas:

Syntax and diction: grammar and style (25 points)

Organization: paragraphs, transitions, introduction, et al. (25 points)

Argument (50 points)

Chapter 33 Test

I. Place these events in the order in which they occurred. (55 points)

_____ In Lake-town, Bard holds his ground. He kills the dragon with his last arrow and escapes before Smaug falls, smashing the town.

_____ Bilbo tries to end the dispute by stealing the Arkenstone, the piece of treasure most valued by the leader of the dwarves. He gives the jewel to Bard, hoping it can be used to force the dwarves to negotiate.

_____ Bilbo Baggins and the dwarfs, with Gandalf's help, plans to travel to the Lonely Mountain to recover the treasure that a dragon named Smaug stole from their people long ago.

_____ Just as war begins to break out, an army of goblins and wild wolves attack. The dwarves, elves, and men forget their differences and join together to keep from being killed.

_____ Bilbo himself isn't sure that he's happy about this arrangement.

_____ Bilbo's bravery wins him praise from all but the dwarves, who are furious with him. When more dwarves arrive from the north, they are determined to fight.

_____ Bilbo finds a magic ring that makes him invisible, and has several opportunities to use it to rescue the dwarves from danger and imprisonment.

_____ Bilbo and the dwarves finally reach Lonely Mountain.

_____ Furious that someone has dared steal a piece of his treasure, Smaug attacks the mountainside where the dwarves have their camp and Lake-town.

_____ Bilbo wants none of the treasure and returns home with Gandalf.

_____ Believing the dwarves are dead, an army of men, led by Bard, and an army of elves find to their surprise that the dwarves are still alive.

_____ Bard, because he killed the dragon, claims his rightful share of the treasure. When the dwarves refuse to surrender it, the army besieges the mountain.

_____ Bilbo has more confidence in himself now and not only steals a cup, but converses with the tricky Smaug.

II. Discussion Question (45 points)

Explain why Tolkien chose Bilbo Baggins as his protagonist.

Chapter 34 Test

Write a play about the *Hobbit.* (100 points)

Unlike prose fiction (novels, short stories) and poetry, drama is to be performed, and the creation of a play performance is a joint work, involving input from producers, directors, actors, choreographers, and in some cases, such as Tennessee Williams's *The Glass Menagerie*, the audience. Even though a play has a written script, every performance of a play is different, involving a unique interpretation of the play text. Casting, set, and costume design, the "blocking" or physical interaction of the actors, and the timing, phrasing, and tone of every speech affect the outcome. Prose fiction and poetry do not allow for such interpretative latitude.

Generally speaking drama has no point of view, no narrator. This is significantly different from prose fiction. Description in drama is determined by stage directions, the set, characters, and props.

In prose fiction, exposition may occur in any number of different milieus, such as dialogue, narrative descriptions, plot action, and so forth. In drama, exposition generally emerges only through dialogue. In other words, the story, unless it is mime, is told by the characters to other characters.

A character is an imaginary person who takes part in the action of a play. Drama tends to simplify the personalities of characters, often relying on stereotypes quickly to reveal and draw contrasts among characters. A playwright does not have 400 pages to tell his story. He needs to identify and to develop all his literary elements with a few lines, or he will lose his audience.